The Fringes of Belief

The Fringes of Belief

*English Literature, Ancient Heresy, and the
Politics of Freethinking, 1660–1760*

Sarah Ellenzweig

STANFORD UNIVERSITY PRESS

STANFORD, CALIFORNIA

Stanford University Press
Stanford, California

Printed in the United States of America on acid-free, archival-quality paper

Library of Congress Cataloging-in-Publication Data

Ellenzweig, Sarah.
The fringes of belief : English literature, ancient heresy, and the politics of free-thinking, 1660-1760 / Sarah Ellenzweig.
    p. cm.
Includes bibliographical references and index.
ISBN 978-0-8047-5877-2 (cloth : alk. paper)
1. English literature—18th century—History and criticism. 2. English litera-ture—Early modern, 1500-1700—History and criticism. 3. Free thought in literature. 4. Christianity and literature—England—History—17th century. 5. Christianity and literature—England—History—18th century. 6. Free thought—England—History—17th century. 7. Free thought—England—History—18th century. I. Title.
PR445.E45 2008
820.9'382—dc22
2008011777

Typeset by Bruce Lundquist in 10/12 Sabon

For my parents,
Harry and Judy

Tho' the *Art of Poetry be Divine*, we have had but very few *Divine Poets*.

—*Weekly Miscellany* (1734)

Contents

Acknowledgments

This book began in very different form as a dissertation under the guidance of Michael McKeon and Jonathan Kramnick at Rutgers University. Since then, their keen criticism, professional savvy, and friendship have continued to nurture the project's growth and maturation more than I can possibly express, and my debt to their generous and ongoing willingness to serve as readers and advisors is tremendous. Several people at Rice University have also offered vital support and mentorship. Jack Zammito provided intellectual fellowship and encouragement at a crucial juncture in the project's history. Caroline Levander, Helena Michie, and Robert Patten read and commented on drafts, helping me immeasurably to clarify my thinking and sharpen the book's focus and direction. Thanks are due to the Department of English, Gary Wihl in the School of Humanities, and the Jon and Paula Mosle Faculty Research Endowment for making invaluable research support available. Terry Munisteri supplied expert and much-needed copyediting services while I prepared the final manuscript. Victoria Ford Smith has proven an exacting and indefatigable research assistant, without whose diligence and energy the project would have progressed far more slowly.

A fellowship from the UCLA Center for Seventeenth- and Eighteenth-Century Studies and the William Andrews Clark Memorial Library in 2002 played a pivotal role in turning the dissertation into a book. Thanks and appreciation are owed to Kirstie McClure, Peter Reill, Jason Frank, and Kinch Hoekstra for stimulating discussion on Hobbes, Spinoza, and related topics. An earlier version of Chapter One grew out of these conversations, appearing in *Journal of British Studies* 44 (2005). I thank the journal for permission to use this material. I am indebted to my editors, Norris Pope and Emily-Jane Cohen, for believing in the book and marshaling it seamlessly through the publication process. A special word of thanks goes to Dror Wahrman and Laura Rosenthal for their perspicacious readings of the manuscript and judicious suggestions for revision.

I am grateful to many family members, friends, and colleagues who have sustained and buoyed my mind and spirit throughout the life of this project. Lisa Ellenzweig, Rebecca Ascher, Miriam Klapper, Mely Santizo, Bonnye and Bob McGill, Caroline Levander, Tanya Agathocleous, Rachel Williams, Jody Radoff, Rachel Buchman, Corrinne Harol, Kimberly Latta, Rachel Zuckert, Elora Shehabuddin, Ussama Makdisi, Harvey Yunis, Caroline Quenomoen, Julie Fette, Cameron Gearen, Kirsten Ostherr, Daniel Cohen, Farrah Braniff, Jane Greenberg, Christopher Kelty, Hannah Landecker, Meredith Skura, Betty Joseph, Marcia Carter, Carl Caldwell, Joachim Coelho, and Gordon Schochet provided inspiration and support in one way or another: some intellectual, some emotional, and some both. My warmest thanks go to Hilda Diaz, Jeanice Davis, Dania Dueñas, Alma Barron, and the wonderful teachers at the Shlenker School in Houston. Their caring work has transformed book writing, assistant professorship, and parenting two small boys from an insurmountable challenge into a possible reality. My deepest debt of gratitude is to my parents—Harry and Judy Ellenzweig—to whom this book is dedicated. Thank you for a lifetime of unstinting love and encouragement. Finally, my husband Scott McGill has been tireless in his willingness to translate Latin passages from the seventeenth and eighteenth centuries. He and our sons, Charlie and Alexander, keep my heart joyful every day.

The Fringes of Belief

Literary Culture, the Classical Past, and the Rise of Restoration Freethinking

> As we think for ourselves, we may keep our thoughts to ourselves, or communicate them with a due reserve, and in such a manner only, as it may be done without offending the laws of our country, and disturbing the public peace.
> —Henry St. John, Viscount Bolingbroke,
> *Letters, or Essays, Addressed to Alexander Pope* (1754)

☾

When Henry St. John, Viscount Bolingbroke, wrote to Alexander Pope that "things the most absurd in speculation become necessary in practice," his subject was the recent "noise made about free thinking" among his contemporaries, and his aim was to redeem the spirit of freethought from its many vociferous detractors. Suspicion of revealed religion, Bolingbroke insinuates, did not necessarily lead to an open denigration of Christianity and its laws. However absurd according to the rigors of speculation, orthodox religious practice takes precedence over the disenchanted truths revealed by freethinking. "Let us not imagine," he continues,

that every man, who can think and judge for himself, as he has a right to do, has therefore a right of speaking, any more than of acting, according to the full freedom of his thoughts. The freedom belongs to him as a rational creature. He lies under the restraint as a member of society.[1]

It is a long-standing truism that the critique of religion and religious knowledge was a fundamental feature of the Enlightenment. And yet, if the Enlightenment was the epoch of "freethinking" (defined as a skeptical religious posture that saw Scripture and the truths of Christian teaching as idle tales and fables), Bolingbroke's emphasis on the demands of practice, or the need for conformity to the laws and opinions of one's

ancestors, would seem to point in a different direction. Indeed, Bolingbroke declares that he "should fear an attempt to alter the established
religion as much as they who have the most bigot attachment to it, and
for reasons as good as theirs, though not entirely the same."[2] This book
contends that in the English imagination it was possible to reject Christianity as divine truth while defending the necessary authority of the Anglican Church. This curious rapprochement between religious skepticism
and the interests of the Protestant establishment represents a crucial and
untold chapter in the larger history of secularization, and one that forms
the subject of the ensuing pages.

My thesis grows out of an examination of the literature of English
freethinking, a body of writing that has been overlooked, I contend,
because it unexpectedly supported aspects of institutional religion. With
chapters analyzing poetry and prose by John Wilmot, Earl of Rochester, Aphra Behn, Jonathan Swift, and Alexander Pope, I foreground an
unexamined strand of the English freethinking tradition, one that was
suspicious of revealed religion yet often strongly opposed to the open
denigration of Anglican Christianity and its laws. This distinct incarnation of English freethinking, though engaged with a range of philosophical radicals including Lucretius, Montaigne, Lord Herbert of Cherbury,
Thomas Hobbes, Spinoza, Charles Blount, and Bolingbroke, was marked
by a predilection to reinvest in religion pragmatically as a series of heuris-
tic fictions. By exposing the volatility of categories like belief and doubt,
this book participates in the larger argument in Enlightenment studies—
as well as in current scholarship on the condition of modernity more
generally—that religion is not so simply left behind in the shift from
the premodern to the modern world.[3] In its broadest formulation, then,
my project aims to contribute to efforts to reconsider the secularization
thesis, marshaling evidence from English literary culture to support the
claim that modernity is less fully secular than formerly imagined.

The most recent historiographical work on English freethinking has
demonstrated, for example, that the radical republican thought of figures like Henry Stubbe, John Toland, Anthony Collins, and Matthew
Tindal relied on a revived notion of civil theology for its formulation
of a renovated and liberalized state.[4] This study argues that the freethinkers' project to adapt religion to serve the needs of the state had
an intellectual history more diverse and complicated than the familiar
narratives of radical republicanism indicate. Also rejecting religion as
transcendental truth, the literary freethinkers this book examines held
up deference to traditional religious laws as an expedient fundamental
to the stability of customary social and political forms. I thus attempt to
show the centrality of literary culture to the paradoxical way in which

the most radical and modern of religious postures—unbelief—was frequently deeply ambivalent about the democratization of both religious and political institutions. Through delineating the singular literature of English freethinking, my interest is to shed light on a central yet neglected feature of the history of secularization; namely, that what will become modern atheism shares a surprising legacy with aspects of early conservative thought.

Within the particular terms of Enlightenment studies, my book follows the lead of historians such as Margaret Jacob and Jonathan Israel on the complex relationship between mainstream and radical elements of the European Enlightenment tradition.[5] Israel's recent groundbreaking study, *Radical Enlightenment*, has established definitively for the field the magnitude and surprising cohesion of what had formerly been seen as a peripheral fringe to larger more moderate currents. This book attempts to show how in the English experience deeply radical elements inhered within and were not always separable from establishment forces. Thus, though I am indebted to previous historians' inclusion of England as a critical player in what is now seen as "a single highly integrated intellectual and cultural movement" across Europe, I also seek to emphasize the particularity of the English engagement with the radical thought of the period.[6] As J. G. A. Pocock has argued in a series of seminal essays, the Enlightenment in England is defined most enduringly by its historical contiguity to an age perceived by contemporaries as one of deep fanaticism and disorder.[7] In consequence, the English Enlightenment is shaped above all by its animus against religious enthusiasm in all guises as well as its association between radical religious expression and civil anarchy. Much of existing historiography on freethinking and skeptical religion in the period has tended to limit its focus to the radical legacy of the Civil Wars and Interregnum.[8] By contrast, this book shows how Anglican Christianity could be defended as precisely the antidote to the civil unrest produced (some insisted) by the extremes of both Catholic and Protestant fanaticism. When manipulated properly, religion, the argument went, enjoyed a matchless capacity to serve the interests of a stable, sovereign state.

Also central to the argument of the book is the way in which English freethinking's emphasis on the utility of religious observance looked back to the theological inheritance of the ancient pagan philosophers. Whereas Peter Gay's influential work *The Enlightenment: The Rise of Modern Paganism* argues that the *philosophes* appealed to antiquity for a "signpost to secularism," I demonstrate that the English freethinkers used the classical heritage as a model for reconciling the institution of religion with unbelief.[9] The English tradition uncovers an antiquity conspicuous not so much for its subversive incredulity as for its sociological investment in religion's function as a pious fraud, a ruse that artfully preserved civic order. Ubiquitous in the writings of ancient philosophers ranging from Plato to Polybius to Plutarch to Cicero, the pious fraud taught that unbelief, however true, was not to be promulgated among the multitude. From these ancients, the modern freethinkers learned that the fictions of religion functioned as an indispensable undergirding for the civil polity.

This argument begins later in this chapter with a broad contextual overview of English freethinking in the late seventeenth and eighteenth centuries, one that considers didactic pamphlets, theological polemics, and philosophical writing as well as current historiography. The book then proceeds to detail four case studies of freethinking in Restoration and eighteenth-century literary culture. Through revisionist readings of Rochester, Behn, Swift, and Pope, my project seeks to interrogate the received parameters of English literary classicism by considering the classical theology of three important literary "ancients." This project contends that it is by bringing literary culture into the conversation about Enlightenment religion that the peculiar radical-conservatism of English freethinking comes to light.

Though religious enthusiasm has received extended treatment as a context central to our understanding of literary modernity, the evolution of English freethinking has been virtually undocumented in literary criticism of the period.[10] Author studies have largely isolated literary figures from the cultural and theological shifts identified in this book, just as work on the history of religion in the period, by turn, has overlooked literary culture's participation in the critique of religion. The idea that religion is a fictional and imaginative construct is crucially bound up with theories of the aesthetic, thus justifying a literary examination of the critique of religion. Indeed, it has long been recognized that the rise of the aesthetic in the eighteenth century is coincident with the decline of a traditional religious worldview.[11]

Charging his *Essay on Man* (1733–34) with religious heterodoxy, Pope's detractors expose this trajectory, complaining that "the reader, carried away by the beauty of the poetry, reads with eagerness, and supposes, often contrary to truth, that facts are as the poet represents them." As another warns, "Whatever is read with so much Pleasure, should be read with as much Caution." When Swift comments of Bolingbroke's freethinking paraphrase of Horace that "the goodness of the poetry convinces me of the truth of your philosophy," he emphasizes (less censoriously) the way in which the power of the literary is inextricable from philosophy's incursions on time-honored assumptions about faith and belief.[12] According to Annabel Patterson, moreover, the various arts central to the literary—devices such as irony, ambiguity, and veiled and coded meanings—developed precisely out of the early modern culture of religious and political censorship. To say what they wanted to say without provoking the authorities, writers learned to take refuge in the (relative) safety of the fictional.[13] Hobbes notably made use of such a ruse in his heterodox *Historia Ecclesiastica* (1688), written unprecedentedly in verse. About this unexpected turn to the literary, Hobbes's English translator claims, "But this may be urg'd in His Defence, that he often-times delivers himself rather in a Poetical, than in a Catholick Manner; and there, ought rather to fall by a Jury of Criticks, than be clapp'd into the Inquisition by a Bench of Prelates."[14] Swift's reminder in his 1710 "Apology" to *A Tale of a Tub*, "that some of those Passages in this Discourse, which appear most liable to Objection are what they call Parodies, where the Author personates the Style and Manner of other Writers, whom he has a mind to expose," seeks a like protection in the impossible ambiguity of his satiric virtuosity.[15] This connection between the critique of religion and the aesthetic realm suggests that the latter might well constitute a vital and overlooked archive for an investigation of freethinking more generally. Such is the informing premise of this book.

I

In a letter to Swift in 1724, Bolingbroke attempts to rectify his culture's partial understanding of what is meant by the term freethinker, or what he calls "Esprit fort." According to Bolingbroke, freethinkers are commonly lumped together as "the Pests of Society," men who wickedly seek to "take att least one curb out of the mouth of that wild Beast Man when it would be well if he was check'd by half a score others." This customary view, however, overshadows the contrary tendency of another set of men, largely misconstrued. "The persons I am describing," Bolingbroke writes, "think for them selves, and to them selves. Should they unhappily not be convinc'd by yr arguments, yet they will certainly think it their duty not to disturb the peace of the world by opposing you." To think freely, on this view, is to seek truth discreetly and privately.[16]

As early as 1710, Richard Steele's *Tatler* delineated a similar taxonomy of freethinking, one that makes explicit the intellectual heritage of Bolingbroke's cohort of "Esprit forts." Here Steele, like Bolingbroke, denounces the shallow infidels of the age for recklessly publishing and advertising their skeptical doctrines abroad, and thereby "harden[ing] the Hearts of the Ignorant against the very Light of Nature, and the common received Notions of Mankind." Though deeply critical of these modern unbelievers, Steele suggests that the venerable sages of the classical world, including Socrates, Cicero, Seneca, and all "the Philosophers of Note" in Greece and Rome, provide another perspective on religious doubt. These "Free-Thinkers of Antiquity," Steele asserts, both fought against "the Idolatry and Superstition of the Times in which they lived" and "complied with the Religion of their Country, as much as possible."[17] The ancient freethinkers might unite with the modern debauchees Steele denigrates in their essential skepticism about a supernatural order, yet Steele suggests that the ancients shrewdly knew better than to promulgate their unbelief among those not morally equipped to handle the implications of a nonprovidential worldview.[18]

In his introduction to "Letters or Essays Addressed to Alexander Pope," likely composed in the early 1730s, Bolingbroke again articulates the dilemma of the civic-minded freethinker of the age, this time invoking the wisdom of Steele's ancient freethinkers: "Truth and falsehood, knowledge and ignorance, revelations of the Creator, inventions of the creature, dictates of reason, sallies of enthusiasm, have been blended so long together in our systems of theology, that it may be thought dangerous to separate them." For this reason, Bolingbroke argues that from Plato on, the ancient Greeks and Romans wisely apprehended that "things evidently false might deserve an outward respect, when they are interwoven into a system of government." Though unbelievers in private, the best of the ancients thus supported the concept of a state religion— one that transmitted a set of (supposedly) divine truths—for the stability it encouraged in the civil order.[19]

Bolingbroke traces the practice of what he calls the "pious fraud" to "the days of primitive simplicity," as does William Warburton's *The Divine Legation of Moses* (1738–41), the period's preeminent discussion of the modern reception of ancient theology.[20] Like Bolingbroke, Warburton suggests that the notion that religion was a fiction manipulated by the civil power in the interests of the state was pervasive among the ancient writers and philosophers, entailing the practice of a "Twofold Doctrine." As he explains,

The Genius of their national Religions taught them to conclude, that Utility and not Truth was the End of Religion. . . . From this Principle, a third necessarily arose, That it was Lawful and Expedient to Deceive for the Public Good. This all the ancient Philosophers were full of: And Tully, from Plato, thinks it so clear, that he calls the doing otherwise *Nefas*. . . . The ancient Sages did actually say one thing when they thought another. This appears from that general Practice . . . of a Two-fold Doctrine. The External and the Internal. A vulgar and a secret One. The first openly taught to all; and the second confined to a select Number.[21]

According to Warburton, the ancient freethinkers recognized religion's tremendous influence on the minds of the people, an insight that inspired their practice of public deception. In Polybius' words, "If indeed one was to frame a Civil Policy only for wise Men, 'tis possible this kind of Institution might not be necessary. But since the Multitude is ever fickle and capricious, . . . there is no way left to keep them in order but by . . . the pompous Circumstance that belongs to such kind of Fictions." As Warburton comments, this wisdom stood as a warning against an increasing "Libertinism, that had spread amongst the People of Condition (who piqued themselves on a Knowledge superior to . . . the People) of regarding themselves, and preposterously teaching others to regard the Restraints of Religion as visionary and superstitious."[22]

In Steele's and Bolingbroke's sense of the word, then, it is only those more rarefied moderns who, following the ancients' example, deserve to be counted as "Free-thinkers" rightly considered.[23] A true freethinker wisely hides his private doubts, striving not to disabuse the credulous of religion's cheats and imposture. In 1711 the Earl of Shaftesbury baldly presented the logic behind this position, observing that among the vulgar "A devil and a hell may prevail where a jail and gallows are thought insufficient."[24] The casual hauteur informing Shaftesbury's remark points to an important and often neglected distinction between mid and late seventeenth-century religious radicalism, and one that will occupy the attention of this book. While the mechanic sectarians coupled their censure of religious tyranny with a republican attack on hierarchical social and political structures more generally, the Restoration and eighteenth-century unbelievers, this book argues, were frequently conservative in their sociopolitical allegiances.

This conservatism, as Shaftesbury's example indicates, led to a revived interest in the ancient practice of the twofold philosophy, for despite its radical skepticism, the notion that religion should be propagated as a pious fraud was fundamentally supportive of a stratified social structure. As Steele suggests in the *Guardian* in 1713, although the educated elite may succeed in controlling their baser passions without the fictions of religion, "the bulk of mankind who have gross understandings . . . and strong passions" are incapable of embracing virtue for its own sake: "the fumes of passion must be allayed, and reason must burn brighter than ordinary, to enable men to see and relish all the native beauties and delights of a virtuous life." Lacking this refinement, the masses, it was thought, require the hope of future rewards and the threat of future punishments to divert them from a life of lust, fraud, and violence. With such practical social considerations in view, many elite freethinkers in the period acknowledged, as Samuel Parker describes, that "Princes may wisely make use of the Fables of Religion to serve their own turns upon the silly Multitude."[25] Precisely because it is the greatest "politick invention" in history, religion, the freethinkers confess, "hath the greatest power to keep the World in awe and order." A "fence" designed wisely "to secure the peace and comfort of the world," religion dupes the vulgar in the service of the greater public good.[26]

II

The tendency for Restoration and eighteenth-century freethinking to resurrect the classical world's concept of the pious fraud begins with two men of quality, Edward Lord Herbert of Cherbury (1583–1648) and Charles Blount (1654–93), separated by the notorious favorite of the gentry, Thomas Hobbes (1588–1679). In two investigations of ancient religion, *De Religione Gentilium* (*The Antient Religion of the Gentiles*) and *A Dialogue between a Tutor and His Pupil*, both published post-humously, Herbert began a reevaluation of ancient religion that profoundly influenced the status of Christianity for the educated religious skeptics of his age. First published in Latin in 1663 and again in 1665 and 1700, *De Religione Gentilium* went through four English editions between 1705 and 1711. Though the first official edition of *A Dialogue* did not appear until 1768, evidence suggests that the work circulated in manuscript form as early as 1680, as well as in several plagiarized versions in three of Blount's freethinking writings.[27] Arguing that the ancient philosophers and wise men were monotheists who practiced a simple religion of virtue and piety, Herbert implies that even Christianity was an unnecessary accretion to this earlier and purer tradition, itself long obscured by the numerous superstitions associated with paganism. According to Herbert, ancient priests and governors conspired to perpetuate religious fictions as a mechanism of social control. Herbert suggests that much of religion colludes with civil power, manipulating the people's credulity to further the authority and advantage of a select few. In his account of the priests' cunning orchestration of pagan oracles, for example, Herbert argues that their supposed revelations tended to represent the agenda of the magistrate, who, in alliance with the priests, used sham auguries to trick the masses into a fatuous deference.[28]

And yet, though the people were frequently abused for corrupt ends, Herbert emphasizes that in some instances they were beguiled by fictions "that might relate to some publick good."[29] Herbert here implicitly defends the twofold philosophy's dictum that wise men should not necessarily seek to demystify the ignorant credulity of the vulgar.[30] Although the religion of the best of the ancients was importantly natural and unrevealed, most wise men "did not so publickly declare themselves" or "openly publish" their views to "the vulgar sort."[31] Indeed it is through a tacit acceptance that fraud can be pious that Herbert comes to understand why so many wise men through the ages seem to have abided by the false doctrines of the priests: "the magistrates, and those of quality," he explains, "might perchance think that the common people could not be well governed, unless first they were so much fooled, as to renounce their understanding, and resign it up wholly to the arbitrement of others."[32]

Given the emphasis on political peace and stability in the doctrine of the pious fraud, it should come as no surprise to discover references in Hobbes to religion's historical status as a stratagem of the State. To contemporaries, Hobbes's definition of religion as "*Feare* of power invisible, feigned by the mind, or imagined from tales publiquely allowed," necessarily entailed the view that all religions, even those useful to the ends of government, "are in reality nothing but Cheats and Impostures."[33] In his *Leviathan*, Hobbes is clearly suspicious of the manifold ways in which rulers appropriate religious discourse to serve their own private ends in governing.[34] And yet he also allows that even those rulers who have manipulated religion as a device of politics "have done it with a purpose to make those men that relyed on them, the more apt to Obedience, Lawes, Peace, Charity, and civill Society."[35] The ancient founders and legislators of commonwealths in particular are not to be blamed if they sought to instill peace and obedience among the people by letting them believe that the state's religion proceeds, not from their invention, "but from the dictates of some God, or other Spirit." Hobbes thus believed in the productive possibilities of religion's fictional power, remarking that "it is with the mysteries of our Religion, as with wholesome pills for the sick, which swallowed whole, have the vertue to cure; but chewed, are for the most part cast up again without effect." Religion's sway, Hobbes here suggests, is effective only as long as its supernatural truths are not pried into, at which point belief ostensibly is no longer possible. The ancients, once again, serve as our model on this point, appreciating religion's unique power to inspire the imagination when they "chose to have the science of justice wrapped up in fables, [rather] than openly exposed to disputations."[36]

Hobbes has long been received as England's most formidable opponent of orthodox religion, yet the writings of Charles Blount, though

frequently dismissed as unoriginal, also served as highly effective pub-
licity for a wide range of radical religious thinking, linking ancient unbelief to modern. Following Herbert and Hobbes, Blount forthrightly
claimed that it was political tyrants who first "made the Idol" and the
priestly class who later "ordain'd the worship of it."[37] This was the infamous argument of Spinoza, a favorite source for Blount's radicalism,
who declared in the preface to his *Tractatus Theologico-Politicus* that
"the supreme mystery of despotism, its prop and stay, is to keep men in
a state of deception, and with the specious title of religion to cloak the
fear by which they must be held in check, so that they will fight for their
servitude as if for salvation." Needless to say, Spinoza did not hesitate
to proclaim that the use of religion as policy was "incompatible with
the freedom of the people" and thus a reprehensible strategy to attempt
in any free commonwealth.[38] On this view, to practice any form of religious fraud or twofold philosophy was to surrender to the perfidy of
priestcraft.

In his *Great Is Diana of the Ephesians* (1680), however, an attack
upon heathen sacrifice that covertly held up ancient freethinking philosophy against both pagan superstition and Christianity, Blount asserts that
"Our Saviour himself found how improper it was to unfold his Sacred
Mysterys to the ignorant Multitude." Indeed, upon closer inspection,
Blount admits that "the wisest among the Heathens followd this Rule in
their Converse, Loquendum cum vulgo, sentiendum cum sapientibus; &
si mundus vult decipi, decipiatur" (One must speak with the multitude,
think with the wisemen, and if the world wants to be deceived, let it be
deceived). Blount's *Oracles of Reason* (1693), a collection of writings in
support of natural religion, argued similarly that it was possible to "pay
a just deference to the Church, and yet at the same time raise scruples
for information sake." On the one hand, Blount clearly scorns the way
in which religion has functioned historically as "a political Trick for the
Convenience of Government and Humane Life," deriding the defenders
of the faith as "Whole-sale Merchants of Credulity." On the other hand,
he commends Pliny's comment that belief in divine Providence, while ridiculous, is nonetheless useful to life ("Ridiculum est agere curam rerum
humanarum, Quicquid est Summum; sed credi usui est Vitae").[39]

While the contributions of these first fathers of elite unbelief are examined in the ensuing pages, my primary focus will be on the ways
in which their ancient biases in religion were taken up by the literary
culture of the period. Inspired by the writings of Herbert, Hobbes, and
Blount, among others, the writers this project examines shared a propensity to look to the political and social function of religion in the
classical past as a model for how Christianity might operate in the mod-

ern age. Indispensable to their freethinking initiative was the general revival of classical learning that began in the Renaissance and reached its culmination in the literary classicism of the Restoration and eighteenth century. Among historians, the early moderns' elevation of classical philosophy and literature is seen to be a vital precursor to "intellectual irreligion." The recovery of ancient skepticism was a crucial component of this development.[40] Beginning in the sixteenth century with the first Latin translations of the writings of Sextus Empiricus, ancient skepticism found a notably receptive audience in sophisticated and educated circles of the Renaissance, leading the way for the skeptical efflorescence of the seventeenth century.[41] For many contemporaries, indeed, the greater part of ancient philosophy exhibited signs of a dangerous skepticism. Daniel Whitby argues that "for the Heathen Philosophers, let it be noted . . . that among the generality of them, all things were counted dubious and uncertain; the common issue of their search after their Duty to God and Man, and the foundation on which they do entirely depend, was mostly Scepticism, and the most knowing Men were they who did renounce all knowledge of them."[42]

Skepticism's implications for orthodox religion were notoriously ambiguous. Since Pyrrho, the initial founder of the Greek sect, had taught that the search for knowledge was vain and futile and that reason was incapable of discovering truth or moral certainty, the Christian skeptic was forced to accept his religion on faith alone. Though some did so with genuine piety, others, following Averroës' notion of a double truth, submitted to ecclesiastical authority out of compliance to skepticism's unyielding dictum that the wise man (precisely because he cannot know with certainty) will conform to the official worship of his country.[43] Though skepticism's emphasis on the inviolability of the laws and customs governing religious practice would seem to ensure proper religious observance and mitigate transgression, for Whitby and others, its rejection of certain knowledge could only "weaken all Piety and Holiness . . . ; for if we cannot perceive what is so, if, as to these things, we are wholly in the dark . . . what reason can we have to be Pious, Just, or Virtuous?"[44] It is in this way, then, that the legacy of ancient skepticism, like much of Restoration and eighteenth-century freethinking more generally, was simultaneously radical—linked closely, for example, to the libertine movement of the late seventeenth century—and deeply traditionalist.[45] That skepticism made religion a matter, at best, of faith and not reason is itself an enduring paradox in the history of secularization.

Orthodox contemporaries, indeed, universally registered the anxiety that, however incomparable the ancients were in the domain of the arts, their religious attitudes were theologically suspect and not to be imitated. Thomas Sprat, for example, bemoans the tendency among his generation to mimic the "Fatal condition . . . of the Ancient World" by limiting religion to a show of outward conformity. Though in public, both ancient and modern freethinkers might "observ[e] [religion's] Rules with much solemnity, . . . in privat [they] regarded it not at all."[46] Hobbesian materialism was often seen as a revival of the ancient heresy that conflated nature and the divine. As Robert Boyle attests, "Even in these times there is lately sprung up a sect of men, as well professing Christianity as pretending to philosophy, who . . . do very much [sympathize] with the ancient heathens, and talk much indeed of God, but mean such a one as is not really distinct from the animated and intelligent universe." In a sermon of 1696, Richard Bentley also decries the classical leanings of the gentlemanly unbelievers, insisting that "the whole body of these Men's Religion is no more than what even Heathens attain'd to: the modern Deism being the very same with old Philosophical Paganism." Daniel Waterland similarly asserts that the freethinkers "have Pagan Historians to rest their Faith upon, instead of Moses and the Evangelists," and "Pagan Morals to answer to the divine Sermon on the Mount."[47]

Warburton's *Divine Legation of Moses* argues that "the heathen philosophers of our times" are "displeased to see their ancient brethren shown for knaves in practice, and fools in theory." The freethinkers, he explains, inveigh against Christianity's censure of classical philosophy as "a condemnation of human learning in general."[48] It will be my argument that among the period's intelligentsia, the classical influences long said to inform the literature and intellectual life of the period could lead, as contemporaries suspected, to a dangerous tendency to distrust revealed religion.[49] The celebrated English "ancient," Sir William Temple, provides a useful example.[50] In his "Essay upon the Ancient and Modern Learning" (1690), Temple makes clear that his preference for all things ancient is inspired by the absence of religious strife in the classical world. The inadequacies of the modern age are thus the inevitable product of "the abyss of disputes about matters of religion" from the Reformation onwards. When religion is a matter of private faith and revelation, as it is in modern Christianity, it is difficult, Temple implies, to avoid the "violent heats" and "litigious quarrels" over doctrine that have characterized religious politics in the modern age.[51]

In a veiled critique of Christian revelation, Temple suggests in his "Observations upon the United Provinces of the Netherlands" (1673) that the honor of a religion, on the contrary, is not diminished if it has been "planted in a country by secular means." By emphasizing the secular over the spiritual uses of religion, Temple indicates his approval of the ancients' propensity to conceive religion in terms of its civil efficacy for the state, an efficacy greatly undermined by the seditious enthusiasm unique to the modern Christian world. This preference for religion's public rather than private uses is the more appreciated, he continues, when we recognize that the end of religion is to promote "those manners and dispositions that tend to the peace, order, and safety of all civil societies and governments among men." The modern sectarians that the world calls "religious men" are consequently misguided to "put so great weight upon those points of belief which men never have agreed in," thereby inciting civil strife and faction.[52] Temple here implies that religion's proper function is not to provide transcendental truths but rather to foster social and political cohesion in the state. This was the laudable wisdom of ancient theology, which tended to worship as Gods "the first authors of any good and well instituted civil government in any country, by which the native inhabitants were reduced from savage and brutish lives to the safety and convenience of societies."[53] National religion and civil policy, on this view, were one and the same. What is more, although the vulgar of the ancient civilizations were frequently idolaters, the fact that religious worship was fundamentally oriented around the prosperity and stability of the commonwealth meant that religion was not the divisive force that it had become in modernity. Temple's writings on the superiority of ancient civilizations make clear as well that the educated classes were free from the gross superstitions of the masses.[54] Invoking the tradition of the pious fraud so central to Bolingbroke's and Steele's accounts of freethinking, Temple upholds the necessity of religion as an agent of social control for the ignorant, while endorsing the skeptical unbelief of intellectuals through the ages.

Current work on the reception of the classics has done much to dispel the long-held view that to revere the ancients was to be stodgily reactionary in letters, philosophy, and politics.[55] And yet, while recent accounts of freethinking in the period have emphasized the importance of the classical tradition to radical writers from Harrington to Toland to Walter Moyle, the literary tradition remains unexamined.[56] This oversight stems in part from the tendency to divorce aesthetics from the broader context of classical thought.[57] Dryden and Pope, for example, may have translated Virgil and Homer respectively and imitated the satires of Horace, but their reverence of the ancients is seen to end with literary influences. Swift seems to suggest as much when he refers in a letter of 1723 to Pope's involvement "in an Art where Faction has nothing to do." Since "Virgil . . . and Horace are equally read by Whigs and Toreys," Pope has "no more to do with the Constitution of Church and State than a Christian at Constantinople."[58]

However, as Pope's *Essay on Man* suggests, by 1733–34 his interest

in the classical past was vastly more wide-ranging. In a letter to Swift
six years later, Pope describes the poem as "a system of *Ethics* in the
Horatian way," a characterization that importantly stresses the nonliter-
ary content of the poem's classicism.[59] What is more, this emphasis on
ancient ethics and morality not coincidentally provoked a mild firestorm
of protest over the poem's perceived neglect of revealed religion. Indeed,
as I argue in the concluding chapter, it was Pope perhaps more than any
other English "radical" whose perceived deism garnered the endorsement
of the French *philosophes*, linking England to the continental freethinking movement of the later eighteenth century. Famously regarding the
Christian dispensation as outside of its plan, *An Essay on Man* advocates
a common and wholly natural religion of conduct that would rise above
the sectarian animosities of modern Christianity:[60]

> For Modes of Faith, let graceless zealots fight;
> His can't be wrong whose life is in the right:
> In Faith and Hope the world will disagree,
> But all Mankind's concern is Charity:
> All must be false that thwart this One great End,
> And all of God, that bless Mankind or mend.[61]

Like Pope's, Dryden's literary classicism also betrays evidence of a
broader commitment to the intellectual life of the ancient world, particularly early in his career. In his play *Tyrannick Love* (1670), set in the time
of the Roman Empire, a Christian saint appears successfully to convert
a heathen philosopher from a natural religion of virtue to Christianity,
though only through convincing the latter that Christianity's promise
to reward virtue in the next life leads to the stricter practice of morality
in this one. Louis Bredvold points out that the saint thus persuades the
pagan to embrace Christianity without ever calling upon revealed religion, a detail that asks us to question the authenticity of the conversion.[62]
As a result of this emphasis on the utility as opposed to the transcendent
character of religious truth, the pagan's invocation of religion's "pleasing fables" is equally applicable to his new religion: "In all religions, . . .
there are / Some solid truths, and some things popular."[63]

In his preface to the play, Dryden similarly claims not so much an
intrinsic faith as a respectful reverence for the religion that he publicly
professes and to which "all men, who desire to be esteemed good or honest, are obliged." His "outward Conversation," he insists, "shall never
be justly taxed with the Note of Atheism or Prophaneness."[64] Though
Dryden's later writings drop reference to the ancient practice of the pious
fraud, they continue to emphasize religion's political uses. As Steven
Zwicker observes of Dryden's Horatian "Religio Laici" (1683), "At the

poem's close we discover that 'common quiet' and not salvation is mankind's concern."[65] It is arguable that Dryden's conversion to Catholicism in 1685, perhaps paradoxically to some, was inspired by precisely this political emphasis on civil stability, for the Anglican Church, as figured in his elusive poem "The Hind and the Panther" (1687), fails adequately to control the subversive potential of private judgment.

III

My case studies of English freethinking begin with an examination of Restoration libertinism as exemplified by the Earl of Rochester and Aphra Behn. Typically, studies of the Restoration libertines, most of whom were skeptics in their religious biases, have been removed from examinations of freethinking. This is partly due to the critical emphasis on sexuality over religion in much of current criticism; trends in Restoration scholarship have inclined to privilege sexual libertinism over its religious variants. By joining the libertine traditions of Rochester and Behn to the larger initiative of English freethinking, the first part of the book aims to broaden our sense of the significance of libertinism beyond the precinct of the sexual. Libertinism, I hope to show, had more philosophical and theological complexity than tends to be appreciated. Indeed, it is arguable that one reason for the dearth of studies of English freethinking in the literary tradition is critics' propensity to neglect libertinism's contribution to the critique of religion in the period. Though studies of Restoration England generally understand libertinism to signify promiscuous or free sexuality, in the period the term also denoted a challenge to orthodox religion. According to the *Oxford English Dictionary* (*OED*), "libertinism" indicates "the views or practice of a libertine in religious matters; freedom of opinion or non-recognition of authority as to religion; freethinking." The sexual definition then follows: "disregard of moral restraint, especially in relations between the sexes; licentious or dissolute practices or habits of life."[66] One recent critic has argued that the sexual meaning "is of course the one we now apply . . . when we describe the literature of Rochester and his circle," but this assumption is likely anachronistic.[67] A full and historically accurate appreciation of the phenomenon called libertinism thus requires that we take its religious facets into account. Once we do this, a new sense of the writers connected to this tradition emerges. Indeed, as I argue, Rochester's and Behn's freethinking religious tendencies are perhaps more central to their thought and writing than their libertine critique of Christian sexual morality.

Recent criticism has thus been almost exclusively concerned, in one form or another, with Rochester's bawdy verse, his explicit, often obscene, depictions of sexual acts.[68] And yet the poem his age knew best, "A Satyre against Reason and Mankind," is the least lewd in Rochester's canon and seriously engaged with the freethinking critique of orthodox Christianity. Attentive, to be sure, to his infamous carryings-on with wine, women, and boys, the poet's own generation was even more focused on the religious libertinism from which the former behavior was perceived as inextricable. This feature of Rochester's libertinism is most apparent and most fully articulated in the "Satyre," a verse satire modeled on the classical example of Horace, which circulated in clandestine manuscript until its first broadside edition of 1679.[69] To many contemporaries, religious libertinism developed as a necessary defense of sinful living; the Anglican divine John Tillotson observed that "Men of dissolute lives cry down Religion, because they would not be under the restraints of it."[70] In a certain sense, however, such a view was merely an earlier version of the modern tendency to give sexuality precedence over theology and philosophy. In exploring the freethinking that fueled Rochester's most widely read poem, Chapter One argues not only that Rochester's religious stance deserves an attention it has not yet received, but also that his condemnation of religion, evident also in his conversations with Burnet, is less starkly iconoclastic than it initially seems. An examination of the "Addition" to the "Satyre," particularly, reveals that Rochester's religious doubt is closer to the conservative skepticism of Swift than we have previously recognized.[71] His classicism in religion, I suggest—manifest in his "Satyre against Reason and Mankind" and also in his translations from Seneca and his favorite poet, Lucretius—is inextricable from this radically conservative doubt.

If the theological aspects of Rochester's libertinism have been neglected in scholarship, discussions of Aphra Behn's connections to English freethinking are almost nonexistent.[72] For some time, critics have attempted to reconcile Behn's staunch royalism with her progressive view of gender relations, but in the eyes of contemporaries, her religious libertinism was a far more threatening royalist bedfellow.[73] Behn's biographer, Janet Todd, suggests that Behn was not aware of any incompatibility between the two: "Behn seems to have felt she could be daring in religion without impinging on politics, so that destabilising the Christian God did not necessarily destabilise Charles II."[74] As I argue, freethinking in the Restoration began as a reaction against the religious zeal of the Civil War sectarians, whose godliness served as the legitimating agent of their revolutionary doctrine. In its early stages at least, religious skepticism could thus function as a marker of one's allegiance to the monarchy in opposition to the parliamentarian cause. It is unclear, then, to what extent royalism was fueled by political allegiance to traditional monarchal authority, and to what extent by resistance to the perceived alternative—religious fanaticism.[75]

Chapter Two examines evidence of Behn's religious skepticism in many of her best-known works, including her pastoral poem "The Golden Age" (1684); her play *The Rover* (1677); and her novels *Oroonoko* (1688) and *Love-Letters between a Nobleman and His Sister* (1684–87). Behn's attraction to freethinking is complicated, I argue, by her sense that religious heterodoxy is inextricably bound up with male attempts at sexual conquest. Behn thus insists that we bring an awareness of gender politics to our assessment of freethinking doctrine, asking us to proceed cautiously in dismantling the traditional categories of love and faith. This caution, however, is itself always informed by a prior skepticism, one that leads her by the end of her career to explore the philosophy of freethinking as separate from the critique of Christian sexual morality. Her much-neglected translations of two iconoclastic works by the French philosopher Bernard de Fontenelle—*Entretiens sur la pluralité des mondes* (1686) and *L'histoire des oracles* (1687)—provide her with this opportunity and form the central subjects of the chapter. *A Discovery of New Worlds* and *The History of Oracles* both appeared in 1688, the latter anonymously. The former included a preface that tackled disquieting questions about the relationship between materialism, Enlightenment science, and Christian theology.

Summarizing the content of Fontenelle's *Entretiens*, Behn asserts boldly that Fontenelle "ascribes all to Nature, and says not a Word of God Almighty, . . . so that one would almost take him to be a Pagan."[76] While such a remark would appear to indicate Behn's criticism of Fontenelle's thoroughgoing materialism, what follows comprises a stealthy refutation of revealed religion. Central to this covert denial, however, is Behn's adherence to the twofold philosophy. The initiated know that Scripture speaks in allegories designed to inspire the vulgar and encourage their obedience. Miracles can be explained according to natural laws, but the function of religion is not to teach philosophy. In order to foster public virtue and morality, then, the knowing must respect the decrees of the Church, despite their skepticism regarding revelation. This inclination to support the institution of religion on pragmatic as opposed to spiritual grounds, as an unparalleled source of social stability, draws from the ancients' sense of religion as a practice that one performs (rather than believes in) for the greater good of the public. Behn's translation of the more radical *Oracles* served as her entry into the world of ancient theology. The debate over the oracles was itself an offshoot of freethinking's fascination with ancient religion generally, a fascination that Behn evidently shared, and that linked her to Herbert of Cherbury's *De Religione Gentilium*, the several writings of Charles Blount, and the later critique of the spirit in Swift's *Tale of a Tub*.

♉

The second part of the book turns to an extended examination of Jonathan Swift's writings on religion. Though Swift faced intense charges of heterodoxy and impiety in the reception of his *Tale of a Tub* (1704), the dominant tradition of Swift criticism continues to take his defense of his orthodoxy in the "Apology" of 1710 at face value. In chapters Three and Four, I argue that Swift's theology was simultaneously skeptical of revelation and the supernatural and supportive of the social and political utility of Christianity. To be sure, Swift condemns the unbelievers' view that religion was a purely human invention, particularly when such a view informs their conviction that religion functions as a corrupt fraud. In this view, religion was "a Creature of Politics," invented by legislators "to mislead the Vulgar and Prophane (as they are pleased to term them) into a Blind Implicit Obedience."[77] Swift indeed parodies this position in his preface to "Mr. Collins's Discourse of Free-Thinking" (1713), in which his freethinking narrator explains that "Crafty designing Men, that they might keep the World in Awe, have, in their several Forms of Government, placed a Supream Power on Earth, to keep human Kind in fear of being Hanged; and a Supream Power in Heaven, for fear of being Damned."[78]

In the freethinkers' wily hands, Swift emphasizes, the argument that religion was a political invention necessarily leads to a wholesale rejection of Christianity, including its ethics and morality.[79] The libertine narrator of "An Argument against Abolishing Christianity" (1708) suggests this trajectory when he famously asks, "For, of what Use is Freedom of Thought, if it will not produce Freedom of Action; which is the sole End, how remote soever, in Appearance, of all Objections against Christianity?" (2:38; see also 2:70). Impersonating Collins's heterodoxy in "Mr. Collins's Discourse," Swift's narrator declares with grim irony that "There is not the least hurt in the wickedest Thoughts, . . . nor in telling those Thoughts to every Body, and endeavouring to convince the World of them; for all this is included in the Doctrine of *Free-thinking*" (4:30).

Much of the critical resistance to the idea that Swift harbored a radical religious skepticism thus stems understandably from his numerous writings against religious radicals of all kinds. How could Swift have been an unbeliever when he wrote such passionate condemnations of

freethinkers? Part of this dilemma results from the complexities in terminology indicated by Steele's and Bolingbroke's writings on freethinking. Both imply, as I have suggested, that there are virtuous as well
as depraved freethinkers. As Bolingbroke comments, the depraved infidels, "by a presumptuous, factious spirit under that of liberty," attempt
to "destroy at once the general influence of religion," while the honest
"Esprit fort" understands that truth must be sought quietly, without
disturbing the minds of the untaught multitude.[80] In his various writings
on freethinking, Swift stresses precisely Bolingbroke's distinction between freethought, strictly speaking, and freedom of speech and action,
making evident that his main contention with the so-called freethinkers of the time is their refusal to separate the former from the latter.
"*Free Thinking* signifies nothing," he satirically observes, "without
Free Speaking and *Free Writing*. It is the indispensable Duty of a *Free
Thinker*, to endeavour *forcing* all the World to think as he does, and by
that means make them *Free Thinkers* too" (4:36). With those, on the
contrary, who are "so wise as to keep their sentiments to themselves," he
importantly has no problem (4:49). Like Bolingbroke, Swift emphasizes
indeed that men should be free to hold whatever opinions they would in
private, as long as they don't "disturb the public" (9:261). The truth of
religious doctrine, then, is beside the question if its civic endorsement
promotes the interests of morality and religion in general.

In his "Thoughts on Religion," Swift contends that though belief is
private and thus outside of state control, men can and should be forced,
"by interest or punishment, to say or swear they believe, and *to act as if
they believed*" (9:261, italics mine). It is because our thoughts and beliefs
are "the seeds of words and actions," he argues in his "Some Thoughts
on Free-Thinking," that they "must be kept under the strictest regula-
tion." One of the most important and difficult tasks we face as moral
subjects, therefore, is to choose among "the great multiplicity of ideas,
which one's mind is apt to form, . . . those, which are most proper for
the conduct of life" (4:49; see also 9:163–64). Doubt, skepticism, and
unbelief, Swift implies, are a part of what it means to be human and
flawed, and our objective as a society should not be to attempt to control belief, an impossible task in the best of circumstances, but rather
to regulate action. As he admits, unprecedentedly, of his own spiritual
struggles, "I am not answerable to God for the doubts that arise in my
own breast, . . . if I take care to conceal those doubts from others, if I use
my best endeavours to subdue them, and if they have no influence on the
conduct of my life" (9:262).[81]

Those few critics who have continued to find a critique of the spirit in
Swift's writings on religion tend not to connect Swift's more heterodox

theological positions to the broader context of freethinking in the period.[82] Claude Rawson brilliantly examines the "restlessness and doubt" that pervades Swift's work as well as the "self-implicating" tendencies of his critiques of freethinkers and other subversive types, with whom he seems to experience "a kind of sympathetic involvement."[83] In analyzing the notoriously slippery speaker of *A Tale of a Tub*, John Traugott argues similarly that, although he is an irreverent madman whose attitudes we are meant to disavow, "distinctions between Swift and his speaker collapse." With covert intensity, Traugott suggests, Swift "conjures up his repertoire of voices in the *Tale* and speaks his deepest thoughts in their tongues."[84] Though both critics have set the agenda for future students of Swift, requiring that we grapple with his "paradoxical qualities— the strange mixture of institutional piety with a subversive and fundamentally pyrrhonistic imagination"—they have left open the question of whether a larger intellectual tradition, embodying just this paradoxical set of motivations, may have informed Swift's peculiarly radical conservatism.[85] My aim in Chapters Three and Four is to read Swift's mixture of conformity and doubt not so much as an example of idiosyncratic iconoclasm, but rather as definitive of conservative, neoclassical unbelief in the period.[86]

In its concluding chapter, the book moves beyond the particularities of the English experience to consider Britain's links to the continental Enlightenments that follow later in the eighteenth century. My point of connection is Pope's *Essay on Man*, a work whose participation in the European Enlightenment has been greatly underappreciated by modern scholarship. Arguably the most important literary text to come out of the English context for the wider international milieu, Pope's poem, I contend, points up the broader significance of the Tory neoclassical heritage investigated in this book. Taking from the mix of skepticism, antienthusiasm, and naturalism emphasized in Rochester, Behn, and Swift, Pope also moves beyond his predecessors by largely dispensing with the mask of the pious fraud and more explicitly embracing natural religion. It is for this reason, I argue, that *An Essay on Man*, though nurtured in a Tory-radical literary tradition, appealed uniquely to the *philosophes* on the Continent. More philosophically daring than what came before it, the poem articulates an ethical and moral scheme from which Christianity is conspicuously absent. Thanks to the enduring success of William Warburton's defense of Pope against charges of irreligion and impiety, the freethinking implications of his great philosophical poem remain unexamined.

The chapter shows how the continental reception of *An Essay on Man* illustrates England's unique role in the European Enlightenment—both as a noteworthy and early participant in its own right and as a tradition with distinct limits to its radicalism. Upon its translation in the mid 1730s, the poem generated an outcry among the French religious establishment, providing an occasion for Voltaire to hone the French freethinking platform in response to its critics. Whereas Pope's French attackers complained that his deistic credo, "Whatever IS, is RIGHT," opened the door to Spinozist fatalism and libertine immorality, Voltaire insisted, rather, that its more apposite failure was an inability to contend responsibly—both socially and politically—with the problem of evil in the world. Pope's deism rejects the notion of special Providence (miracles and other spectacular divine interventions for the advantage of man), but his theodicy continues to affirm the existence of a general Providence—understood as God's necessary and immutable laws, established at the Creation. For Voltaire, however, the existence of evil, upon consideration, forces us to confront the likelihood that the universe operates wholly at random, without the benefit of even the most general divine superintendence. Such is the conclusion reached in *Candide* (1759), a recognition that motivates the *philosophes'* turn away from England's perceived quietism in favor of a radical attempt to make man a productive agent in a world devoid of supernatural order.

IV

Current historiography on freethinking and skeptical religion in the English Enlightenment is marked by a proclivity to concentrate on the radical, republican heritage of the seventeenth century, and literary scholarship has largely followed suit. Contemporary polemics, I contend, belie this bias on several counts, calling into question the supposedly skeptical tendencies of the sectarians as well as commonplace associations between religious doubt and the lower classes. Indeed, by most accounts, freethinking, in all its manifestations, was seen to be a phenomenon peculiar to the Restoration, a direct reaction against the perceived fanaticism (not atheism) of the Civil War sects, and, importantly, most prevalent among the upper ranks of society.[87]

Beginning in the 1660s, Anglican apologetics reveal an important shift in the character of religious heterodoxy from the previous era. Whereas the threat of the Civil Wars and Interregnum had come from plebeian religious enthusiasm and its strong ties to republican politics, the Restoration and early eighteenth century appeared to face "a new Generation of Atheists risen up" among the privileged and educated classes. In one of the first didactic pamphlets devoted to this development, Clement Ellis contends that "an Atheist and a Gentleman in the

opinion of many, have for a long time been either Synonymous, or at
least Convertible termes."[88] Not limited to the strict nobility, freethinking tendencies, described variously as atheism, libertinism, freethinking,
and deism, were seen, moreover, as "the Blemish of these Inquisitive
Times."[89] Increased knowledge and cosmopolitanism, in other words,
purportedly encouraged the view among educated sophisticates that religious belief was "the mere Effect of Credulity and Ignorance" and, therefore, an affront to the discernment of men of wit and understanding.[90]

Though contemporary theological polemic was admittedly alarm-
ist about what it perceived as an epidemic of elite religious skepticism,
it nonetheless betrays a shift in cultural anxiety (from enthusiasm to
skepticism) that tells us something about how the period understood
the legacy of the revolutions of the 1640s. Rather than seeing freethinking as an organic extension of seventeenth-century religious radicalism,
contemporaries appeared to blame Restoration freethinking on the destructive example of the midcentury sects. In his *History of the Royal
Society* (1667), Thomas Sprat claims that while "the fierceness of *violent
Inspirations*" is largely spent in England, whatever remains of it "will
be soon chac'd out of the World, by the remembrance of the terrible
footsteps it has every where left behind it." The present escalation of
incredulity, he continues, represents a backlash phenomenon, responding to "the late extravagant excesses of *Enthusiasm*": "The infinit pre-
tences to *Inspiration*, and *immediate Communion with God*, that have
abounded in this *Age*, have carry'd several men of wit so far, as to reject
the whole matter."[91] Reflecting in 1712 on the English tendency toward
"Bashfulness in every thing that regards Religion," Addison posits the
same explanation for the infidelity of his age. Targeting "Those Swarms
of Sectaries that over-ran the Nation in the time of the great Rebellion,"
Addison contends that their "Jargon of Enthusiasm" caused "the Restoration Men" to recoil from the "Behaviour and Practice of those Persons,
who had made Religion a Cloak to so many Villanies."[92]

How do we explain this apparent discrepancy between the contemporary perception of the origin of modern unbelief in England and the view
of recent historiography? Looking back on the early stages of freethought
in England, Philip Skelton suggests that while "libertinism" in religion
began in earnest at the Restoration, there may have been some inchoate
stirrings among the sectarians:

Libertinism had no considerable footing in England before Cromwell's time, when
it was covered, down to the very cloven foot of contradictory absurdities, in the
long cloak of cant, hypocrisy, and enthusiasm. During this dark and stormy night
of troubled dreams, Hobbes set up a standard for Deism, or rather Atheism; to
which in a little time resorted all such as were willing to think there was nothing

more in religion than hypocrisy or fanaticism. These sort of men in the reign of Charles the Second, which was the reign of luxury and debauchery, taking that to be religion, which had worn such a fool's coat in the preceding times of confusion, made a jest of all religion.[93]

Like Sprat and Addison, Skelton attributes the emergence of unbelief to the critique of fanaticism and religious hypocrisy, associated here with Hobbes. While this movement is seen to coalesce in the debauched and skeptical court of Charles II, Skelton suggests that an inchoate, even covert, version of religious libertinism can indeed be detected in the preceding decades, though mixed up and "covered" with "cant, hypocrisy, and enthusiasm." Historians, it seems, have seized upon these incipient traces of mid-seventeenth-century irreligion, noting in particular the anticlerical character of the sects, their criticism of the Bible, their suspicion that religion was a political ruse to subjugate the masses, and their skepticism about heaven, hell, and future rewards and punishments.[94]

Though these heterodoxies indeed became definitive of late seventeenth-century freethinking, some important differences tend to be overlooked. As Jonathan Scott argues, "religion was the umbilical cord by which the radical groups were born into the world and remained to some extent connected." Robert Zaller points out that the sectarians' "radical disaffection" was from organized religion, not belief itself, and it thus continued to express itself in religious, even millenarian, terms.[95] Their anticlericalism and antiscripturism, for example, made way for the enthusiastic tenet that the spirit dwelled in all men. Gerrard Winstanley, the man who according to Christopher Hill "carried the attack on existing religion the furthest," also believed that God "dwells every where" and thus "manifests himselfe in mankinde."[96] The radicals who scoffed at Scripture and priests did so, in other words, because God was within them, thereby rendering intermediaries such as the clergy and the Bible unnecessary and corrupting of one's private relationship with the divine. Definitive of midcentury radicalism, then, as Scott submits, is "the very passion of [the radicals'] religious convictions—the value they set on their personal relationship with God." Traditional external authorities were pushed aside in favor of a fervent individualism of religious experience.[97]

Whereas the sectarians, however heterodox, were thus "extreme spiritualists," seeking to make "the distance between the human and the divine much smaller than before," the late seventeenth-century freethinkers, on the contrary, aimed to increase that distance to the point that the divine presence in the Creation was virtually nil. As several historians of religion have argued, the question comes down to the often-slippery distinction between heresy and unbelief, between heterodoxy within Christianity and a rejection of the truth of the spirit *tout court*.[98] David

Wooton suggests that the Reformation was a pivotal precursor to the genesis of unbelief precisely because it emphasized "an interior personal commitment, and not merely an outward conformity and attendance at Church ceremonies." It was at this moment, then, that the beginning of "a new preoccupation with faith" emerged, allowing "the unbeliever to be distinguished for the first time from the heretic."[99]

This important distinction between the heretic who revolts against orthodox belief and the unbeliever who lacks faith is critical to a right understanding of the history of religious radicalism in England. It is crucial, moreover, to our assessment of the argument that Restoration and eighteenth-century unbelief was a logical extension of radical sectarianism. According to Wooton's taxonomy, the sectarians of the mid seventeenth century were heretics rather than unbelievers. Although they flagrantly bucked conformity to Anglican rituals and practice, their private faith remained vital, despite its heterodox character. For Wooton, unbelief is thus marked not so much by the degree of one's rejection of the teachings of the church as by the character of one's internal commitment to religion.[100] Indeed, he leaves open the possibility that an unbeliever could well be one who was nominally conformist in his practice, though still deeply skeptical in his private thoughts. As it turns out, Wooton argues, unbelief frequently coexists with "a political commitment to the preservation of religion," for without the assurance of a divine authority, "the state loomed larger in the mind of the unbeliever as the only defensible bastion of order."[101]

Wooton acknowledges, to be sure, that unbelief is also linked to political and social radicalism in the early modern period, as was clearly the case in France.[102] Yet in England, particularly in the late seventeenth century, religious skepticism, far from entailing a republican irreverence for monarchy, often went hand-in-hand with support for an absolutist state.[103] The strange alliance between skeptical unbelief and political conservatism is perhaps best exemplified by a satirical "autobiographical" account of Charles II's infamous conversion to Catholicism:

and though it should be true what I have learned from my Tutor *Hobbs*, (and am indeed inclin'd to believe) *that all Religion is but a Trick of State to keep the People in obedience*; yet a Profession of Religion is necessary for a Prince as well as others, according to *Machiavel's* Maxim, *Plebem dum vis fallere, singe Deum*: and certainly that Religion of which it is a Fundamental Principle, that *Ignorance is the Mother of Devotion*, is most agreeable to a Prince who would maintain or advance his Prerogative: for where it is allowed, as amongst all Protestants, to examine the Dictates of their Ghostly Fathers, in relation to the Church, it must unavoidably follow, that the People will also claim the like Privilege to canvass the Orders of their Civil Fathers, in relation to the State.[104]

With its emphasis on implicit faith as opposed to rational belief, Catholicism, in contrast to Protestantism, puts a premium on obedience and conformity, and is thus Charles's religion of choice. The fact that Charles is seen to choose his religious affiliation out of motives of political expediency rather than authentic belief, however, is the apposite point, for since *all* religion, Catholicism included, is "but a Trick of State," the savvy ruler will ally himself with the one most conducive to a docile populace.[105]

Current historiography on eighteenth-century freethinking has picked up on this conservative element in the tradition by showing the extent to which religion is reformed rather than jettisoned by the English radicals. Several historians have recently argued that freethinkers strived to purge religion of priestcraft (ecclesiastical tyranny) and unnecessary recourse to mysteries and the supernatural, with the aim of serving the moral and ethical interests of an enlightened state.[106] The English freethinkers, on this view, are once again the inheritors of a republican, Commonwealth tradition dating back to the mid-seventeenth-century sectarians. J. G. A. Pocock argues, for example, that in James Harrington's millenarian republic of Christ, "the magistrate took precedence over the priest, and the clergy could lay claim to no authority, even at the point where their mission expressed most perfectly the union of God with man, which did not come to them from the political relations between men."[107] To suggest otherwise would be to flout the Revolution's principles by reestablishing a hierarchy of elites. Pocock points out, however, that this privileging of the political over the spiritual and other-worldly, though necessary to a republican vision, also existed in tension with the "saints of the inner light," who tended to assert the authority of private judgment and private spirituality over *any* secular authority, whether kings or parliaments.[108] In this sense, then, seventeenth-century republicanism's championing of the ancient tradition of "civil religion," or religion in which private conscience and personal faith were made subservient to the political needs of the state, was an ambivalent one, always in potential conflict with its spiritual commitments. It is significant, then, that the figure in the period perhaps most famous for subordinating theology to the state was the notorious arch-absolutist Thomas Hobbes.[109]

Identified in Philip Skelton's *Ophiomaches: or, Deism Revealed* as the first in England to distinguish himself "as a successful adversary to religion," Hobbes was the target of the vast majority of attacks on atheism from the 1650s through the early decades of the Restoration.[110] His commitment to the civil function of religion, moreover, grew out of his animus against fanaticism and sectarianism in religion. As J. M. Robertson argues, "It is in fact by way of a revolt against all theological ethic, as demonstrably a source of civil anarchy, that Hobbes formulates

a strictly civic or legalist ethic, . . . rejecting all supernatural illumina-
tion of the conscience."[111] Like Harrington, Hobbes derives his model for
civil religion from classical antiquity, referring in *De Cive* to the peaceful "golden age" of the ancients, when "subjects did not measure what
was just by the sayings and judgements of private men, but by the laws
of the realm."[112] Since classical Greek and Roman religion was a wholly
practical and performative activity, centered on public rituals rather than
private and subjective states of consciousness, "their several civil laws
were the rules whereby not only righteousness and virtue, but also . . .
the external worship of God, was ordered and approved."[113] For the ancients, in other words, religion, piety, and belief were not distinguishable
from politics and practice: "in all Common-wealths of the Heathen, the
Soveraigns . . . had the name of Pastors of the People." There was no
danger of enthusiastic sectarianism of the kind that plagued the English
Commonwealth.[114] Hobbes and other conservatives thus had good reason for looking back to the ancients for a concept of religion in which the
claims of politics mandate those of the spirit.

What is more, Hobbes was alert to precisely those tensions between
state and spirit that plagued the sectarian commonwealthmen. In his
Leviathan, he argues that the republicans of his day were wrong to uphold the ancient republics of Greece and Rome as sympathetic to their
own political visions. Their mistake rests on a misunderstanding of the
meaning of liberty and a failure to distinguish between "Private Inheritance" and what is "the right of the Publique only." "The Libertie," he
explains, "whereof there is so frequent, and honourable mention, in the
Histories, and Philosophy of the Antient Greeks, and Romans, and in
the writings, and discourse of those that from them have received all
their learning in the Politiques, is not the Libertie of Particular men; but
the Libertie of the Common-wealth."[115] Hobbes hereby makes classical republicanism both consistent with his own defense of monarchism
and wholly inconsistent with the sectarian nonconformity of his more
radical contemporaries; for as Warburton points out in his own discussion of civil religion among the ancients, when religion becomes "one
of the most necessary and essential Parts of the Civil Policy, we are not
to wonder that it should become an universal Maxim . . . that every
one should conform to the Religion of his Country." The Hobbesian
tradition of freethought, then, was particularly well suited to produce a
theory of civil religion free from the difficulties posed by enthusiasm. Indeed, to the extent that the sectarians frequently emphasized systems of
faith, however heretical, over systems of practice, the later freethinkers'
privileging of the notion of a utilitarian, largely natural "civil religion"
is uneasily linked to a heritage of enthusiastic belief.[116]

As this book aims to demonstrate, the project to adapt religion to serve the needs of the modern state is importantly informed by the genteel unbelief of the Restoration and eighteenth century, whose commitment to civil religion and its agent, the pious fraud or "twofold philosophy," was motivated by its horror of fanaticism—both enthusiastic and papist. Even the freethinking republican John Toland makes clear that "all the *religious Liberty*, that is any where now a Days to be met with," has derived not from the radical efforts of "spirit-haunted Enthusiasts" but rather from the wisdom of those politicians and "Men in Power" who have "stud[ied] the Safety of the Republick, and the common Good of Mankind." Whereas the former are to be blamed for "Feuds, Animosities, [and] Mutinies," the latter oppose themselves to "Debates and Parties" and are thus responsible for "the great Advancement of Letters, Commerce, and Civil Concord."[117]

Pocock and other historians have identified two "distinguishable if overlapping" groups of critical intellectuals in the English Enlightenment: the republican commonwealthmen about whom we have heard much, and a less documented "Tory" fringe of malcontents.[118] Toland's above remarks indicate that these groups may have had more familiar ground than we previously imagined, both manifesting a self-consciousness about the need for religion in a cultural context otherwise marked by disenchantment. Isaac Kramnick's study of "the politics of nostalgia" in the eighteenth century has shown that the commonwealthmen are less simply radical than has been thought, sharing a discontent with the establishment with Bolingbroke's circle, including the Augustan satirists and "the reactionary Tory gentry and intellectuals."[119] As is well known, both groups objected to the corrupt rule of Sir Robert Walpole, England's tyrannical prime minister, who threatened the freedom and liberty of the commonwealth through bribing members of Parliament with place and pensions, suspending frequent parliamentary elections, and generally favoring the interests of the new "monied" men over the gentry and landed interest. The eighteenth-century commonwealthmen, Kramnick argues, exhibit "both a radical Whiggism and a nostalgic conservatism that lashes out at the new economic and social order." This double character, he suggests, is indeed definitive of English radicalism, which retained, however ambivalently, "aristocratic alliances" and allegiances to a hierarchical social order.[120] Though historical analyses of the phenomenon of "Tory radicalism" have generally left religion out of their pictures, recent work on the religious radicalism of the Commonwealth tradition in the eighteenth century has, by turn, failed to acknowledge the place of the Tory intelligentsia.[121] Taking this latter group as its object of study, *The Fringes of Belief* seeks to detail the contribution of four of its constituents to the broader history of freethinking in the English Enlightenment. The elite, often conservative element to unbelief peculiar to the English experience has long been neglected in historiographies of religion, and the project of this book is to demonstrate that literary culture is central to its heritage.

That my investigation of English freethinking ends with an examination of Pope's *Essay on Man* is thus a fitting conclusion to a literary study of the critique of religion in the Enlightenment, for more than any other writer from the English tradition, Pope was the consummate man of letters—England's first professional author and the period's famed poetic virtuoso. Celebrated by Voltaire and other intellectuals as the "*poète-philosophe*," Pope and his great philosophical poem serve as a reminder of the instrumental and still underappreciated role played by English literary culture in European modernity's clash with a religious worldview.

Since E. P. Thompson's lively and aptly named article "The Peculiarities of the English," first published in 1965, scholars of the English tradition have battled against the dominance of the French model of unbelief. And yet, beginning with Arthur Wilson's brave declaration that "the Enlightenment came first to England," the standard lineup of agitators has been steadily expanding: nationally, philosophically, and chronologically. Though the British intelligentsia is increasingly heralded as trailblazers and instigators, recently receiving more extended and careful treatment by historians and critics alike, the *philosophes'* intrepid war against Christianity has nonetheless continued to set the terms of debate.[122] This book attempts to contribute to the larger scholarly effort to redress the long standing absence of scholarship on English freethinking. If much of this recent effort has focused on continuities between the English Commonwealth legacy of the 1650s and the High Enlightenment in eighteenth-century France, my book seeks to complicate this picture by shifting the genealogical emphasis from radical republicanism to radical conservatism. As Thompson observed years ago, "The point is not to rush in to the defense of British intellectual traditions, or to minimize their characteristic limitations. It is to call for a more collected and informed analysis, and one which takes some account of their historic strengths."[123] There is more to be said on all fronts.

PART ONE

Libertine Precursors

CHAPTER ONE

Rochester, Blount,
and the Faith of Unbelief

But he often confessed, that whether the business of Religion was
true or not, he thought those who had the perswasions of it, and
lived so that they had quiet in their Consciences, and believed God
governed in his Providence, and had the hope of an endless blessed-
ness in another State, the happiest men in the World: And said, He
would give all that he was Master of, to be under those Perswasions,
and to have the Supports and Joys that must needs flow from them.
—Gilbert Burnet, *Some Passages of the Life and Death of the
Right Honourable John Earl of Rochester* (1680)

This study begins with a figure few would consider as a defender of
Christianity and institutional religion. Rochester spent his short life as
one of the most notorious infidels of his day, a deathbed conversion to
Christianity notwithstanding. Critics have been divided on how serious
an intellect Rochester was—how much and what he actually read. Most,
however, have agreed that whatever thinking he did was decidedly heterodox, and that his freethinking poem, "A Satyre against Reason and
Mankind," generally thought to have been composed before June 1674,
supplies the evidence. And yet many readers have sensed that despite
surface appearances to the contrary, Rochester's poetry is deeply preoc-
cupied with and ambivalent about matters of faith. James Turner has
astutely noted, for example, that libertinism in Rochester's poetry is frequently "transcended or undermined by some distinctly nonlibertine attitude."[1] Certainly, most recent studies of Rochester's erotic poetry agree,
as Jonathan Kramnick suggests, that "sexuality turns into a drawn out
mistake."[2] Indeed, the poems most noted for their explicit content—"A
Ramble in St. James's Park" and "The Imperfect Enjoyment" among
others—more often than not demonstrate the failure of sex to provide

pleasure or fulfillment. As has been noted, moreover, many of these same poems articulate a longing for love that is only partially ironic or satirically mawkish.[3] If Rochester is not a libertine in quite the ways we have assumed, it is likely the case, as I will argue in this chapter, that he is also not a freethinker as that identity has previously been understood. My concern in these pages will thus be to arrive at some provisional conclusions about the variable content of Rochester's infidelity and to ask how it changes our sense not only of Rochester's attitude toward religion but also of the character of English freethinking more generally.

Resolving the dilemma of Rochester's attitude toward Christian faith requires at the outset that we further examine both the occasion that produced Rochester's "Satyre" and his wider intellectual sympathies. Gillian Manning has contended that the poem participated in an explosion of animated debate about unbelief in the 1670s. Rochester was "one of the chief spokesmen for the unbelievers in their quarrel with the orthodox, and . . . his best-known poem featured prominently in the controversy."[4] Manning's detailed placement of the "Satyre" in its contemporary milieu marks an important turn in scholarship on the poem, for while previous examinations of the poem's heterodoxy have explored its debts to Montaigne and ancient skepticism, Hobbes, and the Epicurean tradition, when pursued, the specific nature of these debts has been only cursorily linked to religion.[5] A proper understanding of Rochester's freethinking, however, requires that we not bracket the range of philosophical texts and traditions to which the "Satyre" alludes from what appear to be its more topical concerns. Making sense of the problem of belief in the poem demands recognition of the interplay between Restoration heterodoxy and the heterodoxy of the philosophical tradition.

The poem begins with a critique of reason that became the defining feature of Restoration infidelity:

> Were I (who to my cost already am
> One of those strange prodigious Creatures Man)
> A spirit free to choose for my own share,
> What case of flesh and blood I pleas'd to wear;
> I'de be a Dog, a Monky, or a Bear.
> Or any thing but that vain Animal
> Who is so proud of being Rational.[6]

$$(1-7)$$

The proposition, it would seem, is logically unacceptable: if the speaker could exercise the defining attributes of man—his rationality and free will—to choose his species, he would essentially decide *against* rationality and free will, for to elect to be a beast rather than a man is to relinquish these specially human attributes. To use reason to oppose reason is the famous paradox upon which the poem seems to hinge. This much has become a critical commonplace. But as both David Trotter and Dustin Griffin have pointed out, paradox had another usage in the seventeenth century, one not so familiar to modern readers. According to the *OED*, paradox also meant "a statement or tenet contrary to received opinion or belief; . . . sometimes with unfavourable connotation, as being discordant with what is held to be established truth." Hobbes used the word in this sense, observing that "a judicious reader knows that a paradox is an opinion not yet generally received." On this account, Trotter observes, "Rochester thought his poem paradoxical . . . in the sense that it defied the *doxa* (or accepted wisdom) of the age." Edward Stillingfleet's response to Rochester's "Satyre," in "A Sermon Preach'd before the King, Feb. 24. 1674/5," makes this latter connotation clear: "It is [a] pitty such had not their wish, *to have been Beasts rather than men,* . . . that they might have been less capable of doing mischief among mankind; by representing all the excellencies of humane nature, which are *Reason,* and *Vertue,* and *Religion,* but as more grave and solemn fopperies."[7]

Most accounts of the poem's immediate context have noted that by the time the "Satyre" was written, the application of reason to religion had become the new Anglican *doxa.*[8] Stillingfleet's remarks thus bring us to another paradox relevant to the content of the poem's freethinking: the peculiar switching of sides that forms the history of "rational religion." As Manning explains, the typical unbeliever was seen to reject Christianity on the grounds that it lacked rational proofs. Moderate theologians therefore attempted to meet the enemy on his own ground by wielding his own weapon—reason—against him.[9] However, the more the orthodox produced rational defenses of Christianity against the doubts of the infidels, the more the infidels rejected reason itself as merely another instance of doctrinal humbug.[10] Referring to Rochester's "Satyre," Stillingfleet expresses the culmination of this predicament thus: "And because it is impossible to defend their extravagant courses by *Reason,* the only way left for them is to make *Satyrical Invectives* against *Reason*; as though it were the most uncertain, foolish and (I had almost said) *unreasonable* thing in the World."[11] In this rendering, the unbelievers' heterodoxy turns out to lie more in their dismissal than in their glorification of the powers of reason.

Late seventeenth-century religious controversy is characterized by a series of unexpected reversals. On one side, moderate or latitudinarian Anglicanism embraced reason, historically associated with the tactics of the unbelievers, while on the other, the infidels abandoned what was now the tool of the church.[12] A related reversal has been left out of this analysis, however. Though initially accused of marshaling reason to the destruction of belief, freethinking's distrust of reason came oddly to resemble an increasingly outmoded fringe of Anglicanism. Indeed, by the 1670s it was largely High Church traditionalists who remained dubious about the place of reason in religion. One unyielding divine protested that his more moderate fellows made "*Reason, Reason, Reason,* their only Trinity." In response to such objections, Joseph Glanvill asked his fustier brethren to "consider . . . what ends of Religion, or Sobriety, such vehement defamations of our faculties could serve? And what Ends of a Party they did?" Like it or not, Glanvill concluded, "the enemies of Reason most usually serve the ends of the Infidel, and the Atheist." Henry Hallywell similarly railed against the "stupidity" of "some who . . . make the choicest of [Religion's] Articles so incomprehensible as to be elevated above Reason . . . : Then which certainly nothing can . . . give greater Ground to the bold Cavils and Pretensions of . . . disguised Atheists."[13] According to the new moderate orthodoxy, then, to rail against reason's part in religion would only play into the hands of the unbelievers.

An "Addition," or in some editions "Epilogue" (lines 174–225), to the main text of Rochester's "Satyre" illustrates this unusual convergence of doubt and traditional belief, revealing a distinct nostalgia for something akin to an outmoded, reason-free faith:[14]

> Is there a Churchman, who on God relies,
> Whose life his Faith and Doctrine justifies;
> Not one blown up with vain Prelatick pride,
>
> 　　　　. . .
>
> But a meek humble Man of honest sense,
> Who Preaching peace does practice Continence;
> Whose pious life's a proof he does believe
> Mysterious Truth's, which no man can conceive.
> If upon Earth there dwell such God-like men,
> I'le here Recant my Paradox to them;
> Adore those Shrines of Virtue, homage pay,
> And with the rabble World, their Laws obey.
>
> 　　　　　　　　(191–93; 216–23)

On one level, readers have been correct not to take the freethinking speaker at his word here.[15] Certainly his intent is still satiric: since the "God-like" churchman represents an impossible ideal, the speaker's offer to "Recant [his] Paradox" is disingenuous and merely aims another jibe at Christian belief. But in another sense, the poem allows Rochester to have it both ways, to recant potentially *and* remain paradoxical in Hobbes's sense of the word. Richard Bentley, whose Boyle Lectures against atheism defined Anglican orthodoxy for the Restoration and early eighteenth century, had proclaimed that "Even Revelation itself is not shy nor unwilling to ascribe its own first Credit and fundamental Authority to the test and testimony of Reason."[16] The "Satyre"'s clerical *adversarius*, who enters the poem in line 46 to rebuke the speaker for "rail[ing] at Reason and Mankind" (58), argues similarly that reason enables man to "Dive into Mysteries, then soaring pierce / The flaming limits of the Universe" (68–69). The pious churchman's modest reverence presents a striking contrast to the arrogant enthusiasm of the clerical *adversarius*, who insolently "Think[s] hee's the Image of the Infinite" (77). The contrary suggestion of the "Addition" that true piety requires belief in "Mysterious Truth's, which no man can conceive," thus continues to set the freethinking speaker apart from the reasonable religion that forms the object of the poem's attack throughout. The speaker can defend faith and still oppose the orthodoxy of the time.[17]

I

My argument about Rochester's belief, to which I will return in the concluding pages of the chapter, first requires a more thorough examination of the nature of his unbelief, for as I will demonstrate, the two are more linked than has previously been recognized. Late seventeenth-century irreligion, as Manning attests, was a slippery entity, referring to a continuum of heterodoxy ranging from agnosticism to evil living to frank disbelief in God.[18] While Manning is correct to suggest that Rochester's "Satyre" speaks for the diversity of irreligion in the period, it is nonetheless necessary to specify Rochester's place along the above continuum more particularly. I will pursue this aim through a reassessment of recent approaches to late seventeenth-century religious radicalism. The first approach I consider, characteristic of the research of Christopher Hill, has been to understand the freethinking of the 1670s as a continuation, in modified form, of the radical sectarianism of the Interregnum. Hill thus sees a link between the sexual and religious libertinism of the Ranters, for example, and that of the Restoration rakes. Hill shrewdly points out that "the legend of gloomy Puritans who hated pleasure dies hard"; the Ranters not only glorified sex and sinful behavior as evidence of grace but also denied the immortality of the soul and looked forward to the skeptical antiscripturism that became the distinctive mark of the rake's heterodoxy twenty years later.[19] Hill's analysis is persuasive on several counts: not only does it provide a useful reminder of the irreligious tendencies of the enthusiastic sects; it also brings into focus that crucial and largely neglected aspect of the rakes, namely, their furtive religious inclinations.[20]

This approach to the vestiges of faith in Rochester's verse understands all traces of belief as decidedly antinomian. According to James Turner, Rochester's conversion, for example, is closer to the subversive spirituality characteristic of radical Protestants than it is to "conventional piety." Rochester, both Turner and Hill remind us, was described by a contemporary as an "Enthusiast in Wit."[21] To the extent that any threat to civil and spiritual authority had the potential to raise the dreaded specter of enthusiasm, the freethinker of the Restoration can indeed be viewed as the inheritor of revolutionary religious radicalism. The extension of Civil War antinomianism into Restoration libertinism in this sense is consistent with contemporary usage. As J. G. A. Pocock has shown, the polemic against enthusiasm in the late seventeenth century targeted not only the spiritual pretensions of the godly but also the materialism of the unbelievers; Ralph Cudworth described Hobbesian infidels like Rochester as "Enthusiastical or Fanatical Atheists . . . (how abhorrent soever they may otherwise seem to be from Enthusiasm and Revelations)." What is more, both infidels and enthusiasts were seen to undermine the role of reason in religion, if from divergent angles. While the infidels disparaged reason's supposed support for Christian doctrine as "uncertain, various, and fallacious," the enthusiasts feared reason "would . . . cool the pleasant heats of kindled Imagination . . . and Inspiration."[22] Though the two groups were thus opposite in spiritual inclination, the end result was seen to be the same.

These continuities, however, have a tendency to collapse several important distinctions. Turner himself notes that "the religious meanings of 'libertinism' . . . actually refer to two quite distinct phenomena, the mocking denial of the truth and relevance of Scripture, and the intensification of spirituality among radical Protestants."[23] The one repudiates inspiration altogether, and the other magnifies it beyond allowable measures. The Ranters, in other words, though heretical believers, were inspired ones—men of grace and spirit—whereas the Restoration libertines, however ambivalently, were undeniably skeptical doubters. The link between the aristocratic freethinkers of the Restoration and the Civil War sects can also obscure the knotty problem of status. In an early essay, Hill stresses that the roots of Rochester's various excesses— religious, sexual, and political—must be sought in his position as an "alienated aristocrat." Here Rochester is both a "courtier and friend of Charles II" and the writer of "savage republican verse," his heterodoxy an expression of a complex and volatile "radical royalism."[24] It is in this important sense that Rochester's freethinking is as much a reaction *against* the upheavals of the Civil Wars as it is a continuation of those radical tendencies, an insight that has a way of getting lost in Hill's delineation of Rochester's radical Ranter heritage. As Turner argues, Restoration libertines are not Levellers: "They believe in laws to govern 'the rabble,'" and whatever religious heterodoxy they betray stems from the distinctly upper-class presumption that rules can be broken with impunity.[25] Rochester's irreligion, then, had a distinctly aristocratic, distinctly *antienthusiastic* component even as it threatened to reignite the iconoclasm of the midcentury revolutionaries.

This insight has not been applied to the question of freethinking in the "Satyre." As it turns out, the critique of enthusiasm plays a central role in the poem's attack on speculative reason, though its implications have been largely unexplored:

> Reason, an Ignis fatuus of the Mind,
> Which leaving Light of Nature, sense, behind;
> Pathless and dangerous wandring wayes it takes,
> Through Errours fenny boggs and thorny brakes:
> Whilst the misguided follower climbs with pain
> Mountains of whimseys heapt in his own brain.
>
> (12–17)

The "misguided follower" pursues an "Ignis fatuus," or light that exists only in his own mind. Traveling a circular path of error, he climbs mountains that are actually "whimseys heapt in his own brain." The unmistakable marker of enthusiasm in the late seventeenth century was precisely this self-referential tendency.[26] As the above lines have been read, the privileging of "Light of Nature" over reason's spurious inner light satirizes both the nonconformist claim to private inspiration and Cambridge Platonism's notion that reason is the candle of the Lord.[27] Elaborating on the relationship between these two targets, however, is critical to a proper understanding of Rochester's meaning. The Cambridge Platonists, significantly, were part of the latitudinarian movement in Restoration Anglicanism that privileged reason. Their enemies were materialists and unbelievers, like the speaker of the "Satyre," as well as dissenting enthusiasts. Although the Cambridge divines promoted reason as the *antidote* to all forms of enthusiasm in religion, Rochester's speaker insinuates that their solution is merely another instance of the problem: the reason so lauded by the church party is indistinguishable from the enthusiasm it decries.[28]

Manning suggests that such denunciations of reason's powers were intended to frustrate the churchmen's celebration of reason's divine virtues.[29] While designs of the sort surely influenced the unbelievers' strategy, their distrust of reason's influence in matters of religion is also crucially informed by the philosophical legacy of ancient skepticism, a tradition that both Montaigne and Hobbes, long-acknowledged sources for the critique of speculative reason in "A Satyre," adhered to in matters of theology.[30] The poem's suggestion that moderate churchmen become enthusiastic once reason eschews nature's guidance echoes Montaigne's similar concern in his *Apology of Raymond Sebond* (1580). Following Pyrrho and the school of ancient skepticism, Montaigne argues that superstition, rebellion, and disobedience are the inevitable result of man's mistaken view that he can attain knowledge of divinity. For what is more vain, Montaigne asks, "than to try to divine God by our analogies and conjectures, to regulate him and the world by our capacity and our laws?" Rejecting reason's intrusion in questions of faith, Montaigne instead chooses "the ancient opinions concerning religion, that . . . recognized God as an incomprehensible power, . . . taking in good part the honor and reverence that human beings rendered him, under whatever aspect, under whatever name, in whatever manner."[31] Here, too, nature serves as the corrective to man's self-conceit in religion:

It is more honorable, and closer to divinity, to be guided and obliged to act lawfully by a natural and inevitable condition, than to act lawfully by accidental and fortuitous liberty; and safer to leave the reins of our conduct to nature than to ourselves. The vanity of our presumption makes us prefer to owe our ability to our powers than to nature's liberality.

Reason, or "the vanity of our presumption," once again tends to be the culprit in theological error: our faith does not depend on us, nor can "our efforts and arguments . . . attain a knowledge so supernatural and divine."[32]

Hobbes similarly blames the religious excesses of his day on the arrogance of "human ratiocination," citing St. Paul's rule (Rom. 12.3) "That no man presume to understand above that which is meet to understand, but that he understand according to sobriety." Also turning to classical antiquity for a theological model, Hobbes points out that the ancient Greeks and Romans, as well as the ancient Israelites, never imagined that religion was a matter for man's private reason to question. Beginning with Christianity, however, men have pompously attempted "to take for the sense of the Scripture, that which they make thereof." Since Scripture raises questions about the nature of God to which reason cannot speak, men must take special care not to attempt to examine "those things which are incomprehensible." To do otherwise, Hobbes implies, is to open the floodgates of religious enthusiasm. Men's "owne Dreams" become "the Prophecy they mean to bee governed by, and the tumour of their own hearts . . . the Spirit of God."[33] Though Hobbes and Montaigne wrote before reasonable religion had become the orthodoxy of the day—both targeting radical sectarianism rather than the establishment—Rochester suggests that his predecessors' criticisms nonetheless apply to the current moment.[34]

The rejection of reason in religion thus has a vital philosophical heritage, and one that is markedly linked both to antienthusiasm and to freethinking.[35] For Hobbes, sectarianism inevitably accompanied men's reliance on individual reason to settle theological controversy. His *De Corpore Politico* thus advocated a stripped-down creed inspired by Herbert of Cherbury's study of the best of ancient paganism. Just as the evidence of ancient religion before the advent of priestcraft reveals a unified system that is both perfectly pure and simple and free from excessive dependence on mysteries and supernatural revelations, so should Christianity, on Hobbes's view, be comprised only of the basic theological principles that are fundamental to salvation.[36] Once these essential fundamentals are reestablished, "then all other points, that are now controverted, and made distinction of sects, . . . must needs be such, as a man needeth not."[37] This paring away of religious excess and error is characteristic of the Epicurean religion of nature, or what the period called deism.[38] Formally launched in England by Herbert, deism's anticlericalism, denial of most revealed religion, and skepticism about the truth of Scripture made it a dangerously radical movement and an appropriate second context for Rochester's heterodoxy.

There have been several obstacles, however, to placing Rochester and his "Satyre" properly in Herbert's deist tradition.[39] For Hill, deism's roots are once again to be found in the radical thought of the Interregnum.[40] Though indeed associated in contemporaries' minds with its sister heresy, enthusiasm, deism in fact diverges from the latter in crucial ways. In its suspicion of revelation, most importantly, deism was at root an antienthusiastic initiative.[41] The freethinking writings of Charles Blount, the second English deist after Lord Herbert, for example, explicitly attack "the Fanaticks and others who pleaded a Call from God to do the Work of the Devil, cutting off their Soveraigns Head." Anglicans may have identified "enthusiasts" and "deists" as common enemies of Christian religion, but they also made clear that the one "pretends to immediate Inspiration" while the other "pleads only for a Natural Religion in opposition to any Particular Mode or Way of Divine Revelation."[42] Both the Ranters and the deists rejected institutionalized revelation—the word of God as handed down in Scripture—but the Ranters set up private inspiration, the inner light, in its stead, an even worse error in the eyes of the deists.

There is evidence, moreover, that by the 1670s deism had become the more troubling of the two heterodoxies, especially among the court circles. The religious context of the "Satyre" reveals how contemporaries saw themselves faced with a new menace, different from that posed by the radicals of the revolutionary decades. If the former age was one of unlawful and excessive religious zeal, the present was seen as insufficiently spiritual, at least in any familiar sense. As Samuel Parker lamented, "Prophaness [sic] is in our days become as zealous and implacable a thing as Enthusiasm." Robert South likewise admonished that "Religion is not now so much in danger of being divided, and torn piece-meal by Sects and Factions, as of being at once devour'd by Atheism." And whereas the radicals of the 1640s sprouted from the lower social orders, the 1670s faced an unforeseen and largely novel threat: the heterodox aristocrat. The two united in the danger they posed to civil and ecclesiastical authority; divines such as Richard Allestree and Joseph Glanvill continually figured the libertine scoffer, the Interregnum enthusiast, and even the papist as the latest unholy alliance threatening England's newfound stability. But it was a perverse coming together of opposites—"a *complication* of Enemies," in one writer's words—more than a continuity of the same.[43]

Was Rochester a deist? Blount seems to have thought he was, beginning a correspondence with him in 1679 about a shared commitment to freethinking and ancient skepticism. Notably, in the scandalously heterodox "Philological Notes" of his *Two First Books of Philostratus* (1680), a covert attack on Christian miracles, Blount also echoes skepticism's reservations about reason, observing, after Socrates and Cicero, that "Nothing does more betray the Vanity of Philosophy, than the Insufficiency of man's Reason. . . . For he that thinks he knows any thing, that man knoweth nothing." To illustrate this point, Blount concludes "with so many lines as are to my purpose, out of a late ingenious Copy of verses written upon this Subject, by a Person of Honour." The verses Blount cites comprise a medley of the reflections on reason from Rochester's "Satyre."[44]

Though Rochester's connections to Blount's circle have been briefly acknowledged, another obstacle to viewing the "Satyre" through the lens of Restoration deism has been the assumption that in its rejection of revealed religion, deism necessarily magnifies the role of reason.[45] While the commonplace that deism and reason were necessarily allies is long standing, scholars as far back as Leslie Stephen have pointed out that the more apposite alliance in the period was between reason and Christian theology.[46] While Lord Herbert's *De Veritate* (1624), the first deist manual, indeed begins with a censure of the Pyrrhonist tradition, his later writings on ancient religion locate the origins of religious strife in opposing sects' inflated pretensions to greater knowledge of God.[47] Far from supporting the claims of natural religion as against conflicting claims to revelation, reason is here the enemy of theology. Condemning those who boasted of a special familiarity with the workings of the divine, Herbert supports skepticism's contrary injunction that men humbly "follow the civil laws of their country, which taught them at least the rules of justice and equity."[48] In his *View of the Principal Deistical Writers* (1754), John Leland corroborates deism's link with the skeptical tradition, citing Pierre Viret's description of the early deists in France and Italy. The first deists, Viret explains, "laughed at all religion, notwithstanding they conformed themselves, with regard to the outward appearance, to the religion of those with whom they were obliged to live."[49]

A more accurate description of deism's attitude towards reason might read something like this: though the truths of religion, to be sure, needed to be prudently nonenthusiastic, and in this sense reasonable, what was called for was not always rational arguments in their defense. As I have argued, for Hobbes and Montaigne, as well as for Rochester, reason, in fact, had no place in faith. Next to Hobbes, the radical deist of the period most notorious for separating the realms of reason and theology was Spinoza. Like Hobbes, Spinoza seems to have found a receptive audience among the English nobility. Matthias Earbery, the first contemporary to respond to Spinoza's highly inflammatory *Tractatus Theologico-Politicus* (1670), refers to "he who so long has found a place in the Libraries and Hands of very Learned Men," and Stillingfleet similarly targets Spinoza's early readers as "such who pretend to Breeding and Civility." Acquiring a relatively rare and most likely expensive clandestine copy of the infamous text was, of course, more easily accomplished by the nobility.[50]

In his *Tractatus*, Spinoza declared that "all our understanding of Scripture and of matters spiritual must be sought from Scripture alone, and not from the sort of knowledge that derives from the natural light of reason." The setting apart of faith from philosophy thus "forms the most important part of the subject of this treatise." An anonymous adaptation of the blasphemous chapter on miracles, commonly attributed to Blount, illustrates the use to which the argument was put by Rochester's circle.[51] Blount's text, entitled *Miracles, No Violations of the Laws of Nature* (1683), is largely a straightforward translation of Spinoza with extra emphasis given to man's ignorance. We call strange occurrences miracles, Blount argues, not only out of pious faith, but also out of the impertinent presumption that every phenomenon in the universe must accord to our reason: if *we* don't understand something, then it must be a miracle. This particular attack on revealed religion accentuates our intellectual limitations more than it demands what rational proofs of divinity are possible. Recalling Rochester's substitution of the inner light of the Quakers and the Platonists for the "Light of Nature" (13), Blount's alternative explanation of what have been called "miracles" maintains, on the one hand, that all phenomena proceed from natural causes. This proposition seems to elevate reason or rationality above faith. Yet on the other hand, Blount stresses that many of nature's processes remain outside the scope of human understanding: "Humane Understanding is finite, and consequently incapable to know how far the Laws of Nature extend themselves. . . . I do not measure the Power of Nature by the unequal Line of humane Wit." To say that nothing deviates from the laws of nature, then, is not necessarily to say that a phenomenon is *knowable* by reason. Along these lines, Rochester's other freethinking poem, "Upon Nothinge," replaces Christianity's divine order with a material world that is all chaos and accident: "When primitive nothinge something straite begot, / Then all proceeded from the great united *what*" (5–6). The workings of nature, in other words, can be just as mysterious as the supposed supernatural.[52]

In addition to its distrust of reason and revealed religion, deism's more radical incarnation was characterized by several flagrant heresies, including a denial of the soul's immortality and of God's Providence and future judgment of men's actions. It is for these heresies particularly that this form of deism was so often renamed as atheism. In his inaugural Boyle Lecture of 1692, *The Folly of Atheism, and (What Is Now Called) Deism*, Richard Bentley explains that "to avoid the odious name of Atheists," certain infidels "shelter and skreen themselves under a new one of Deists, which is not quite so obnoxious."[53] For Bentley, certainly, "the Existence of God and his Government of the World do mutually suppose and imply one another." A deity who is excluded "from governing the World by his Providence, or judging it by his Righteousness" thus cannot rightly be said to exist. This more blasphemous tendency seems to have been present from deism's inception. As Viret describes the early deists of the sixteenth century, "Some among them have a kind of notion of the immortality of the soul; others agree with the Epicureans on that as well as on the Divine Providence with regard to mankind: they think he doth not intermeddle with human affairs."[54]

Viret's association of this more dangerous strain of deism with "the Epicureans" is important, for radical deism indeed owes its most far-reaching inspiration to the Epicurean doctrine, laid out in Lucretius' *De rerum natura*, that the Gods were indifferent to and untroubled by human needs, neither ruling nor caring to rule the world of man.[55] Lucretius was Rochester's favorite ancient. His translation of the Roman poet affirmed that

> The *Gods*, by right of Nature, must possess
> An Everlasting Age, of perfect Peace:
> Far off remov'd from us, and our Affairs:

Neither approach'd by *Dangers*, or by *Cares*:
Rich in themselves, to whom we cannot add:
Not pleas'd by *Good* Deeds; nor provok'd by *Bad*.[56]

This bald denial that the Gods did anything in the universe was the fundamental starting-off point for the religion of nature and the rejection of revelation, divine Providence, and rewards and punishments that formed deism's more heretical core. "A Satyre" is unabashedly contemptuous of clerics who, believing in "An Everlasting Soul" (61), presume to "Search Heaven and Hell, find out what's acted there, / And give the World true grounds of hope and feare" (70–71). As Rochester put it to Gilbert Burnet in their conversations about religion, "God had none of those Affections of Love or Hatred, which breed perturbation in us"; such a divinity would not take the trouble to "reveal his Secrets to mankind." Once divinity is thus out of the picture, the universe functions according to nature's necessary and immutable laws. Revealed religion is impossible for Lucretius because nature's first principle is that "Nothing at all is ever born from nothing / By the gods' will." We might posit a divine power when we can't determine the cause of strange events, but the fact remains that things come about without the aid of gods.[57]

In his essay "Of Custom," Montaigne, himself following Lucretius, seems to have been the first modern to articulate the deist heresy for which Spinoza is more commonly known, that "Miracles are according to the ignorance wherein we are by nature, and not according to natures essence."[58] In his *Apology of Raymond Sebond*, he argues similarly that the miraculous is resorted to "by each man and each nation according to the measure of his ignorance." Here naming Cicero's *On the Nature of the Gods* as his skeptical inspiration, Montaigne complains that "our overweening arrogance would pass the deity through our sieve." It is for this reason that every day we "attribute events of importance, by particular assignment, to God. Because they weigh with us, it seems as though they weigh with him, also."[59] The notorious theriophilia of Montaigne's *Apology*, likely the source for the opening paradox of "A Satyre," is itself rooted in the indifference of the Epicurean Gods and linked to a rejection of miracles.[60] Citing Lucretius again, Montaigne explains that he has stressed the equality between man and beasts "to bring us back and join us to the majority. We are neither above nor below the rest: all that is under heaven, says the sage, incurs the same law and the same fortune."[61] It is man's vanity only, on this view, that "picks himself out and separates himself from the horde of other creatures." God awards man no "essential prerogative or preeminence" over beasts.[62] Belief in miracles assumes (falsely) just such a special prerogative from God as well as the notion that nature could deviate from her inexorable order. This connection between theriophilia and natural religion is a critical one, for it reveals that Rochester's speaker's desire to "be a Dog, a Monky, or a Bear" has more subversive implications than have hitherto been acknowledged: the theriophilia of "A Satyre," in other words, launches a direct assault on revealed religion.

Following the wisdom of the ancient world, Montaigne praises beasts for better respecting nature's order than man, for "restrain[ing] themselves with more moderation within the limits that nature has prescribed."[63] Rochester's speaker articulates a similar view in "A Satyre," arguing that man is a "vain Animal" (6) precisely because he thinks himself above nature, erroneously preferring reason to "Instinct" (10) and "Sense" (8, 100). These latter categories comprise the poem's notion of "right reason" (99), a distinctly heterodox glance at Christian humanism's identical term. According to the speaker's definition, "right" or "true Reason" (111) is a faculty shared by man and beast, a natural not a "supernatural Gift" (76). The error of the poem's *adversarius* is to insist alternatively (and wrongly, from the poem's perspective) that God "drest" man's "fair frame in shining reason" in order "To dignify his Nature above Beast" (64–65). As we know, however, the speaker would *choose* to be a beast if he could, not only because beasts lack speculative reason, but also because they wisely follow "necessity" (131) and observe "Natures allowance to supply their want" (134).[64] Men, on the contrary, "betray" (130) one another, "Not through Necessity, but Wantonness" (138).

Rochester's emphasis on necessity here is important, for the rejection of revealed religion and divine Providence from Lucretius down to Spinoza depended upon the view that nature's workings are immutable. God cannot alter these workings (causing miraculous events) because he is not separate from them; he, too, is a necessary and determined being. Indeed, men's belief in miracles, Spinoza argues, stems from an incorrect differentiation between God and nature: "Thus they imagine that there are two powers quite distinct from each other, the power of God and the power of Nature, though the latter is determined in a definite way by God, or—as is the prevailing opinion nowadays—created by God." When Spinoza insists, then, that "the universal laws of Nature are merely God's decrees," what he means is that the two are in the strictest sense the same. Nature's laws are God's decrees so as not to be separate from him. The one is not the effect of the other's will, as conventionally assumed, but rather tantamount to it: "The power of Nature *is* the divine power and virtue."[65]

Pantheism, or the doctrine that nature and God form one substance, was seen as an abominable heresy, whose roots went back to Epicurus and Plato among the Greeks and, of course, to Lucretius among the

Romans.[66] The term "pantheist" was coined in 1705 by John Toland, perhaps the best-known radical deist of the period. Although Toland's *Pantheisticon* (1720) was the first deist book explicitly to promote the doctrine of one substance, it is clear that the writers who influenced Rochester's "Satyre," as well as the Restoration deists themselves, all had tendencies in that direction. Hobbes's Epicurean conviction that we can have no concept of a *"Spirit Incorporeall"* was generally taken by contemporaries to require that God, too, be material, thereby equating God and nature.[67] It was for this reason that Hobbism and Epicureanism generally were so frequently charged with a kind of Spinozistic pantheism.[68] In just such a characteristic merging of Hobbes and Spinoza, Bentley objected that the deists' God was "no more than some eternal inanimate Matter, some universal Nature, and Soul of the World, void of all sense and cogitation, endued with none at all, much less with Infinite Wisdom and Goodness." Bentley's description of deism's divinity may well have had Rochester in mind, for according to Gilbert Burnet, Rochester's "Notion of God was so low, that the Supreme Being seemed to be nothing but Nature." Rochester had appallingly described God as "a vast Power that Wrought every thing by . . . necessity"; his God "had none of the Attributes of Goodness or Justice, we ascribe to the Deity."[69] To contemporaries, this kind of pantheism was tantamount to atheism: to say that there is no God separate from the universe was to say that there is no God at all.

II

I have attempted to demonstrate thus far how the twin emphases of Rochester's "Satyre"—the denial of reason in religion and the equation of man and beast—set off a chain of mounting infidelity, ranging from a rejection of revelation to a refusal of a future state of rewards and punishments to a pantheistic (hence atheistic) conception of the universe. I have also suggested that the poem's attack on reasonable religion is inseparable from its reliance on an ancient legacy of freethought, including Epicurean antiprovidentialism and Pyrrhonist skepticism. Though critics have affirmed the importance of Lucretius, Montaigne, and Hobbes to the poem's general endorsement of freethinking, they have not appreciated the coherency of the unbelieving vision produced through the calling up of such precursors, nor the ways in which this vision is rooted in classical attitudes toward theology. What is more, making sense of the problem of belief with which I began this chapter demands that we recognize the interplay between Restoration heterodoxy and classical thought. Doubt and faith may not be so starkly opposed in the freethinking inheritance I am delineating.

Blount's *Anima Mundi* (1679), a consideration of the pagans' often contradictory views concerning the soul's immortality and future state, provides a useful example. Following Herbert's example, Blount's study of pagan religion attempts to strip back the additions of priests and custom and locate an original purity in an ancient tradition. What he reveals, importantly, is a religion whose content is wholly agnostic: the heathens commendably submit themselves to the will of the deity, yet strictly speaking they don't "believe" in a future state of rewards and punishments. To do so "they held . . . a Presumption in Man," for the knowledge of such things "God had reserved to himself." The "most vertuous and prudent" of the ancient pagans, then, "modestly repose[d] themselves in . . . ignorance of the Soul's future state," hoping with humble deference and piety that God would provide for them "although in some new way whereof they had not yet any experimental knowledge."[70]

It is little wonder that Blount's *Anima Mundi* was decried as a heretical text. Yet this heresy, I want to suggest, was comingled with an unexpectedly opposite inclination. If we remember that the unbelievers and the Anglican traditionalists formed an unusual confederacy in their shared animus against reason in religion, Blount's veneration of the unassuming agnosticism of the heathens also reveals a covertly conservative bias. His argument, indeed, rests on a fundamental opposition to modernity and progress: the further we stray from the men of the first ages, he implies, the more corruption accrues to religious belief and practice. Reason, moreover, provides a conspicuous example of this logic. The best of Blount's heathens refrained from wrangling about theological questions, an activity that for Blount can only breed degradation and error. Philosophy's promise of a surer knowledge, however, eventually led some to become "vain in their Imaginations," specifically by "adventur[ing] to address their Doctrines to humane Reason."[71] What becomes evident here is that reason is one of those vitiations of religion attributable to the progress of theology. Such a view is also evident in Rochester's "Satyre," which denounces the reasoning divine who misguidedly "tr[ies] / To swim with bladders of *Philosophy*: / In hopes still to o'retake th'escaping Light" (20–22; italics mine).

For Montaigne, most familiarly, the logical response to ancient skepticism's commitment to doubt was obedience to established law and tradition. We receive our religion "not by reasoning or by our understanding," he explains, but rather "by external authority and command."[72] It is precisely because we can know nothing of divinity that in matters of religion the best we can do is defer to the judgment of the civil authority and submit to the religious forms of our country. By making religion a matter of conformity to external authority only, Montaigne implicitly rejects the premium the Christian tradition places on the private experience of religious faith, following instead the contrary tendency in ancient religion to emphasize practical activity over introspection and subjective states of belief. The Pyrrhonists in particular, while committed to a "pure, complete, and very perfect postponement and suspension of judgment" regarding all claims to truth, religious or otherwise, in everyday life laudably follow the "common fashion" and "the constitutions of laws and customs."[73]

In his *Anima Mundi*, Blount admits that skeptical thought, illustrated by Democritus' opinion that "Truth is hidden in a Well, that she may not be found by men," is on the one hand "very inconsistent with the light of Christianity."[74] And yet, on the other hand, the ancient skeptics prove exemplary in upholding a particular kind of faithful deference to religious tradition: "Whereupon doubting the sufficiency of humane Reason, they would not venture to affirm or deny any thing of the Souls future state, but civilly and quietly gave way to the Doctrines, & Ordinances under which they lived, without raising or espousing any new Opinions."[75]

Blount's *Anima Mundi* suggests, moreover, that obedience to the religious laws of one's country has a kind of practical motivation as well: "For what can be greater relief to a Man, and comfort to him in affliction, than to have a God to flee to in his distress? . . . The very thoughts that we have a Providence at all times to flee to, animates us with a new Spirit of boldness and resolution."[76] Blount hints here at the wisdom of the ancient twofold philosophy: the ancients obeyed the civil religion of the state, he insinuates, because they knew that the *idea* of Providential care, whether or not that idea was correct, fostered courage and other virtues. In February of 1680, the year after the publication of his *Anima Mundi*, Blount referred again to the moral benefits of belief in a future state in a letter to Rochester. Responding to Rochester's translation of Seneca on the material finality of death, in which Rochester had characterized the future state as "sensless Stories, idle Tales, / Dreams, Whimsies, and no more" (17–18), Blount reminds Rochester that the ancient moralists deemed it expedient, both morally and politically, to posit the immortality of the soul.[77] For while some men are naturally virtuous and thus have no need of the teachings of religion to encourage good behavior, many would be wholly vicious were it not for the threat of future punishments. He continues,

Wherefore . . . lawgivers, considering the proneness of men to evil, and themselves aiming at the public good, established the immortality of the soul, perhaps at first not so much out of a regard to truth as to honesty, hoping thereby to induce men to virtue. Nor are politicians to be so much blamed herein more than physicians, who many times, for the benefit of their patients, are compelled to feign and pretend diverse things, since, in like manner, politicians devise fables only to regulate the people. . . . And therefore, my Lord, besides the authority of the Holy Scriptures, as also the innumerable other arguments which may be deduced as well from philosophy as reason to prove the immortality of the soul, together with its rewards and punishments . . . , there is no argument of greater weight with me than the absolute necessity and convenience that it should be so.[78]

Blount's comments in this passage reflect the coincidence of unbelief and support for the political use of religion that is typical of the elite tradition of freethinking I am outlining. As is well known, Rochester had seemingly spent his life in defiance of all moral and religious law. In his deathbed conversations with Burnet, he spoke candidly about his contempt for religion, his conviction that Christianity was "the invention of Priests" and "Prophecies and Miracles" merely "strange Stories" foisted upon the simple and the credulous by "a mixture of Knaves and Fools."[79] And yet, according to Burnet, Rochester also spoke of Christian morality "as a fine thing," "necessary for humane life" and "the Government of the World." This principle, however, as Burnet tells it, grew not "from any deep sense of a Supreme Being, or another State," but rather from "the study of Philosophy."[80] It has not been fully appreciated that Rochester's conversations with Burnet were contemporaneous with his correspondence with Blount, and that both men, from different vantage points to be sure, attempted to convince Rochester of the necessity of religious institutions. Burnet allows certain practical arguments in favor of religion, yet fundamental to his purpose is the certainty that religious practice must be accompanied by true belief, "an inward Principle" inspired by God.[81] Blount, on the contrary, argues that "honesty" of intention is more important than strict spiritual conviction; we commit ourselves to conscious confirmation of the latter because such support is both necessary and convenient for the "public good."

Betraying, I want to propose, the influence of Blount's correspondence, Rochester told Burnet that "the whole Systeme of Religion, if believed, was a greater foundation of quiet than any other thing whatsoever."[82] From early in their conversations, he spoke often of the happiness of those who were able to believe "since they had somewhat on which their thoughts rested and centred," and he agreed "that the Impressions of God being much in Mens minds, would be a powerful means to reform the World."[83] On closer examination, Rochester's freethinking "Satyre" already exhibits incipient signs of this social investment in religious belief. Indeed, the pure faith represented by the ideal churchman in the "Addition" to the poem is significantly not antinomian, or at least not in the sense that Hill and Turner suggest. Contrary to the enthusiast's self-important insistence that he is divinely visited and inspired, the churchman's religiosity is "meek" and "humble" (216): once again, he who is truly pious believes in "Mysterious Truths, which no man can conceive" (219). As Harold Love points out, the status of the Christian mysteries in these lines is notably ambiguous. If no man can conceive them, the mysteries, Rochester likely suggests, are not "true" in the sense of conforming to factual reality, supernatural or otherwise.[84] Rochester said as much in his conversations with Burnet, noting that "it is not in a Man's power to believe that which he cannot comprehend: and of which he can have no Notion." What is admirable, then, about the pious churchman is his commitment to divine reverence, regardless of the truth status of the spirit. To have faith, finally, as Rochester intuited, is "to be under those Perswasions."[85]

It is crucial to note, however, that Rochester's praise of the honest churchman in the "Addition" is dependent on a rejection of his implied opposite—the covetous cleric who is "blown up with vain *Prelatick* pride, / . . . whose Talents ly / In Avarice, Pride, Sloth and Gluttony" (193, 202–3; italics mine). As Mark Goldie argues, "prelacy" was a loaded term of reproach in the period, signifying a critique of the tyranny and corrupt ambition of the church party that threatened to dominate the king's administration in the 1670s.[86] To complicate matters, then, just as it suggests his nostalgia for a virtuous churchman who "Preach[es] peace" (217) and relies on God (191), the "Addition" to Rochester's "Satyre" appears simultaneously to identify the poet with a coalescing *antichurch* opposition that was increasingly radical in character. It is in this context, perhaps, that we can understand what seems to be the antiroyalist political sentiment of Rochester's infamous satire on Charles II, "In the Isle of Brittain" (1673), in which the speaker dismisses "all Monarchs and the Thrones they sit on" (33). Here again, Rochester may well have sided with Blount's view as later expressed in his pro-Exclusion pamphlet, *An Appeal from the Country to the City, for the Preservation of His Majesty's Person, Liberty, Property, and the Protestant Religion* (1679). As Blount cautions, if papist absolutism were to take hold again in England, the result would be the empowerment, not of the monarch, but rather of the same power-hungry "prelates" condemned in Rochester's "Satyre": under popery, "'tis the Jesuits that govern, and not the King."[87] What looks like political and religious radicalism, in other words, can more accurately be described as a critique of "priestcraft" and its tendency to vitiate the integrity of the civil order.

Can Rochester repudiate the despotic arts of priestcraft and allow for the possibility, however remote, that religion, politics, and morality could in fact be united? It is worth remembering that the "Addition," importantly, presents us with the honorable character, not just of the pious churchman, but also of the "just" (180) and "upright . . . Statesman" (185) who seeks to "protect" (182) and "raise his Country" (188). On one level, indeed, both figures appear to represent an impossible ideal: strictly speaking, belief in the mysterious truths of religion is conceptually untenable, and Rochester's speaker specifies that "In Court a just man [is] yet unknown to me" (180). And yet, if the influence of a sincerely held belief produces one "Whose life his Faith and Doctrine justifies" (192), then the speaker is willing to speculate that the "Holy Cheats and formal Lyes" (177) of religion might function not only "to tyrannize" (178) and enslave but also to ennoble. Religion, on this view, is not merely cant for the credulous vulgar.[88] The same rationale holds for a traditional monarchy. Though it expresses contempt for kings, Rochester's "In the Isle of Brittain" seems more perturbed by Charles's "easiness" (4), his lack of "Ambition" (5), and most memorably, the impotence of his "Scepter" (11).[89] Charles's gravest offense, then, appears to be his egregious neglect of his monarchal duties: his failure to govern with constancy, force, and authority.[90] Such a reading thus supports the speaker's claim in the "Addition" that if truly righteous men in fact exist in Church and State, he will "with the rabble World, their Laws obey" (223).

Reflecting on Rochester's own supposed conversion to faith at the end of his life, Blount suggests that a similar character typifies the views of the historical infidel. In the dying words of Pythagoras,

> Te Pater Alme,
> Expertus fidensq, sequar, quo duxeris ibo.
> (Nourishing Father,
> I, true and faithful, will follow you, I will go to where you have led.)

Blount implies here that like the skeptical faith of the heathens, Rochester's new belief is humble and agnostic, exemplary in its hesitance to "affirm or deny any thing of the Souls future state."[91] In this sense, then, the rake's seeming repentance was not, as Blount contends, "a victory over his former Opinions," but rather is continuous with them. We see the early stirrings here of the "willing suspension of disbelief" that, as I will argue, becomes emblematic of a literary tradition of freethinking in England.[92]

Rochester told Burnet that "he was sure Religion was either a meer Contrivance, or the most important thing that could be," thereby largely supporting Blount's tribute to him.[93] By paradoxically identifying the freethinking position with these opposing stances, Rochester comes close to justifying the orthodox concern that those High Church divines whose traditionalism balked at rational defenses of Christianity fed into the hands of the atheists. This particular coming together of opposites is as central to situating the freethinking of Rochester's "Satyre" as Glanvill's feared alliance between the fanatics and the unbelievers is. It has, moreover, long been a neglected aspect of the history of English freethinking.

Reading Rochester's distinctive aristocratic heterodoxy requires a flexible framework. To place his freethinking in the context of English deism serves a multiple purpose. Not only does it provide a more accurate account of the content of Rochester's ideas about religion; it also affords a more nuanced view of the heterodox aristocrat's always uneasy relationship to a radical tradition. To the extent that the critique of enthusiasm is fueled by class anxiety, it is no coincidence that deism began as a largely aristocratic, even politically conservative, movement.[94] It is also little wonder that Hobbes's distinctive mixture of freethinking and authoritarian absolutism served as an appropriate inspiration.[95] In its antienthusiasm, in its nostalgia for a pure religion untainted by the corruptions of interest and politics, deism was radically conservative, a fitting home for an alienated aristocrat like Rochester.

Deism's radical conservatism and its related ancient bias in matters of theology offer support for Arthur Lovejoy's thesis that there is a parallel between deism and classicism. According to Lovejoy, deism points in two directions. In some respects, he argues, deism, like classicism, is conservative in its sympathies: progress for the former as for the latter is just a euphemism for "changes for the worse." What is oldest is purest and therefore best. And yet deism, as Rochester's case corroborates, also illustrates the way in which being an ancient in religion was dangerous business. Divinity, William Wotton pronounced in his *Reflections upon Ancient and Modern Learning* (1694), was a modern accomplishment. Although "The *Old Testament* . . . has constantly been at hand; . . . yet it is very possible that Modern Divines . . . may be better Work-men than [the] Ancient Fathers." As Pocock has demonstrated, over the course of the eighteenth century, the Church of England learned that it "had good grounds for taking a modernist and not a traditionalist view of the history of philosophy."[96] Rochester and Blount, among others, may well have offered the impetus for this shift. Their writings, indeed, provide evidence of the curious way in which aspects of tradition, by the late seventeenth century, could become radical. In the next chapter, we will see how classical theology as filtered through the heterodox philosophy of Bernard de Fontenelle sparked the freethinking imagination of Aphra Behn, providing her, moreover, with an alternative to the gender constraints posed by Restoration libertinism.

CHAPTER TWO

Behn, Fontenelle, and the Cheats of Revealed Religion

> . . . if we consider the humor of Mankind a little, we shall find
> how much we are taken with any thing that is Miraculous.
> —Bernard de Fontenelle, *The History of Oracles*,
> trans. Aphra Behn (1687)

If Rochester's ties to the freethinking initiative in Restoration England are more intricate than has often been supposed, Aphra Behn's associations with this movement are yet more bedeviled by paradoxes and inconsistencies. For one, establishing Behn's place in a freethinking lineage is complicated by the ambivalent representation of skeptical religious thought in her imaginative works. More often than not, Behn's fictional freethinkers are also sexual libertines, a linkage that tends in Behn's hands to imply that unbelief and religious doubt serve the interested cause of male conquest a little too well to be entirely trusted. This chapter begins by briefly exploring the tangled intersections between freethinking and libertinism in three of Behn's best-known writings: her Restoration comedy *The Rover* (1677), her pastoral poem "The Golden Age" (1684), and her novel *Love-Letters between a Nobleman and His Sister* (1684–87). In bringing gender politics to the foreground of freethinking doctrine, these works imply that religious heterodoxy can function as the latest stratagem in the game of sexual power play. In this way, Behn adds a new layer to the suggestion in Rochester's poetry that traditional categories like love and faith are not so easily dispensed with. Equally suspicious, however, of the sustainability of these earlier modes of fulfillment, Behn, I will argue, experiments toward the end of her career with extricating the philosophy and theology of freethinking from what she sees to be the corrupting influence of the libertine creed. Her greatly overlooked translations of two

iconoclastic works by the French philosopher Bernard de Fontenelle—
Entretiens sur la pluralité des mondes (1686) and *L'histoire des oracles*
(1687)—serve as evidence of this important shift. Behn's foray (through
Fontenelle) into the heart of the early French Enlightenment marks her
determined effort to enter the freethinking conversation as an *intellectual*
libertine in her own right, an effort that has yet to be explored in scholarship.[1] This chapter proposes that Behn's engagement with the classical theology central to Fontenelle's thought provides her with an escape
from a seemingly irresolvable impasse. If libertinism and freethinking are
troubled by intractable struggles for power and dominance between men
and women, while the conventional categories of love and faith, by turn,
prove naïve and outmoded, Behn's solution, as we shall see, is to moderate the radical critique of tradition through a skeptical and self-conscious
reinvestment in its informing assumptions.

In many ways *The Rover* represents Behn's strongest defense of freethinking religious and sexual philosophy. When Angellica Bianca, a
beautiful courtesan in love with Willmore—the play's titular Rover—
finds herself betrayed by his inconstancy, the play suggests that Angellica was in fact foolish to believe in fictions such as constancy in the
first place. Invoking the Epicurean demystification of romantic love and
its conviction that love, like religion, destroys man's most sought-after
good, peace of mind, Angellica laments that "Love . . . has robbed [her
heart] of unconcern," leaving her "undone" (5:5.1.235, 247). The implication here is that one does better not to put faith in what are necessarily
ephemeral vows of fidelity, a position argued persuasively by Willmore:

> Broke my vows! Why, where hast thou lived?
> Amongst the gods? For I never heard of mortal man
> That has not broke a thousand vows.
>
> . . .
>
> Angellica! That beauty has been too long tempting
> Not to have made a thousand lovers languish,
> Who in the amorous fever no doubt have sworn
> Like me; did they all die in that faith? Still adoring?
> I do not think they did.
>
> (5:5.1.248–50, 252–56)

In response to Angellica's mad despair, Willmore points out rightly
that her assumption of his moral perfidy imagines a standard of constancy that no actual man can satisfy. On this view, her misery and
anguish are more the fault of her idealism and credulity than his supposed treachery. Declaring the motive of lust to be both natural and
irresistible, Willmore likens himself to "cheerful birds, [who] sing in all

groves, / And perch on every bough, / Billing the next kind she that flies to meet me" (5:5.1.287–89). Just as Angellica would be ridiculous to expect animals to be monogamous, he suggests, so is she absurd to expect such behavior from him.

The play's position on libertine freethinking becomes more complicated, however, when we consider its lively heroine, Hellena, a young woman designed (by her family's male authority figures) for a nunnery, yet seemingly bent on experimenting with the libertine lifestyle instead. Early in the play's first scene, Hellena informs her brother, Pedro, that he is "mistaken in [her] way of devotion" (5:1.1.139–40), insinuating in an aside to the audience that the "saint" she plans to pray to is a saint of love, not religion (5:1.1.142–43). By Act III Hellena pronounces that she plans to have her choice of men and seems to have found her match in Willmore, claiming that "we are both of one humour; I am as inconstant as you" (5:3.1.169–70). And yet, despite her embrace of the Rover's libertine principles, Hellena, like Angellica, "cannot choose but be angry when I think that mad fellow should be in love with any body but me" (5:3.1.21–24). And when Willmore suggests that they sate their appetites for each other, she appears to fall back upon customary moral and religious law, refusing to "fall to, before a priest says grace" (5:3.1.151).

By the final act, it becomes clear to the audience that Hellena is not so much inconsistent in her libertinism as she is realistic. From the play's early moments we know that she is deeply cynical of marriage as an institution, particularly of the ways in which it tends to exploit women economically and sexually. As she reminds her sister, Florinda, regarding her arranged marriage to a rich old man whom she despises, "And this man you must kiss; nay you must kiss none but him, too—and nuzzle through his beard to find his lips. And this you must submit to for threescore years, and all for a jointure" (5:1.1.118–20). When Hellena insists that Willmore marry her before enjoying her, then, the official sanction of the priest is meant to function pragmatically and wholly without sentiment (not to mention reverence): "Let but old gaffer Hymen and his priest say amen to't, and I dare lay my mother's daughter by as proper a fellow as your father's son, without fear or blushing" (5:5.1.425–27). Hellena's return to marriage as a kind of practical necessity is further revealed in her rejoinder to Willmore's protest against her use of the "bug words . . . priest and Hymen" (5:5.1.428): "No, no," he insists, "we'll have no vows but love, child, nor witness but the lover; the kind deity enjoins naught but love and enjoy! . . . I'll neither ask nor give a vow" (5:5.1.429–31, 434). Indeed, her reminder that Willmore's credo, though appealing in theory, will leave her stuck with "a cradle full of noise and mischief, . . . [and] a pack of repentance at [her] back" (5:5.1.439–40)—shrewdly

exposes the way in which libertine philosophy, and its freethinking rejection of institutions like marriage, is just as guilty of idealism as romantic love. For this reason, the play concludes, both are only uneasily
hospitable to women.

In "The Golden Age," an adaptation from an unidentified French
translation of the opening chorus of Tasso's *Aminta* (1573), Behn seems
even less sanguine about freethinking's possibilities for women. Here the
poem's speaker famously locates pastoral antiquity as a privileged space
of sexual freedom, one that results crucially from the absence of institutional religion and Christian law:[2]

> The Lovers thus, thus uncontroul'd did meet,
> Thus all their Joyes and Vows of Love repeat:
>   Joyes which were everlasting, ever new
>   And every Vow inviolably true;
> Not kept in fear of Gods, no fond Religious cause,
>   Nor in Obedience to the duller Laws.
>   Those vain those Politick Curbs to keep man in,
> Who by a fond mistake Created that a Sin;
> Which freeborn we, by right of Nature claim our own.
>
>   (1:105–15)

These lines would seem to suggest the familiar libertine commonplace,
informed by freethinking's critique of Christianity, that before religion
politicized sex by designating man's bodily appetites as sinful, the "Joyes
and Vows of Love" were merely the guileless dictates of simple nature.
What makes sex sinful, the speaker implies, is the hypocrisy imposed by
the constraints of Christian morality, not the physical expression of love.
Such was the argument articulated by Willmore in *The Rover*.

The example of the honorable promiscuity of the earliest men—
described as "the first race of men, nearest allied to God"—is intended,
we learn, to assuage the scruples of the speaker's more punctilious lover
(1:162–65). We soon realize, however, that the speaker is a man cajoling
a woman to relinquish her chastity, a detail that remains opaque to the
reader until the last fifteen lines of Behn's two hundred line poem.[3] Before this point the poem reads as a straightforward tribute to the sexual
and religious freedoms enjoyed by pagan antiquity before the introduction of Christianity. The speaker's motive is exposed in the final stanza,
when in a conventional carpe diem conclusion, he warns a newly speci-
fied "Sylvia" that once her "Beauties" (1:184) fade, "no kind Spring their
sweetness will supply" (1:188). The belated revelation that the poem
participates in a persuasion-to-enjoy tradition changes, retrospectively,
our assessment of "The Golden Age"; it cannot help but encourage the
reader to suspect that the speaker's condemnation of the tyranny of sex-

ual honor under modern Christianity was calculated to further that one ambition.

The rakish hero of Behn's novel *Love-Letters between a Nobleman and His Sister* engages in a similar strategy, contrasting the empty bond of his marriage to his lover Silvia's sister—"a Ceremony impos'd on man by custome"—to the legitimately sacred, though technically unauthorized, union he hopes to enjoy with Silvia. Once again turning to the ancient pagans as his inspiration, Philander lauds the promiscuous mating of "Father and Daughter, Brother and Sister," who "reap'd the joys of Love without controul, and counted it Religious coupling, . . . encourag'd too by Heav'n it self" (2:11, 12). Philander's speech is intended to placate Silvia, who insists that his marriage to her sister constitutes a sacred bond forbidding their alliance. His radical figuring of marriage as an outmoded custom, a "trick" perpetuated by priests for the base ends of property, would appear to derive from freethinking's anticlerical bias and its rejection of institutionalized religion (2:11). Comparing his promiscuity to that of the best of the ancients, Philander insists that his "coupling" with Silvia constitutes real, uncorrupted religion. Yet Philander proves himself to be just as self-interested and dishonest as the clerics he disdains. Recognizing that religion tends to be his "foe" where women are concerned, he does not scruple to use radical rhetoric to serve his final ends (2:238). Indeed, we soon discover that such rhetoric is merely the "dear dissimulation . . . [that] keep[s] up a good Character of constancy" (2:171).

Both "The Golden Age" and *Love-Letters* can thus seem to argue quite strongly that the critique of organized religion is no more than male hypocrisy writ large. Yet in *Love-Letters*, most poignantly, Silvia's conversion to Philander's doctrine at the end of part 1 recalls the persuasive power, hypothetically speaking, of the libertine challenge to orthodoxy as suggested in *The Rover*:

No, Philander, that's a heavenly match when two Souls toucht with equal passion meet (which is but rarely seen)—when willing vows, with serious consideration, are weigh'd and made; when a true view is taken of the Soul, when no base interest makes the hasty bargain, when no conveniency or design of drudge, or slave, shall find it necessary, when equal judgments meet that can esteem the blessings they possess, and distinguish the good of eithers love, and set a value on each others merits, and where both understand to take and pay; who find the beauty of each others minds, and rate 'em as they ought, whom not a formal ceremony binds (with which I've nought to do; but dully give a cold consenting affirmative) but well considered vows from soft inclining hearts, utter'd with love, with joy, with dear delight when Heaven is call'd to witness; She is thy Wife, Philander, He is my Husband, this is the match, this Heaven designs and means. (2:111–12)

For Silvia, libertinism's attraction lies in its emphasis on sexual reciprocity and gender equality. In her vision of a libertine union, "two Souls" are "toucht with equal passion" and form "equal judgments." What is more, Silvia's model lovers "set a value on each others merits," and appreciate "the beauty of each others minds" as well as the allure of each other's physical charms. Such a vision of mature and enduring passion, free from the desiccating effects of institutional authorization, is notably absent from Philander's creed, in which the rejection of marriage's legal power serves to expedite a steady succession of short-lived intrigues.[4] Silvia quickly learns this painful lesson, accusing Philander of irreligion and godlessness, among other betrayals, and by part 3 of the novel, she has successfully appropriated his Machiavellian strategy to the end of achieving a grand revenge (2:218–19). Transformed into a ruthless virago, Silvia abandons her dream of respectful mutuality for "base interest" and "convenience," remaining dependent on her sexual charms for an always temporary power.

Though Silvia's fate appears to confirm Behn's final sense that libertinism, however attractive in its freethinking philosophy, only reproduces the exploitation of women, Behn does offer us another heroine who comes closer to living out Silvia's libertine imaginary. Hermione, the mistress of Caesario, the leader of the Whig rebellion, "was a Friend as well as a Mistress, and one with whom, when the First Play was ended, [Caesario] could Discourse with of useful things of State as well as Love; and improve in both the Noble Mysteries, by her Charming Conversation." Hermione's power over Caesario is a lasting one, based in friendship and shared interests. Never a great beauty, even when young, "she, whose Charms of Youth were ended, being turned of thirty, fortified her decays with all the Arts her Wit and Sex were capable of" (2:335, 397).

It should be no surprise that Behn, herself long past the flush of youth in 1687, would have been searching for additional avenues of power and emancipation for women, especially within the libertine circles that she inhabited.[5] Materialist philosophy appears to have been one of them as early as 1682.[6] When Thomas Creech came out with the first complete translation of Lucretius' great Epicurean poem, *De rerum natura*, in that year Behn was asked to write a poetic commendation for the second edition.[7] The resulting poem, "To the Unknown Daphnis on His Excellent Translation of Lucretius," thanks Creech for making philosophy accessible to women:

> Till now I curst my Sex and Education,
> And more the scanted Customs of the Nation,
> Permitting not the Female Sex to tread
> The Mighty Paths of Learned Heroes Dead.

The Godlike Virgil and Great Homers Muse
Like Divine Mysteries are conceal'd from us,
We are forbid all grateful Theams,
No ravishing Thoughts approach our Ear;
The Fulsom Gingle of the Times
Is all we are allow'd to Understand, or Hear. (1:25–34)

The comparison of Virgil and Homer to "Divine Mysteries" "conceal'd" from women is appropriately arch in this context, as Lucretius' teachings notoriously dismiss supernatural in favor of purely natural explanation. By translating Lucretius into the vernacular, Behn insinuates, Creech enables women to participate in the freethinking dialogue. The outcome is their rejection of faith-based explanations of the universe—"The Fulsom Gingle of the Times"—in favor of materialist ones.[8]

To Behn's contemporaries, Epicureanism was the first known expression of unbelief, but most dismissed freethinking forays into philosophy—ancient and modern—as puerile efforts to justify debauchery.[9] The libertine reception of Epicurean thought most readily exposed freethinkers to this attack, as Epicureanism's emphasis on freedom and pleasure seemed so favorable to the cause of promiscuity. In the words of Edward Ward's poem, "The Libertine's Choice" (1709),

O great Lucretius, thou shalt be my Guide,
Like thee I'll live, and by thy Rule abide:
Measure my Pleasures by my Appetites,
And unconfined, pursue the World's Delights.[10]

Although Epicureanism was capable of providing as powerful a rationale for philosophical atheism as it did for the indulgence of the appetites, contemporaries consistently characterized the freethinker as incapable of mastering serious speculative thought.[11] Creech himself, in the dedication to his translation of Lucretius, argues that Epicurus purposely "appealed rather to the loose affections of the debauched, than the reason of the Sober." As Joseph Glanvill remarked, "Reason is a severe thing, and doth as little comport with mens Lusts, as Religion: and the same Lusts that make [men] willing to reason against Religion, make them incapable of it: For debauchery is almost as great an enemy to mens intellectuals, as to their morals." Clement Ellis declared similarly that "the very source and spring" of Restoration freethinking was mere licentiousness: "Were your hearts laid open, I doubt not, but we should soon find, that it was not any strength of reason that prevailed upon you to dislike our Faith; but that opposition which it now makes against your darling lusts. 'Tis only your unwillingness to forsake the present sweets of sin, that makes you set so light by the future joys of Heaven."[12]

And yet, even the Anglican apologists were forced to recognize that all unbelief was not reducible to sexual hedonism, and that freethinking was steadily establishing a philosophical armory they could not ignore. While conceding that "scoffing at Religion . . . is no such new thing in the world," John Fell laments the emergence of "a Sect of men" who deny God "as Philosophy." Charles Wolseley describes the freethinker's mandatory education in Democritus, Epicurus, and Aristotle, remarking that "he is thought a novice in knowledge, and an absolute freshman in the highest sort of learning, that has not imbibed some of this kind of Philosophy."[13] After the final book of *Love-Letters*, it appears that Behn's libertinism was headed in this direction. For the following year, she embarked upon her translations of Fontenelle's controversial contributions to the early French Enlightenment. Behn would have been aware that her praise of Lucretius grouped her among the apologists for free love, and her turn to Fontenelle's natural philosophy can be seen as an attempt to overcome the long-standing charge that her writing was merely bawdy.

I

Entretiens sur la pluralité des mondes, translated by Behn as *A Discovery of New Worlds*, is contrived as a series of nighttime conversations between an attractive marquise and a natural philosopher whom she receives at her castle. The philosopher is charmed by the lady, but he prefers the more intoxicating task of "draw[ing] Madam the Marquiese into our party" through showing her that supernatural forces do not control the physical world. While acknowledging that his readers might "expect to hear of Feasting, Parties at play, and Hunting-matches," the philosopher makes clear that his account will concern pleasures of a different sort. In his preface, Fontenelle explains that his purpose in creating the "Fiction" of "Madam the Marquiese" is to provide "the fair Sex" with an example of an ordinary, uneducated woman who nevertheless succeeds in understanding philosophy "without Confusion" (4:92, 88). Natural philosophy, he suggests, has been rendered unnecessarily abstruse, and women assume falsely that its lessons are beyond their comprehension. Like other women of her time, Behn lacked the background to participate on a par with men in current philosophical debates. Translation provided her a way of joining the conversation without education and formal training. It also allowed her to engage with and disseminate radical ideas while remaining at a safe distance from them. Behn made the most of this opportunity, going so far, as Line Cottegnies points out, as to improve on Fontenelle when his argument proved obscure as well as to change the text's references to men in general to "men and women" (4:ix, xiii).[14] In this way, Behn makes explicit Fontenelle's implied invitation to women to participate in the freethinking crusade as informed thinkers in their own right.[15]

A Discovery of New Worlds aims to propagate Copernicus' heliocentric theory of planetary motions as against the ancient system of Ptolemy. As Fontenelle's philosopher tells it, the advocates of Ptolemy believed that "the Earth was immoveably fixed in the Centre of the Universe, whilst all the Celestial Bodies (made only for her) were at the pains of turning continually round, to give Light to the Earth." In Fontenelle's rendering, what is at stake in the debate between the Ptolemaic and the Copernican worldview is not so much science as theology. Indeed, Ptolemy's scientific error is evidence of a prior theological one, namely, man's misguided and "vain" belief "that all this vast Frame of Nature was destined to our use." Copernicus "humbled the Vanity of mankind" by dislodging the earth from the center of the universe and proving that it was no different from the other planets. The somewhat disorienting consequence is that man no longer enjoys any special dispensation. On listening to the philosopher's explanation of Copernicus' theory, the marquise laments, "What shall become of us in the middle of so many Worlds; since the Title you give to the rest agrees to this of ours? And for my Part, I see the Earth so dreadfully little, that hereafter I shall scorn to be concern'd for any part of it." Copernicus' earth, in other words, is no longer the beneficiary of God's divine supervision (4:100, 103, 154–55).

Like all natural philosophers of the seventeenth century, Fontenelle was well aware that his intellectual allegiances threatened Christian belief in Providence.[16] Indeed, careful readers of the philosophical tradition knew that long before the controversies over Copernicanism, Lucretius had asserted his doubt that "our sky / And our round world are precious and unique." Indeed, for Lucretius, the endlessness of space itself served as evidence that "nature has no tyrants over her, / But always acts of her own will; she has / No part of any godhead whatsoever." Which of the Gods, he asks, "is strong enough / To rule the sum of things, to hold the reins / of absolute profundity?"[17] Many of the early virtuosi of the Royal Society managed to reconcile scientific mechanism with orthodox theism through emphasizing that nature's operations, though regular and consistent, were not autonomous and unconscious; the regular motions of nature, in fact, revealed the skillful hand of its Creator. Boyle most famously placed God at the center of an atomistic universe as the ultimate source of all motion and design. Providence thus generated the mechanical laws governing the universe.[18] As Richard Bentley confidently asserts in his Boyle Lecture of 1692, "All the powers of mechanism are entirely dependent on the Deity, and do afford a solid argument for the reality of his nature."[19] Fontenelle, on the contrary, nowhere pays tribute to the Great Author of the machine, a glaring absence given the intensity of theological objections to seventeenth-century science.

Whereas the majority of his contemporaries in natural philosophy bent over backwards to reassure their readers that God operates through the mechanical laws of nature, from which he is wholly separate, Fontenelle makes nature alone a sufficient explanation, independent of all spiritual forces. Comparing nature to a theatrical representation, Fontenelle's philosopher observes that, if we had access to "the hinder part of the Theatre at the Opera," we would learn that the seemingly extraordinary scenes in front of us were in fact the effects of "Ropes, Pullies, Wheels and Weights." In his view, we fall back on a belief in "Secret Virtue[s]," and other "sublime Idea[s]" due to the difficulty of determining natural causes (4:97, 96, 97, 98). The idea that we attribute a supernatural design to nature only because we lack an adequate understanding of its mechanical processes is a consistent theme throughout *A Discovery of New Worlds*. And Fontenelle was not the first philosophical radical to articulate this view. A reigning preoccupation of Montaigne in his *Apology*, the view serves most notoriously as the launching pad for Spinoza's critique of miracles in chapter 6 of his *Tractatus*. "Just as men are accustomed to call divine the kind of knowledge that surpasses human understanding," Spinoza writes, "so they call divine, or the work of God, any work whose cause is generally unknown."[20]

As Richard Westfall has argued, the clash between scientific mechanism and Christianity came down to the problem of miracles, for the mechanistic understanding of nature promoted by Boyle allows for God's creation of the laws of nature, but not so easily for his occasional interruption of those laws. Once Providence is progressively limited to God's general design of nature, the problem becomes how to explain the biblical records of his supernatural interventions in the Creation. Boyle and other natural philosophers of the period got around this problem by making miracles a possible though infrequent exception to a general rule: God has the power to violate his otherwise immutable laws, but acts on this power only rarely.[21] John Wilkins, an early virtuoso and defender of Copernicanism, suggested that miracles were limited to the early days of Christianity, when it needed the support of supernatural testimony.[22] His *Discovery of a New World* (1638) and *Discourse concerning a New Planet* (1640) both sought to popularize Copernican astronomy and clear it from any taint of irreligion. In England, Wilkins's works represented the most influential defense of Copernicanism and were important sources for Fontenelle as well as for Behn.[23]

Although Wilkins aimed to reconcile mechanism with the possibility of miracles, one can see how his tendency to minimize the miraculous could be appropriated for more radical ends. In *A Discovery of a New World*, Wilkins argues that "a Miracle often serves for the Receptacle of a lazy Ignorance," and his *Discourse concerning a New Planet* warns that philosophers should not "fly unto the absolute Power of God" in their efforts to explain unusual natural phenomena. Alexander Ross states the danger inherent in this position, charging Wilkins with "turn[ing] Divinity into naturall Philosophy, and confound[ing] the works of God, and of Nature."[24] Wilkins did not intend to banish divinity from the Copernican universe, but Fontenelle seems to have taken advantage of this potential in his argument.[25] His efforts were aided, moreover, by the Copernican insight that God did not structure the natural world around man and his doings.

As Rochester's "Satyre" attests, this particular lesson had long been invoked by the freethinking tradition to cast suspicion on miracles.[26] Thomas Burnet, another seventeenth-century natural philosopher linked to an atheistic agenda, had warned in his *Sacred Theory of the Earth* (1681) that "we must not by any Means admit or imagine, that all Nature, and this great Universe, was made only for the sake of Man." A proper understanding of "natural Providence," indeed, would protect us from blindly seeking refuge in either the "first Cause" or "Miracles." Charles Blount included Burnet's teaching in his translation of Spinoza, ostensibly to buttress Spinoza's similar claim that mankind has fabricated miracles "[so] that others might believe them to be . . . the chiefest part of the whole creation."[27] Thus when Fontenelle scorns the naïve belief that "the earth was immoveably fixed in the centre of the universe" and the corollary view that "all this Frame of nature was destined to our use," he reveals the link between his Copernicanism and his critique of revealed religion, a critique that forms the tacit subject of *A Discovery of New Worlds*.[28]

Although Behn's translation stays close to Fontenelle's original, it is prefaced by a new contribution entitled "Essay on Translated Prose." As Cottegnies remarks, the title page of the first edition calls attention to the part played by the translator by including Behn's name in capital letters while omitting Fontenelle's entirely. Her prefatory essay is also advertised prominently as a "Wholly new" contribution to the philosophical controversy surrounding Copernicanism, one that promises to answer "the Arguments of Father Tacquet, and others, against the System of Copernicus."[29] Unlike Fontenelle, who addresses and abandons the problem of religion in the final paragraph of his preface, Behn makes the theological objections to Copernicanism her central concern.[30] Most conspicuous in the debate was the charge that Copernicanism contradicted several key passages of Scripture, particularly the text of Joshua 10.12–14, in which Joshua commands the sun to stand still.

The controversy over this text centered on the conviction that a motionless sun was a miracle. As Behn recounts it, traditionalists had cited this extraordinary event as incontrovertible evidence in favor of Ptolemy's earth-centered universe: since Scripture reports the stillness of the sun as a miracle, its normal state must be one of motion, as Ptolemy taught. Fontenelle had indirectly answered such objections to Copernicanism by suggesting that the belief that the sun stands still tells us more about man's vanity and crude misconceptions about the natural world than it does about astronomy. Since man tends "to fansie all things made for himself," he logically imagines that the sun rises and sets on him. In reality, however, "when we see the Moon, Planets and fixed Stars turn round us . . . , all is but bare Imagination." Indeed, it is precisely because we are not in the center of the universe that we lack an objective perspective through which to evaluate the motions of the planets accurately. In a veiled reference to the argument from Scripture that God might choose on occasion to alter the usual course of the planets, Fontenelle's philosopher insists that planetary rotation is consistent and regular: "Any thing that may appear to us to be irregular, . . . is occasion'd by our own Motion meeting theirs in such different manners" (4:104, 105, 142, 106).

Behn's translator's preface, in turn, confronts the argument from Scripture head on, launching a virtual tour de force of biblical criticism. Focusing her attention on the Joshua controversy, Behn makes much of the fact that Joshua commands the moon as well as the sun to stand still. As she explains,

The Reason the Sun was commanded to stand still, was to the end the Children of Israel might have Light to guide them, to destroy their Enemies. Now when by this Miracle they had the Light of the Sun, of what Advantage could the Moon be to them? . . . If the Sun did not move, according to the System of Ptolemy, where was the necessity of the Moon's standing still? For if the Moon had gone on her Course, where was the Loss or Disorder in Nature? (4:83)

Since there is no essential relationship between the motions of the sun and the moon in a Ptolemaic world, if Ptolemy's theory were correct, Behn suggests, then God would not have needed to stop the moon. The light of day could have been extended and the moon could have continued on its usual course without any disruption to nature. According to the Copernican view, however, the motions of the planets are integrally linked, so that any alteration in the movements of one must necessarily affect the others and thus the universe as a whole.[31] The fact that God stopped the moon as well as the sun would seem, then, to decide in favor of Copernicus, for to let the moon continue her rotation "would have occasioned such a Disorder and Confusion in Nature, that nothing less than two or three new Miracles, all as great as the first, could have set the World in Order again" (4:84).

Since God, as the argument went, designed nature to function with only his occasional intervention, Copernican theory would *seem* to support the miracle described in Joshua: if God had the choice to work one or three miracles, he would surely choose the most efficient alternative. As Behn's exegesis continues, however, it becomes clear that even the Copernican principle of relative motion fails to explain how the natural world could possibly have borne the cessation of the sun's and the moon's habitual rotation. Indeed, Behn ends her examination of Joshua 10.12–14 by concluding that all of nature—not just the sun and the moon—must have been stopped in its tracks:

So that I doubt not but when this stupendious Miracle was performed by the Almighty and Infinite Power of God, his omnipotent Arm did in an Instant stop the Course of Nature, and the whole Frame of the Universe was at a stand, though the Sun and Moon be only named, being, to vulgar Appearance, the two great Luminaries that govern the Universe. (4:84)

Behn craftily turns Spinoza's heresy, popularized by Blount and Burnet, on its head here. As we remember, the freethinking position claimed that the miracles related in Scripture are natural occurrences described as supernatural in an effort to accord "to vulgar Appearance." Yet Behn asserts, on the contrary, that the miracle in Joshua, in fact, involved *more*, not *less*, supernatural intervention than Scripture reports. In her account, Scripture tells of God stopping the sun and the moon because the illiterate masses believe these planets to "govern the Universe." In truth, however, God's "omnipotent Arm did in an Instant stop the Course of Nature": the entire universe, not just the sun and the moon, came to a spectacular halt.

Why would Behn seek to amplify God's intervention in the natural world in this manner? As Jonathan Israel has recently argued, even the mainstream, moderate camp of Newton and Boyle was attempting "to narrow the gap between the supernatural and natural as much as possible, virtually denying that there was any great difference."[32] Miracles, according to this accommodationist view, operate largely through God's manipulation, not suspension, of the laws of nature. This kind of emphasis on the "argument from design"—the notion that God foresaw all possible permutations and contingencies when he created his laws—became the basis for reconciling scientific mechanism with faith in Christian Providence. The fight against philosophical irreligion, then, was waged through making science the ally, not the foe, of theology.[33] In Behn's hands, however, the attempt to explain the miracle in Joshua 10.12–14 according to the scientific principles of Copernicus breaks down. Science, in this instance, notably fails to support theology, and we appear to be left with a supernatural explanation so improbable as to render belief impossible. Behn's foray into scriptural exegesis thus offers a sly parody of scriptural commentary and of conventional belief in revealed religion. The implication, I would argue, is that any rational investigation into a supposed miracle ends in absurdity. Since recourse to the miraculous, even in orthodox circles, was becoming less, not more, strident by the late seventeenth century, Behn's exaggeration of God's interventions in the natural world asks to be read satirically.[34]

Looking back, Behn prepares the careful reader for this conclusion. For her argument at the outset of the translator's preface is not that Scripture decides in favor of Copernicus, but rather that "this Text of Scripture is at least, as much for Copernicus as Ptolemy." Behn's point here is subtle: if Scripture appears to provide evidence for conflicting theories, it actually decides for neither. Even though the Copernican theory of planetary motions is scientifically correct, one should not look to Scripture to find proof of its rightness. Here Behn rests her reading of Joshua on the principle, newly circulating in freethinking circles, that Scripture adapted its message to the limited aptitudes of the common people, never intending to teach philosophy:

Therefore, with all due Reverence and Respect to the Word of God, I hope I may be allowed to say, that the design of the Bible was not to instruct Mankind in Astronomy, Geometry, or Chronology, but in the Law of God, to lead us to Eternal Life; and the Spirit of God has been so condescending to our Weakness, that through the whole Bible, when any thing of that kind is mentioned, the Expressions are always turned to fit our Capacities, and to fit the common Acceptance, or Appearances of things to the Vulgar. (4:79)

As it turns out, Blount's "Premonition to the Candid Reader," prefacing his unattributed translation of Spinoza's chapter on miracles, begins by borrowing a passage to the same effect from Burnet:

It is the Judgement of most of the ancient Fathers of the Christian Faith, and of the most learned Theologues among the Moderns; that the Authors of the holy Scriptures, when they speak of natural things, do not design to instruct men in Physical Speculations and the Science of Natural Philosophy; but aim only to excite pious Affections in their breasts, and to induce them to the Worship and Veneration of the true God.[35]

In Burnet's and Blount's hands, the theological position that Scripture's purpose is to teach faith, not philosophy, forms the backbone of the rejection of miracles.[36] The clue is the emphasis on the way Scripture "speak[s] of natural things," or in Behn's version, of "Astronomy, Geometry, or Chronology." Instead of telling the truth about nature's operations, the argument went, Scripture aims to excite wonder and awe in the minds of its readers by referring causality to a supernatural power, or, in other words, by claiming that God works miracles. The lesson was indispensable to Spinoza, for central to his confidence that events supposed to be supernatural or accomplished by God were, in fact, natural occurrences is the prior conviction that "it is not the part of Scripture . . . to teach things through their natural causes or to engage in pure philosophy."[37] Scripture attributes acts to God in its efforts to strike the imagination and instill piety in the minds of the masses, all the while knowing that these same acts in fact come about in accordance with nature's immutable laws.

Spinoza had already singled out the Joshua miracle in the second chapter of the *Tractatus*, arguing, like Behn after him, that both the Ptolemaists and the Copernicans are wrong to look to Scripture for confirmation of their theories. In his chapter "Of Miracles," moreover, the Joshua miracle stands as unique evidence of how Scripture relates an event "quite differently from the way it could really have come about." As he explains it, since the Hebrews were Ptolemaists, believing that the sun circled a motionless earth, when the day in question seemed longer than usual, their primitive ideas about astronomy caused them to imagine that God had stopped the sun's usual motion, or worked a miracle.[38] Blount, too, invokes the Joshua miracle in his *Oracles of Reason* to demonstrate that "there is often times great Errors committed in the manner of reading Scripture." In the case of the sun supposedly standing still for a whole day in Gabaon, Blount refers to the "able Interpreters" who have shown that, in fact, "the Light of the setting Sun after he was himself gone down, was only the Reflection of his Beams, remaining as yet in the Atmosphere." Because of the "favourable Situation" of the hills surrounding Gabaon, the sun's beams "reverberated longer than ordinary," making it appear to the ignorant that the sun had miraculously failed to set.[39]

The correct way to read the extraordinary events recounted in Scripture, Behn asserts, is allegorically. As she comments of Joshua 10.12–14, "This was the space of a Day in Time, yet can be called no part of Time, since Time and Nature are always in motion, and this Day was a stop of that Course" (4:84). And the alleged miracle in Joshua is not the only evidence Behn supplies to support this claim. The Bible, she argues, is rife with inaccuracies, from the implausible dimensions of Solomon's molten brass sea to the inconsistent chronology of King Solomon's reign

(4:84, 79–82). After Spinoza, any attempt to divorce theology and philosophy demands scrutiny for latent irreligious intent, for the result of his separation would appear to be theology's relegation to the realm of fiction, fantasy, and, ultimately, falsehood. In the meantime, all matters of truth are accorded to philosophy.[40]

The notion that Scripture was a pious allegory, accommodated to the weak understandings of the vulgar, was itself importantly informed by the tradition of twofold philosophy so central to the elite freethinkers of the period. Blount's *Oracles of Reason* contends that Moses himself was conscious that his representation of the beginning of the world in Genesis "followed the popular System" and thus went against "Physical Truth." Blount insinuates here that Moses knew perfectly well that the earth was not at the center of the universe, or man its primary beneficiary, but rather that he described "the first Originals of Things after such a method as might breed in the minds of Men Piety, and a worshipping of the true God." Blount even goes so far as to say that buried in its (often marvelous) accounts of natural things, Scripture contains a hidden element of philosophy, "sometimes accommodating it self to the capacities of the People, and sometimes to the real but more clouded truth."[41]

In the spirit of this peculiarly heterodox tradition, Behn concludes her translator's preface with a defense of submission to the ruling directives of the Church. Despite her own implicit skepticism about the possibility of supernatural intervention in the natural world, her explicit position is that "all good Christians" should "acquiesce in the Opinion and Decrees of the Church of Christ, in whom dwells the Spirit of God, which enlightens us to Matters of Religion and Faith" (4:85). Such a surrendering of the field, in the final hour, to traditional religious authority may appear paradoxical, given what would seem to be the essay's evident demystification of divine Providence. And yet, closer examination reveals that Behn's preface is not only informed by twofold philosophy; it is also itself a masterful example of its processes in action.[42] Indeed, a right appreciation of Behn's strategy in the translator's preface requires our insight that her curiously heightened account of the Joshua miracle reads skeptically only to those in the know. This inner circle is uniquely aware that the enlightened age, if it believes, does so reasonably, not credulously, and is therefore too savvy to accept the divine excess her version of events would seem to suggest. It is precisely such heightenings, on the contrary, that continue to appeal to the naïve belief of the uneducated masses, distinguished by their enduring predisposition toward the marvelous.[43] In their case, the more fabulous the account, the greater is their pleasure and enthusiasm in the tales of religion. The unenlightened reader is thus never meant to recognize Behn's exposure of the fictional nature of the miraculous. But what about the enlightened reader who knows that miracles contradict the laws of nature? The current age, Behn argues, is characterized by a dangerous mixture of unbelief and enthusiasm, both of which stances wrongly use religion "as a Foundation and Ground for Rebellion." To turn the Scripture into "Ridicule," on the one hand, or to "give the Word of God only that Meaning and Sense that pleases their own Humours," on the other, are thus equally destructive of civil peace and thereby equally to be avoided (4:85). Behn's solution, then, as Cottegnies suggests, is to advocate religious obedience more as a matter of form and duty than as a concern of faith and belief.[44]

For Behn, the fact that the masses show themselves to be so unfailingly stirred by the cant of religion makes it of paramount importance that they continue to be inculcated with "good wholesome Doctrine, that teaches Obedience to . . . King and Superiours."[45] Her 1682 play *The Roundheads*, a royalist satire against the hypocrisy and corruption of "Good Old Cause" republicans, throws this lesson into relief by demonstrating how religious frauds "pass for Gospel with the common Rabble" and prevail more "than all the Rhetorick of the learn'd or honest" (6:3.1.233, 382–83). Behn stresses repeatedly the way in which the Commonwealth men have relied on cant and "Gadly cozenage" to delude the masses into treason and sedition (6:3.1.132). By the end of the play, though the mob abandons the cause and proclaims its fidelity to the king, its return to a lawful allegiance is shown to be equally tinged with religious enthusiasm.[46] Freeman, one of the play's royalist heroes, proclaims nervously that "their zealous Loyalty admits no Bounds," and the play concludes with the honorable Captain of a band of armed apprentices directing his gang to go home "and to the Powers Divine, Pray for the King, and all the Sacred Line" (6:5.1.524–25). Though praying for the king and his sacred line assumes a religious posture that is just as fraudulent as the sanctified sedition of the "Good Old Cause" rebels, Behn's point is that the former position supports loyalty, civil peace, and stability, while the latter fuels an unwarranted rebellion marred by greed and self-interest. In this way, fidelity to royal and ecclesiastical authority becomes, as Eliot Visconsi argues, "a legitimate and virtuous means of disciplining a volatile populace dangerously susceptible to the influence of demagogues and enthusiasts."[47]

II

As we have seen, this propensity to support the institution of religion on pragmatic rather than spiritual grounds, as an unrivaled source of social stability, derives from the skepticism of the best of the ancients and their sense of religion as a practice that one is required to perform (for the greater public good) rather than subjectively to believe. It thus comes as no surprise to discover that Behn had been working on a translation of Fontenelle's *L'histoire des oracles*, a detailed investigation into the varieties of ancient pagan religion, simultaneously with her translation of *Pluralité des mondes*. Before Herbert, the starting-off point for the field was Gerard Vossius' magisterial *De theologia gentili* (*Origins of Gentile Theology*) (1641), significantly reprinted eight times by 1700. With Vossius' massive achievement began a series of learned researches into the beliefs, rites, and superstitions of the pagans, all with the ostensible aim of distinguishing between the errors of idolatry and true religion.[48] As we recall, Herbert's *De Religione Gentilium* was translated into English in 1705, with a second edition in the same year and two subsequent printings in 1709 and 1711. After Herbert, Blount published no less than three studies of ancient religion in the 1670s and 1680s, with more writings collected in his posthumous *Oracles of Reason* of 1693. John Toland and Matthew Tindal followed the trend well into the eighteenth century.[49] As the above names might suggest, however, the investigation of pagan superstition tended to function as a "grand subterfuge" through which all revealed religion could be theoretically discredited.[50] For Vossius' research had unearthed evidence that made it increasingly difficult to differentiate false pagan superstition from true Christian revelation. Though Vossius was a Christian apologist who insisted on the necessity of revealed truth, his research nonetheless suggested (to those willing to go the distance) that Christianity's special revelation was at best unnecessary and at worst yet another instance of superstition.[51] As Frank Manuel argues, "Throughout the eighteenth century no discussion of pagan or exotic religion ever lost its heretical overtones, however fervid the philosophers' protests that they were only combating the false gods of the gentiles and were not impugning the established truth of Christianity."[52]

The notion that the various supernatural occurrences described in Scripture are fraudulent indeed forms the tacit subtext of Fontenelle's *L'histoire des oracles*. Although the book takes the tricks of pagan religion as its subject, ostensibly reserving Christianity as an exception, few were fooled by this tactical ploy. Fontenelle had clearly raised the bar of heresy, and Behn's translation, *The History of Oracles and the Cheats of the Pagan Priests*, appeared anonymously and without a publisher's imprint on the title page. In another effort at popularizing somewhat arcane material, Fontenelle's work was itself borrowed from Anthonie Van Dale's *De Oraculis Ethnicorum* (1683). Van Dale, a Dutch physician, had felt little compunction in implying that the frauds of ancient oracle priests were no different from various bogus miracles of the Christian tradition, and his audacity produced a flurry of charges of heresy and atheism. Aware of the explosive nature of his material, Fontenelle offered a softer version of Van Dale's thesis. Whereas Van Dale had boldly asserted that the professed magical power of the ancient oracles was fraudulent because all supernatural power was a myth, Fontenelle attempted to distinguish between the possibility of real magic and the deceit of the oracle priests. Although Fontenelle's modifications proved largely effective—the first attack against him not appearing until 1707—knowing readers were nonetheless aware of the implicit message: there is no supernatural presence in the world of man.[53]

Once again the debate hinged on the reality of miracles. For the orthodox view, introduced by the Church Fathers and disseminated over centuries of Christian tradition, was that the greatest miracle of Christianity was Christ's silencing of the heathen oracles. It was this miracle, indeed, that marked the establishment of Christian religion, "an Event," in one divine's words, "so remarkable, that it was almost one continu'd Miracle, during the first Ages of the Church, and an evident Proof of the Truth of the Christian Religion."[54] To call this miracle of miracles into question thus cuts to the core of all faith. In Van Dale's and Fontenelle's account, the heathen oracles were nothing more than an elaborate and longstanding hoax, orchestrated through the self-serving machinations of the pagan priests. The oracles did not, in fact, cease miraculously with the coming of Christ; their eventual demise was the purely political result of the antipagan decrees of later Christian rulers (4:257–66).[55] The cessation of the oracles, in other words, could not have been less extraordinary.

This critique of the oracles' supposed supernaturalism began, importantly, in antiquity itself. Indeed, a significant subtext of both Van Dale's and Fontenelle's work is the skepticism of "some Grand Sects of the Pagan Philosophers" about the supernatural nature of the oracles (4:201). As Fontenelle comments,

If in the midst of *Greece* it self, where all place resounded with their *Oracles*, we had maintained that they were but Impostures, no one would have been astonished with the Boldness of the *Paradox*. . . . For *Philosophers* were divided about the Subject of *Oracles*. . . . The Wonders of the *Oracles* were not so great, but that half the Wise Men of *Greece*, were still at Liberty to believe nothing of them. (4:201–2)

We arrive here at freethinking's ancient bias. Implicit in Van Dale's and Fontenelle's suggestion that the best of the pagans remained untouched by the corrupting effects of the oracles is the prior notion that an older, purer religion preexisted priestly efforts to perpetuate superstition. The idea began with Herbert's *De Religione Gentilium,* which went back beyond the Church Fathers, the Gospels, and even the Old Testament, to locate an untainted "primordial tradition" in the worship of antiquity. Here was the origin of the five Religious Common Notions, introduced in Herbert's earlier philosophical treatise, *De Veritate* (1624), which he hoped would serve as the foundation for a universal religion and encourage an end to sectarian strife. Because Herbert's Religious Common Notions are innate, and therefore predate the establishment of institutional religion, ancient religion provides the best evidence of their content in pure and simple form. Over time, Herbert argues, the Common Notions became obscured by an overgrowth of superstition and priestly corruption. By creating a variety of rites, ceremonies, and mysteries, the priesthood gained control over the minds of the people, and "the purest and most chaste parts of divine worship were neglected." And yet, the fraudulent priestly doctrines "did not dazzle everyone." "Educated" and "perceptive" people doubted what they said, and the philosophers likewise stood fast in their resistance to all forms of superstition.[56] The examination of ancient pagan religion thus reveals not only the roots of priestcraft and the evils of institutionalized religion, but also the merits of the old religion of simple virtue, piety, and rational worship.

An even more important precursor to Van Dale and Fontenelle on the oracles was Herbert's more radical *Dialogue between a Tutor and His Pupil,* a work suspected to have circulated in manuscript in the seventeenth century. Much of Herbert's *Dialogue* was also disseminated in Blount's *Great Is Diana of the Ephesians: or, the Original of Idolatry* (1680), though Blount never attributes his material to Herbert.[57] In this later work, Herbert argues forcefully that the heathen priests were frauds who deluded the vulgar with fabricated fictions concerning God. In mercenary league with princes and magistrates, the priests exploited the oracles for the purposes of social control, deluding the people "when any business of importance did occurr in the commonwealth." Here again Herbert attempts to resurrect a purer pagan past, before the introduction of priestcraft, in an effort to remind the corrupt present of what an uncontaminated religion might look like:

Before religion, (i.e.), rites, ceremonies, pretended revelations, and the like, were invented, there was no worship of God but in a rational way, whereof the philosophers pretending to be masters, did to this end, not only teach virtue and piety, but were great examples of it in their lives, whom also the people chiefly followed, till they gave ear to the covetous and crafty sacerdotal order; who, instead of the said virtue and piety, introduced fables, and figments of their own coining, and together persuaded the vulgar sort, that as men could not know the best manner of serving God, by any natural abilities of their own, so it was necessary he should reveal the same to the priests, in some extraordinary kind, for the better instruction of them.[58]

All true virtue and morality, Herbert suggests, was taught by philosophy, not theology. The philosophers of antiquity, indeed, were called *Hierophantae*, or "teachers of holy doctrines," and unlike the priests, they not only taught piety; they also practiced it. The wise and prudent among the heathens followed their example in rejecting superstition and priestly impostures.[59]

At the same time, however, Herbert acknowledges the ancients' insight that an exclusively natural religion was not for everyone: "some of the most penetrating and intelligent minds" even submitted to the superstitious worship of the priests, but they did so "in order that the lewd and debauched, who could not distinguish truth from falsehood, should not completely reject or condemn all [genuine] worship."[60] Fontenelle also betrays an awareness of the benefits, when necessary, of twofold philosophy. The ancients, he relates, adopted a divided consciousness regarding the truth content of the oracles, consulting them as a matter of ritual and performance, on the one hand, all the while knowing, strictly speaking, that they were "absolute impostures," on the other (4:204). Once we understand the definitive separation between belief and practice in ancient religion, we are in a position to appreciate its peculiar mixture of radical skepticism and conservative conformity. Since the ceremonial performance of religious duties had no intrinsic relationship to faith (as Fontenelle argues, "*Religion* was a practice, the speculation of which was very indifferent"), the ancients lost little by complying with the religious customs of their country. Cicero, most notoriously, was free to vent his doubt among his fellow philosophers without the threat of persecution precisely because he "profess'd" the state religion when necessary.

We have no translator's preface accompanying Behn's *History of Oracles*, a choice likely determined by the subversive nature of Fontenelle's material. As Janet Todd has argued, however, Behn's decision to translate this work "must suggest something of her attitude to religion in general."[61] We do know, moreover, that Behn was aware of the charges that Van Dale's thesis amounted to heresy and atheism, for Fontenelle's preface refers to an account in a recent journal of the incriminating attack of the German scholar George Moebius, and Behn adds the exact reference to her translation (4:173n*b*). In her dedication to George Lord Jeffreys, a Tory distinguished for his loyalty to the Stuarts, Behn suggests that her offering forms part of the celebration of tranquility in the aftermath of the Popish Plot and Exclusion Crisis.[62] On such an occasion, Behn affirms, the poets should express their pleasure through the writing of panegyrics. In her case, however, "the Muses have all taken Wing, and are fled to Climates more encouraging and kind . . . so that instead of Nobler numbers, they are necessitated servilely to creep after the fence of foreign Authors, stinting the Generous fancy to anothers thought." Behn takes refuge in the role of mere translator here, emphasizing that all inspiration and intention must be attributed to Fontenelle. Though she identifies her subject as "only . . . the Pagan Religion," the interest for contemporaries, as Behn knew well, lay precisely in the implications the critique of the pagan oracles had for Christianity (4:170–71).

Indeed, Behn explains that she writes on religion "in a time when we have scarce any other Theme" (4:171). The study of pagan religion, in other words, cannot help but tell us something about our own (4:170–71). And if the ultimate lesson to be gleaned from this study is that religion, as Fontenelle suggests, should be understood as "meer Ceremony, in which the mind [bears] no part," then the same insight should ostensibly apply to Christianity (4:206). Once again, the implications of this lesson are twofold. While the emphasis would seem to fall on unbelief, orthodox practice, or what Fontenelle calls "outward Respect," is equally commanded of each citizen (4:208). The key to a right understanding of religion's function, whether paganism or Christianity, is to "[do] as others did" (4:206). With this deference to traditional observance, one is then free to believe what one pleases.

The notion that the best of the pagans preferred a simple virtue and piety to the more flagrant aspects of ancient superstition is central to the ancient bias of English freethinking. And since it was the priests who debased what was a worthy practice into a set of barren rites and hollow performances, detaching moral principles from their true ethical center, the cure for today's theological ills was to remember that religion's end was not the rightness of a particular doctrine but rather the practice of virtue and good conduct. This is precisely the view affirmed in Behn's novella *Oroonoko*, written in the same period as the *Oracles* translation. Here the Indians of Surinam, existing in a pagan, golden-age setting, enjoy the absence of ecclesiastical law:

And these People represented to me an absolute *Idea* of the first State of Innocence, before Man knew how to sin: And 'tis most evident and plain, that simple Nature is the most harmless, inoffensive and vertuous Mistress. 'Tis she alone, if she were permitted, that better instructs the World, than all the Inventions of Man: Religion wou'd here but destroy that Tranquillity, they possess by Ignorance; and Laws wou'd but teach 'em to know, Offence, of which now they have no Notion. (3:59)

In a reversal of the orthodox position, Behn here suggests that modernity, or man's "Inventions" (namely theological rule), only perverts nature's sufficiency. With nature as man's God and sovereign, the Surinam natives remain virtuous and innocent. Indeed, the novella's titular hero, another instance of an exemplary pagan whose goodness derives from his roots in a primitive, premodern culture, attributes his ignoble treatment at the hands of greedy Europeans entirely to Christianity's tendency to sacrifice real virtue and moral probity for empty doctrine. One can put "no Faith in the White Men, or the Gods they Ador'd," as Christianity "instructed 'em in Principles so false that honest Men cou'd not live amongst 'em; though no People profess'd so much, none perform'd so little" (3:109).

The Christian investment in rewards and punishments in the afterlife becomes the perfect example of this hypocrisy. When the English captain who tricks Oroonoko into captivity insists upon distinguishing between "the Word of a Christian, . . . sworn in the Name of a Great God" and the necessarily unreliable promise of a godless heathen, he explains that the Christian's word is trustworthy because to break it would be to "expect eternal Torment in the World to come" (3:84). As Oroonoko points out, however, the postponement of punishment until the afterlife is in fact no punishment at all; the man of true honor knows that the consequences of betraying an oath must be faced in life to have any definite meaning:

Punishments hereafter are suffer'd by ones self; and the World takes no cognizances whether this God have revenged 'em, or not, 'tis done so secretly, and deferr'd so long: While the Man of no Honour, suffers every moment the scorn and contempt of the honester World, and dies every day ignominiously in his Fame, which is more valuable than Life. (3:84–85)

Christianity, on Oroonoko's account, gives man license to behave dishonorably in earthly existence, as it provides no tangible check in the here and now against wrong action. "Deferr'd so long," the moral and ethical teachings of Christianity become disingenuous abstractions (3:65). As the narrator remarks, "Ill Morals are only practis'd in Christian-Countries, where they prefer the bare Name of Religion; and, without Vertue or Morality, think that's sufficient" (3:81). Both Oroonoko and his French tutor exemplify the pagan alternative: the tutor is described as a heretic and Oroonoko rejects both the Trinity and the Christian emphasis on faith, yet they nonetheless exhibit "admirable Morals, and a brave Soul" (3:93).[63]

This emphasis on honorable, righteous living should remind us of the pure faith of Rochester's pious churchman, "Whose life his Faith and

Doctrine justifies" (192), and warn us again of his opposite, the pompous prelate who displays a florid yet barren sanctimony. As "A Satyre" teaches, the pious churchman's estimable faith should also not be confused with the extravagant and aggressively private spirituality of dissenting Protestantism. As we remember, Blount disdained the enthusiasm of the Civil War crusaders who claimed that divine inspiration sanctioned regicide. Indeed, for Blount, the "Fanaticks" serve as the preeminent instance of religious corruption more generally, as they are the lowest among "all manner of Hypocrites, who counterfeiting the true Religion, are as much Traytors to Heaven as those counterfeiting Coyns, venting False Metal for true, are Traytors to the King."[64] Oroonoko, Behn's narrator tells us, bemoaned the death of Charles I, "and wou'd discourse of it with all the Sense, and Abhorrence of the Injustice imaginable" (3:62). Though Behn does not here specify the link between Charles's deplorable fate and Protestant fanaticism, we know from *The Roundheads* that the Civil Wars provide a glaring example of Christianity's tendency to use godliness as a screen for reprobate action. Oroonoko's royalism, then, as well as his good breeding and civility, are of a piece with the "more refined and speculative Doubts" of the genteel freethinker.[65]

III

To see freethinking, as Behn's translations of Fontenelle suggest, as the impetus behind her political conservatism—and not, as commentators have believed, as a negation of it—sheds new light on long-standing tensions in Behn criticism on the ambiguous status of her politics after 1685.[66] Criticism on *Oroonoko*, in particular, has been divided on whether the novella defends the inviolability of royal authority—invoking sympathetic parallels between the increasingly unpopular James II and the besieged Oroonoko—or whether it meditates the possibility of just resistance, offering the hero's gruesome and tragic death as a lesson against the brutal autocracy of James's regime.[67] I would like to suggest that both readings are partly right, that Behn's royalism indeed becomes notably less strident toward the end of the 1680s, but that she nevertheless continues to affirm the necessity of submission to existing lines of authority.

Her freethinking, once again, informs the doubleness of this stance, for central to her movement away from the unequivocal Toryism of her earlier works was the perception that James's administration was leaning toward religious absolutism in the form of the Church of Rome.[68] As we remember, Blount had warned as early as 1679 that popery made monarchs less, not more, absolute, insofar as "no School boys have been greater slaves to their Masters, than many of our English kings were to the Pope."[69] Popish absolutism, in Blount's framing, was nothing less than ecclesiastical tyranny, a position confirmed to all appearances by James's establishment of a Court of Commissioners for Ecclesiastical Causes in 1686, a despotic arm of the Church that had been virtually outlawed since 1641.[70] Compounding this manifestation of religious absolutism were James's spurious Declarations of Indulgence of 1687 and 1688, ill-disguised tactics that used the pretense of religious toleration to place Catholics in prominent government positions from which they would otherwise be prohibited.[71] Cottegnies has pointed out that Lord Jeffreys, the royalist dedicatee of Behn's *History of Oracles*, was notorious for his brutal persecution of dissenters just when the so-called official policy of the administration was one of tolerance. To dedicate a work that denied the special revelations of any particular religious tradition to Jeffreys, then, as Cottegnies suggests, is to insinuate a powerful critique of James's regime.[72] Though Behn was certainly no friend to dissent, she was even less of a friend to hypocrisy in any form. As Melinda Zook has discovered, political doggerel copied in Behn's personal chapbook from 1685 to 1689 warns Whigs and Dissenters not to trust James's Declarations of Indulgence, bearing testament to her mounting suspicion that these sham policies smacked of the very corruption and self-interest previously found so detestable in Whig political stratagems.[73]

If the politics of *Oroonoko* remain in some sense undecidable—both voicing and at the same time troubling an apology for Stuart kingship, the penultimate play of Behn's career, *The Widow Ranter*, also likely written, as *Oroonoko*, just before James II's departure from England, offers somewhat clearer ground.[74] Like *Oroonoko*, the play grapples with the notion of a defensible rebellion, basing its plot on a largely sympathetic interpretation of Nathaniel Bacon's uprising in the colony of Virginia in 1676. According to historical accounts, which Behn's play corroborates, Bacon and other Virginians had complained that the colonial government refused to protect them against marauding Native Americans, insinuating that the government sought to preserve their private trading interests over ensuring the safety of their subjects. Behn's primary historical source for the play appears to have been the official report of the King's Commission, entitled *A True Narrative of the Rise, Progresse, and Cessation of the Late Rebellion in Virginia* (1677).[75] In this document Bacon is condemned for his "pestilent and prevalent Logical discourse tending to atheisme in most companyes," a propensity that is matched by his commonwealth politics. According to the report, Bacon was a charlatan who cried up the cause of "Lives and Estates, Libertyes, and such like fair fraud . . . , which he seduced the Vulgar and most ignorant People to believe."[76] Given this emphasis on Bacon's hypocrisy and his evident dependence on republican rhetoric, it is noteworthy that Behn, unprecedentedly, chooses not to translate Bacon into a Whiggish opportunist.[77] As Chrisante, one of Bacon's supporters, laments, "What pity 'tis there should be such false Maxims in the World, that Noble Actions how ever great, must be Criminall for want of a Law to Authorise 'em" (7:1.3.124–26).

Since law ostensibly originated as a way to reinforce noble action, Chrisante's complaint shows up the depravity that results when the one is divorced from the other, for despite the fact that Bacon "has serv'd the King and our Country, and preserv'd all our Lives and Fortune," the Virginian authorities insist that "if he did it against Law, 'tis Lawful to hang him" (7:1.2.105–6, 109–10). What is more, the logic of Chrisante's complaint mirrors that of the freethinking critique of institutional religion. Both expose the disconnect in modernity between honor, virtue, and piety and the official doctrine that is meant to support them. In the play's dedication to "Madam Welldon," written by George Jenkins after Behn's death, Jenkins praises Welldon for "Qualities that carry much more of Divinity with them, than a Puritanicall outward Zeal for Virtue and Religion" (7:292). Welldon's "Divinity" without outward religion serves as a parallel to Bacon's honor without law, thus preparing us for the play's insinuation that Bacon is a freethinker. Described by one of the corrupt councilmen as "fear[ing] neither Heaven nor Hell," Bacon is in love with Semernia, the Indian queen who is herself a pagan and "stud[ies] the Lives of the Romans." Like Oroonoko, he is "by Nature Generous," and he puts an absolute faith in the truth of another man's word (7:1.2.60–61; 1.1.114–15; 1.1.114). The Christian councilmen, on the contrary, once again invoke religion as a screen for their duplicity. In a nearly parallel scene to Oroonoko's betrayal by the ship captain who sells him into slavery, the councilmen's promise of Christian fidelity—"Now Heavens forbid, are we not Christians Sir, All Friends and Countrymen!"—becomes the now-familiar signal that foul play is soon to be acted against the hero (7:2.1.72–73).

The Widow Ranter would seem to suggest, then, that if lawful power becomes corrupt and abusive, resistance in the form of a populist leadership might prove an acceptable alternative after all. Though it seems clear that Behn, however tentatively, was considering the virtue of something approaching republican politics after 1685, the play ultimately forecloses such a possibility. Not only must Bacon, the rebel, die; he also importantly fails to provide a workable alternative to the statecraft of the upstart colonists. Indeed, Bacon's final moments on stage call into question the much vaunted public-spirited nature of his rebellion when his anguish over the loss of his beloved Semernia betrays love to have been a motivating interest in his taking arms against the Indian king (see 7:4.2.30–44; 7:5.1.203–43).[78] Bacon's dying words ask his generals, Dareing and Fearless, to "make a Peace—with the English Councel," warning them not to forget "your Duty—And Allegiance" (7:5.1.306–8). Forgiven for their disobedience, Dareing and Fearless are granted legitimate commissions and become part of the official council, thereby emphasizing the fundamental value of law's proper channels.

An alternative to Bacon is represented, moreover, by the English gentleman Friendly, an honorable man who admires Bacon, though "resolve[s] to be of the Contrary Party" (7:1.1.134–35). Despite his respect for Bacon's bravery and acknowledgment of the "Service" he has done "to the Country," Friendly refuses publicly to support actions performed against "Authority" (7:1.3.122–23). Just as he respects Bacon's principles, if not his actions, Friendly defers outwardly to the base and servile councilmen in their capacity as "Magistrates," while implicitly disdaining them as cowards and fools (7:2.2.118). A similar compromise is suggested by the union between Bacon's right-hand man, Dareing, and the eponymous Widow Ranter. Committed to the "Primitive Quallit[ies]" of generosity, hospitality, and good nature, the Widow offers a less idealistic, more pragmatic, version of Bacon's freethinking radicalism. Employing the language of traditional faith blasphemously, she jokes with friends that the sight of a man at her door would count as "a Miracle," sent to cure her of her skeptical "infidel[ity] in affairs of romance" (7:1.1.84–85; 1.3.52–56).[79] A confirmed unbeliever in love (7:1.3.107–8; 7:2.2.60–62), the Widow nonetheless learns to suspend her disbelief in the institution of marriage. Though far from perfect, marriage and its official status comes closest to ensuring that Dareing will "love no bodies Body besides my own" (7:1.3.51). The Widow is a minor character, yet the play, significantly, is named for her. Behn's return here to the public/private parallel so famously employed in *Love-Letters* is instructive, for as that novel teaches, "'tis in Love as in Religion too, there's nothing makes their votaries truly happy but being well deceiv'd" (2:226). Traditional institutions, whether marriage, religion, or government, may well be "contrived to satisfy the Ignorant" and "the musty Rules of Law and Equity" (2:280, 399), but more often than not, we find that observing their ceremonies is more convenient than the alternative. Such instrumentalist strategies, indeed, become increasingly central to the philosophy of freethinking in English literary culture, as the example of Jonathan Swift will illustrate.

PART TWO

Skepticism and Piety

CHAPTER THREE

Swift's *Tale of a Tub* and the Anthropology of Religion

Natural Religion was easy first and plain,
    Tales made it Mystery, Offrings made it Gain;
    Sacrifices and Shows were at length prepar'd,
    The Priests ate Roast-meat, and the People star'd.
          —John Toland, *Letters to Serena* (1704)

Beginning with William Wotton in 1705, numerous contemporary readers questioned Jonathan Swift's piety, faith, and proper Anglican orthodoxy. From the distanced perspective of France, the first translator of *A Tale of a Tub* mused that "pious people in England regard [*A Tale*] as the extreme effort of a libertine imagination, whose sole intention is to lay the foundations of irreligion on the ruin of all Christian sects."[1] To contemporaries, then, the distance between the freethinking productions of Rochester and Behn and the early religious satire of the man ordained as Dean of St. Patrick's in 1713 is less than much of modern reception would have it. Swift's lifelong support of the Church of England as an institution has never been in doubt, but the thornier matter of his belief remains as contested today as it was in Swift's own lifetime. For this reason, my investigations into Swift's links to English freethinking will unfold over the course of two related chapters. This first one will explore the evidence of Swift's infidelity as exhibited in *A Tale of a Tub*. In the previous section of the book, I proposed that a closer examination of Rochester's and Behn's writings yields a growing sense of both authors' interest in preserving some vestiges of a religious fabric in a context otherwise marked by skepticism and unbelief. In this chapter I will argue that an equally surprising and pervasive sense of Swift's doubt is the fruit of a careful study of his belief. Despite this doubt, however, as the following chapter will argue, Swift remained profoundly committed to safeguarding religion's place in the social and political institutions of eighteenth-century England. In Swift's various writings on religion, fictional and nonfictional, we see the full efflorescence for the English Enlightenment of religion's status as a pious fraud, a strategy that was crucially informed, once again, by a theory of religion rooted in ancient theology.

As Michael DePorte points out, Swift's writings as well as the stories about him, "tell us less about Swift's spiritual life than about his sense of duty." An Anglican priest for fifty years and a staunch champion of the Test Act, Swift was determined to defend Anglican doctrine against the attacks of radical freethinkers, and to urge the necessity of Christianity as the foundation of moral life. And yet, we know virtually nothing of his individual relationship to God, except what we can infer from his impatience with others' "qualms of conscience."[2] It is this ambiguity that no doubt fueled the oft-cited remark of the Archbishop of York that it was "a Scandal . . . to Church and State to bestow Preferment upon a Clergyman, who was hardly suspected of being a Christian."[3] A similarly puzzled sense of Swift's belief informs the infamous "Verses," reputedly affixed to St. Patrick's Cathedral upon Swift's ordination as Dean:

> This Place he got by Wit and Rhime,
>   And many Ways most odd;
> And might a Bishop be in Time,
>   Did he believe in G—d.
>
>   . . .
>
> Look down St. Patrick, look we pray,
>   On thine own Church and Steeple;
> Convert thy D—n on this great Day,
>   Or else God help the People.[4]

The debate concentrates, then as now, on *A Tale of a Tub*, and the notorious difficulty of Swift's irony has rendered general critical agreement still out of reach. From Wotton to now, critics have differed over how to interpret the narrative personae through whose profane voices Swift works his satiric magic.[5] Is the impious speaker of *A Tale* straightforwardly the object of Swift's parody, a view supported by Swift's clerical status, or is his diabolical heterodoxy a hidden facet of Swift's own troubled belief?[6] The latter reading, put forward most persuasively by John Traugott and Claude Rawson, attends more satisfactorily to the ingenious virtuosity of Swift's satire: the paradoxical process by which Swift's "invention takes fire and he becomes his enemy, working out his own sceptical ideas in the enemy's guise." It also accounts for most readers' instinctive sense of the deeply subversive character of *A Tale*, particularly the ineffable way in which its most outrageous parodies of religious experience "have a habit at odd moments of sounding like Swift himself."[7] The technique, as Irvin Ehrenpreis suggests, remained essentially foolproof. Swift's irreverent musings about the absence of spirit are still arguably the abhorrent mistake of a profane madman, and therefore his holy office and public orthodoxy remain for the most part unscathed.[8]

The *Apology* appended to the fifth edition of *A Tale* (1710) pleads this defense. Swift here explains that "some of those Passages in this Discourse, which appear most liable to Objection are what they call Parodies, where the Author personates the Style and Manner of other Writers, whom he has a mind to expose" (7). Swift famously insists that his aim had been to expose "the Follies of Fanaticism and Superstition," or abuses in religion "such as all Church of England Men agree in" (5, 8). Beginning with Wotton, however, readers have intuited a tendency in *A Tale* toward a broader assault on Christianity, the spirit, and religion more generally. As Wotton declares,

I would not so shoot at an Enemy, as to hurt my self at the same time. . . . But our *Tale-teller* strikes at the very Root. 'Tis all with him *a Farce, and all a Ladle*. . . . The *Father*, and the *Will*, and *his Son Martin*, are part of the *Tale*, as well as *Peter* and *Jack*, and are all usher'd in with the Common Old Wives Introduction, *Once upon a Time*.[9]

More recently, Traugott and Rawson have drawn attention to the same sweeping attack on religion in *A Tale*. Rawson refers to the "strange universalizing tendency which . . . turns the specific types Swift is castigating . . . into examples of a radical human perversity, common to all." The threats posed by superstition, sectarian enthusiasm, atheism, etc. "are the threats posed by human nature itself." Traugott argues similarly that the allegory of Peter and Jack exposes the "radical realities of religious egotism." This egotism is not particular to papists and fanatics but is rather an inescapable aspect of the human psyche. "Swift's satire goes into the inevitable psychology of the religious personality, and raises ultimate questions."[10]

If the satiric butts of *A Tale* represent universal corruptions inherent in the human condition, then its subject in Traugott's view is no less than "the psychopathology of religious experience." Leo Strauss has argued that "the explanation of religion in terms of human nature . . . is the complement and culmination of critique of religion." Once religion is approached as a psychological phenomenon, Strauss suggests, we are no longer in the thrall of belief. To see religion as an aspect of such universal facets of mind is to seek to expose its root cause on the most fundamental level; the critic "finds himself compelled to uncover the origin from which the whole complex of fallacious thinking characteristic of religion arises."[11] As the debate over the pagan oracles indicates, explorations into religion's earliest stirrings were not unfamiliar to the late seventeenth century. The period's attempt to lay bare the origins of religious error provides an important and neglected context, I will suggest, for understanding the radical representation of religion in *A Tale*, alerting us as well to the ambition and reach of Swift's critique. What is more, this context incorporates the emphasis of Traugott and Rawson on the universalizing momentum of *A Tale*—a momentum whose psychological energy transcends "the parochial quarrels of the Restoration"—as well as the importance critics like Philip Harth and Roger Lund have placed on late seventeenth-century theological debate.[12] If we agree with Wotton and Traugott that Swift's critique of religion was far deeper and broader than the surface details of the allegory indicate, it is possible to see *A Tale* as taking part in the period's fascination with the history of superstition. As Richard Popkin has argued, the seventeenth century witnessed the beginnings of an "anthropology of religion," a movement that developed out of a growing interest in the comparative study of different religions, both historically and geographically.[13] In its effort to locate the root of religious corruption and a true worship, the anthropology of religion was invariably forced to contend with the relationship between Christianity and ancient theology.

Radicals and orthodox alike initially undertook this effort. Anglicans and freethinkers for a time inveighed equally against the influence of pagan superstition on Christianity and advocated a return to an original purity in religious practice.[14] The distinction was often one of subtle emphasis. Whereas churchmen like Gilbert Burnet and freethinkers like Hobbes and Toland agreed that the plain doctrine of the first Christians was preferable both to the extravagant rites of the pagans and to later degradations within the Christian church, the churchmen made clear that this plain doctrine relied crucially on a legitimate (Christian) revelation. Hobbes and Toland, alternatively, tended to emphasize the extravagance of *all* claims to revealed religion, pagan and Christian. In his *Historia Ecclesiastica*, Hobbes argues that primitive Christianity distinguishes itself by a simple worship: "Christ's easy Yoke,"

> . . . sets no glitt'ring Pomp before our Eye,
> No costly Shew, nor gilded Majesty;
> With gaudy Pageantry the World's allur'd,
> Whereby the Pope his Vot'ries has secur'd:
> Christ, chiefly urges us to mutual Love,

And in all moral Virtues to improve:
Not to offend, or do our Neighbour Wrong,
From Lies, and Slander, to refrain our Tongue;
No Gold, or Treasure, wrongfully t'attain,
Nor vilely covet, what's thy Death to gain.

Early Christianity, Hobbes suggests, eschewed mysteries, rites, and ceremonies, in favor of a plain and natural religion of morality and civic virtue. Its later supernatural elements were thus corruptions stemming from
the infiltration of pagan superstition: "New Miracles were wrought, and
new, old Lies devis'd, / . . . Thus still Idolatry the Faith invades, / And,
more than Truth, a gilded Lye perswades."[15]

For Toland, following Herbert and Blount, this primitive form of
Christianity was importantly rooted in an earlier unrevealed ancient
tradition. Toland's "Origin of Idolatry and Reasons of Heathenism,"
for example, commends the ancient religions of the Egyptians, Romans,
and Hebrews for avoiding the idolatry of the later pagans. These early
religions, he states, predated superstition and "had no sacred Images or
Statues, no peculiar Places or costly Fashions of Worship." Toland here
alludes to Herbert's thesis that modern religion should return to the best
of ancient paganism for a model of pure worship. Like Herbert, he argues that "the more learned and virtuous had many times better Notions
of Things" and "ought not to reckon for Heathens, by which Expression
is properly understood Idolators."[16] It was examples like Hobbes's and
Toland's that motivated William Warburton's comment that orthodox
efforts to champion reformation Anglicanism through recourse to the
primitive ran into trouble when "the Infidels . . . joined Issue with them,"
using the adequacy of ancient simplicity to "shew . . . that therefore
Christianity was not necessary."[17]

♉

In his *Complete Key to the Tale of a Tub* (1710), Edmund Curll sets
out to correct the record regarding the controversy over the representation of religion in Swift's *Tale*, a controversy informed by seventeenth-
century debates over the status of the primitive. Curll believed that the
consensus was wrong, insisting instead "that the true Intent and Aim
of the Authors was not to ridicule all Religion, but to assert and defend the Purity of our Church's Doctrine."[18] To support his case, Curll
reminds us of the immediate occasion for the production of *A Tale*:
Wotton's acrimonious debate with Swift's patron, Sir William Temple,
over the respective merits of ancient and modern learning. Swift's *Tale*,
Curll affirms, entered the fray in defense of Temple on the side of the

ancients. Believing *A Tale* to be the shared project of Swift and his nephew Thomas Swift, Curll provides the following account of the history of the controversy:

The one of 'em began a *Defence* of Sir *William* under the Title of *A Tale of a Tub*, under which he intended to couch the General History of Christianity; shewing the Rise of all the Remarkable Errors of the *Roman Church* in the same order they enter'd, and how the Reformation endeavoured to root 'em out again, with the different Temper of *Luther* from *Calvin* (and those more violent Spirits) in the way of his Reforming: His aim is to Ridicule the stubborn Errors of the *Romish Church*, and the Humours of the *Fanatick Party*, and to shew that their Superstition has somewhat very fantastical in it. . . . The Author intended to have it very regular, and withal so particular, that he thought not to pass by the Rise of any one single Error or its Reformation: He design'd at last to shew the Purity of the Christian Church in the primitive Times, and consequently how weakly Mr. *Wotton* pass'd his Judgment, and how partially in preferring the *Modern* Divinity before the *Ancient*, with the Confutation of whose Book he intended to conclude.[19]

We need no reminding that Swift's *Tale* made part of the English phase of the quarrel of the ancients and the moderns. And yet it is Swift's *Battle of the Books*, appended to *A Tale*, and the various digressions on modern learning in *A Tale* proper that are typically cited as Swift's contribution to the ancient cause on the side of Temple. Curll's comments, however, highlight an aspect of that quarrel that has gone relatively unnoticed, particularly in current scholarship. Circumventing the quarrel's contentions over philosophy, science, and even aesthetics, Curll instead locates the ancients/moderns controversy squarely within the realm of divinity.[20] To contemporaries, this was no idiosyncratic reading. Wotton's *Observations upon the 'Tale of a Tub'* were appended to *A Defense of the Reflections upon Ancient and Modern Learning*, his second response to Temple, so his readers would necessarily have associated his attack on the irreverence of *A Tale* with his preference for modern over ancient learning. What is more, Wotton's initial sally against Temple in 1694 had explicitly defined the quarrel as a war of faith, associating "ancients" in religion with Epicurean libertines.[21] For Curll, then, the religious allegory of *A Tale* is centrally concerned with this debate. Swift's defense of Temple and the ancients takes the form of a "General History of Christianity," one that seeks to document the "Errors" and "Superstition" of the Catholic Church as well as the radical Protestant reaction against it. As Curll recognizes, this is a history of religion in modernity, a narrative of the Reformation and its aftermath. And yet the ascendance of the Church of England, a distinctly modern institution, involves a return to "the Purity of the Christian Church in the primitive Times." The superiority of ancient to modern Christianity, then, serves to prove "how weakly Mr. *Wotton* pass'd his Judgment, and how partially in preferring the *Modern* Divinity before the *Ancient*."

Wotton himself picks up on this ambiguity in his *Observations upon the 'Tale of a Tub.'* Commenting on the allegory of the coats in *A Tale*, Wotton notes that Swift describes Christianity before the introduction of superstition as "very plain, with little or no Ornament." In glossing this reference, Wotton writes, "*Christiana Religio absoluta & simplex* was *Ammianus Marcellinus's* Description of it, who was himself a Heathen."[22] Though Wotton does not specify the implications of his gloss, I want to suggest that they are central to our understanding of the relationship between divinity and the ancients/moderns controversy in *A Tale*. If Swift's aim is to promote the church in its primitive purity—to revivify ancient Christianity—he necessarily runs the risk, as Wotton's remark intuits, of brushing up against paganism.[23] Indeed, Marcellinus' praise of the simplicity of ancient Christianity is of a piece with the now familiar freethinking view that revealed religion adds insignificantly to the moral and ethical code taught by the classical philosophers. If simple is tantamount to better, the argument goes, then early Christianity is little different than the best of ancient paganism.[24]

The relationship between paganism and Christianity is a major preoccupation of Swift's writings on religion, particularly the deist objection that the ancient philosophers exhibited greater wisdom and virtue—on the strength of nature and reason alone—than their Christian counterparts.[25] Characteristically, Swift's handling of this objection is ambiguous and inconsistent. "A Letter to a Young Gentleman, Lately Entered into Holy Orders" (1719–20), "A Sermon upon the Excellency of Christianity, in Opposition to Heathen Philosophy," and "On the Testimony of Conscience" all ostensibly hold up the preeminence of Christian revelation as delivered in the Gospels.[26] And yet, Swift's defense of revealed religion is persistently undermined by his irrepressible admiration of pagan virtue. In "A Letter to a Young Gentleman," he complains about "the common unsufferable Cant, of taking all Occasions to disparage the Heathen Philosophers," adding that "I am deceived, if a better Comment could be any where collected upon the moral Part of the Gospel, than from the Writings of those excellent Men" (9:73). And though it argues strongly that religious conscience is an essential foundation for morality, "On the Testimony of Conscience" also admits that the heathens' rigorous education of their children, their estimable patriotism, and the belief in rewards and punishments among the better sort—all of which are largely absent among modern English Christians—serve to explain their exceptional virtue (9:155–56).

As these examples attest, the insufficiency of heathen morality is far from a self-evident proposition in Swift's sermons. The ancient sages enjoyed an innate moral sense not yet to be equaled or surpassed, but Christianity is to be preferred, Swift argues, because it provides "principles and doctrine" through whose teachings less exalted minds might be encouraged to embrace virtue (9:249, 74). Swift makes clear that without the support of official theological principles, the early Christians, missing the natural morality of the best of the pagans, would have been far less virtuous, if at all (9:249). For though "our lessons are . . . better," our "practices . . . fall short" (9:243). If the pagans suffered a theological deficit, Swift concludes, it was more political than spiritual; "the true Misery of the Heathen World" was precisely the absence of formalized doctrine, or what Swift describes as "the Want of a Divine Sanction." Lacking this sanction, the wisdom of the philosophers, however laudable, "failed in the Point of Authority" (9:73). Swift's criteria for the choice of Christianity over the ancient theology are thus secular and pragmatic.[27] Such an instrumentalized view of the role of revealed religion, to which I will return in the next chapter, cannot but raise doubts about the nature of Swift's belief.

If Swift's design in *A Tale* was, as Curll contested, "at last to shew the Purity of the Christian Church in the primitive Times," the question thus remains whether he defined this primitive purity in terms of a revealed tradition, or whether—like Herbert, Blount, Hobbes, and Toland—his effort to pare away false belief strikes at the category of spirit itself. This question is complicated by the fact that by the start of the eighteenth century, mainstream Christianity was beginning to distance itself from its earlier appeals to the primitive.[28] Claiming divinity for the moderns, Wotton argued in his *Reflections* that right religion requires progressive learning: ancient divines "seem in several Places not to have found out the true Original of many things in the New Testament which have been discovered since."[29] Other orthodox divines followed suit. William Warburton, Joseph Butler, John Edwards, and William Nichols all argued similarly that like natural knowledge, religious knowledge was gradual, developing over time through man's ever-increasing wisdom and effort. As Edwards claimed, "a more setled Knowledg of Religion" prevails now than in the days of the primitive Church.[30] By 1700, then, the modern doctrine of progress was fully integrated into Anglican theology. This retreat away from the primitive, moreover, was largely a reaction against the perceived radicalism of the ancient biases of writers like Blount and Toland, particularly against the freethinking truism that the earliest instances of religion were purer because they were natural and thus undefiled by claims to revealed truth.[31]

I

Swift's allegory of the Reformation opens in section II of *A Tale* with the establishment of primitive Christianity. As is well known, the allegory unfolds through the story of three brothers: Peter, Martin, and Jack, who eventually come to represent Catholicism, the Church of England, and Protestant dissent respectively. In the beginning, however, the brothers' practice is not distinguished according to differing creeds. They are each given "a new Coat" by their "Father" (God), who on his deathbed provides a "Will" (Scripture) detailing how the coats are to be worn and managed (73). According to Swift's own gloss in the fifth edition of *A Tale*, the coats stand for "the Doctrine and Faith of Christianity" (73), and they are meant to be preserved plain and unadorned (82). Unfortunately for the brothers, however, competing and more anciently established sartorial habits, or systems of worship, contradict their father's counsel on the prudence of a simple coat. As the narrator recounts, the "sartorist"[32] sect

worshipped a sort of *Idol*, who, as their Doctrine delivered, did daily create Men, by a kind of Manufactory Operation. This *Idol* they placed in the highest Parts of the House, on an Altar erected about three Foot. . . . This God had a *Goose* for his Ensign; whence it is that some Learned Men pretend to deduce his Original from *Jupiter Capitolinus*. At his left Hand, beneath the Altar, *Hell* seemed to open, and catch at the Animals the *Idol* was creating; to prevent which, certain of his Priests hourly flung in Pieces of the uninformed Mass, or Substance, and sometimes whole Limbs already enlivened. . . . The *Goose* was also held a subaltern Divinity, or *Deus minorum Gentium*, before whose Shrine was sacrificed that Creature, whose hourly Food is Human Gore. . . . Millions of these Animals were cruelly slaughtered every Day, to appease the Hunger of that consuming Deity. The chief *Idol* was also worshipped as the Inventor of the *Yard* and the *Needle*, whether as the God of Seamen, or on Account of certain other mystical Attributes, hath not been sufficiently cleared. (76–77)

This grotesque chronicle invokes the standard excesses of pagan superstition familiar to any contemporary reader: idolatry, human and animal sacrifice, polytheism, and mysterious rites and ceremonies. Swift's point, of course, is that the objects of the sartorists' worship have no true spiritual dimension. According to his notes, the idol they worship is a "Taylor," and the Goose, or minor deity, said to descend from the sacred geese of the temple of Jupiter on the Capitoline Hill in Rome, represents the handle of a tailor's iron (in reference to said handle's resemblance to a goose's neck). The underworld threatening to consume the sect's devotees is the receptacle for the tailor's discarded scraps of cloth, and the mysterious yard and needle are merely the tools of the tailor's trade.[33] All claims to the elevated are thus brought down to their pedestrian roots in material, everyday experience.

Swift's satire becomes yet more fiendish when the narrative voice adopts the persona of a sartorist initiate and turns to detail the system of their belief:

The Worshippers of this Deity had also a System of their Belief, which seemed to turn upon the following Fundamental. They held the Universe to be a large *Suit of Cloaths*, which *invests* every Thing: That the Earth is *invested* by the Air; The Air is *invested* by the Stars; and the Stars are *invested* by the *Primum Mobile*. Look on this Globe of Earth, you will find it to be a very compleat and fashionable *Dress*. What is that which some call *Land*, but a fine Coat faced with Green? Or the Sea, but a Wastcoat of Water-Tabby? . . . . Observe how sparkish a Perewig adorns the Head of a Beech, and what a fine Doublet of white Satin is worn by the Birch. . . . To instance no more; Is not Religion a *Cloak*, Honesty a *Pair of Shoes*, worn out in the Dirt, Self-love a *Surtout*, Vanity a *Shirt*, and Conscience a *Pair of Breeches*, which, tho' a Cover for Lewdness as well as Nastiness, is easily slipt down for the Service of both. (77–78)

As Warren Montag points out, the play between the literal and figurative senses of "invest" in this passage articulates a materialist parody of Creation.[34] Not only is God reduced to a tailor; the divine act of creation, yet more irreverently, becomes the prosaic work of making clothes. What is more, instead of mistaking the material for the spiritual—a tailor for an idol and a goose for a deity—the sartorists' theology here elevates one created entity—the universe, the earth, land, and sea—by way of a metaphorical equivalent that is itself still material: a suit of clothes, fashionable dress, a fine coat, a decorative waistcoat. The sartorists' false pretenses to spirit, in other words, are now merely more elaborated versions of matter. The supposed supernatural content of pagan superstition, the satire suggests, is merely dressed up natural phenomena masking as transcendent properties.

In 1961 Philip Harth argued that the opening paragraph of Hobbes's *Leviathan* provided the source for Swift's parodic account of the sartorists' system of belief. Since then, it has become standard practice to interpret the sartorist cult as a censure of seventeenth-century materialism. Through their impertinent worship of clothes, the sartorists, the argument goes, make everything in the universe sensible and tactile, thus denying the reality of the spirit.[35] Swift's satire, on this view, aims to defend the spirit's integrity against the sartorists' atheistic insinuation (attributed to Hobbes and Descartes, among others) that matter was the only substance in the universe. What this account forgets, however, is that the sartorists are idolaters. Their materialism is thus a spiritual error, not "an antireligious doctrine."[36] Indeed, contrary to the atheistic tendencies in mechanistic materialism, in which the notion of spirit is dismissed entirely, the sartorists make matter an object of *religious worship*, seeking divine favor through absurd and frivolous rites about clothes.[37] When the narrator famously asks, "Is not Religion a Cloak, Honesty a Pair of Shoes . . . , and Conscience a Pair of Breeches?," Swift's point is to expose the way in which pagan idolatry falsely attributes lofty meaning and mysterious significance to ordinary, clearly earthbound objects such as cloaks, shoes, and breeches.[38]

Moreover, the narrator's summary of the sartorists' system of divinity unequivocally provides the context for primitive Christianity's degeneration into popish superstition, a religious corruption in no way equivalent to atheistic materialism. This degeneration is allegorized through Peter's increasingly brazen attempts to adorn the brothers' formerly plain coats based on the pagan fashion trends of the sartorists. Indeed, the narrator explains that he has collected his history of the sartorist cult "out of antient Authors," precisely "to give [the reader] Light into several Circumstances of the following Story: that knowing the State of Dispositions and Opinions in an Age so remote, he may better comprehend those great Events which were the issue of them" (80–81). The sartorists generate a vogue for "Shoulder-knots," "Gold Lace," and other frippery, and Peter finds ways to justify and defend such ornamentation (see 81–91). Peter's embrace of the sartorist system thus indicates paganism's nefarious influence on Christianity and the parallels between pagan and popish superstition.[39]

Such a view was not uncommon in the period during which Swift composed *A Tale*; anti-Catholic polemic in the seventeenth and eighteenth centuries frequently linked popery to ancient paganism. The argument that Catholicism was the heir of paganism also served, however, as support for the freethinking position that *all* Christianity, not merely popery, perpetuated ancient superstition. Most notorious in this tradition was Toland's *Christianity Not Mysterious* (1696), in which the author aimed to trace the rise of institutionalized Christianity, its departure from an original natural worship, and its eventual decline into false mysteries and superstition.[40] Wotton identified Toland as a source for Swift's irreligion in *A Tale*, and, more recently, Kenneth Craven has shown how *Christianity Not Mysterious*, similarly to Hobbes's *Leviathan*, provides a model for several details in Swift's satire on the sartorists and their influence on the purity of primitive Christianity.[41] Continuing the tradition of Herbert, Hobbes, and Blount, Toland charges pagan priestcraft with the introduction of superstition into "the plain convincing Instructions of Christ." Primitive Christianity was clear and reasonable until the priestly class "impudently father'd upon Moses" a set of "nonsensical

Superstitions" and "superadded Fooleries."[42] In this way, what began as a natural religion based in ancient philosophical wisdom became mysterious and degenerated back into the worst of paganism.

As Craven argues, Swift's account of the sartorists' corruption of the plain coats of the three brothers is notably similar to chapter 6 of *Christianity Not Mysterious*, which documents the introduction of mysteries into the easy worship of early Christianity. Here Toland describes the way in which the pagans "were not a little scandaliz'd at the plain Dress of the Gospel, . . . having been accustom'd all their Lives to the pompous Worship and secret Mysteries of Deities without Number." Fearful that the plainness of Christian doctrine would encourage the skepticism of unbelievers, Christianity thus "likewise set up for Mysteries." The "new-coin'd Christian Mysteries," Toland concludes, were "one in Nature" with those of the ancient pagans. "The Garb of their several Sects . . . were appropriated to the Christian Clergy. Nay, their very Habits, as white Linen Stoles, Mitres, and like, were retain'd to bring those, as was pretended, to an imperceptible Change, who could not be reconcil'd to the Christian Simplicity."[43]

Craven maintains that Swift's satire of popish idolatry as a form of pagan clothes-worship was inspired by Toland's emphasis in the above examples on the flamboyant "Garb" and "Habits" of the pagan priests and the way in which their gaudy sartorial tastes debased the heretofore-simple style preferences of the Christian clergy.[44] Toland here uses clothing as a metaphor for the simplicity of Christian doctrine—"the plain Dress of the Gospel"—and as a literal example of luxury and excess—the "white Linen Stoles" and "Mitres" of the pagan priesthood. The pagan priests' passion for ornate clothing, Toland suggests, is reflected in their base tendency to "worship the Creature as well as (and sometimes more than) the Creator." In Swift's account of the idolatrous practices of the sartorist cult, clothing indeed functions similarly to satirize pagan creature worship and the belief "that admirable things were adumbrated by these Externals."[45] As it turns out, Toland was not the first freethinker to employ clothes as a metaphor for religious corruption. In his critique of priestcraft in *Great Is Diana of the Ephesians*, Blount cites the ancient epigram, "Ut melius possis fallere, sume togam" (So that you are able to deceive better, put on the toga). And in *Philostratus*, he cites the epigram yet again, complaining that "he that shews how [religion] is sometimes made a *Cloak for Knavery*, and how some Men fight the Devils Battle under a counterfeit Banner of Christ, . . . Shall render himself a mortal Enemy to Hypocrites."[46] Swift's use of clothes to refer to the debased practices of the sartorists thus alludes to a favorite metaphor for the falsity of religion (derived, once again, from the ancients) among the period's unbelievers.

Implied in Toland's account is the radical claim that revealed Christianity reenacts pagan superstition.[47] As noted, his portrayal of the purity of primitive Christianity is significantly silent on the importance of revelation: early Christianity is a natural religion, its morality easily comprehensible "to the Capacities of all." As Toland infamously proclaimed, Christianity is not mysterious: "what is reveal'd in Religion, as it is most useful and necessary, so it must and may be as easily comprehended, and found as consistent with our common Notions, as what we know of Wood or Stone, of Air, of Water, or the like." What we have thought of as mysterious is in truth "any thing sacred or profane that is design'dly kept secret."[48] Revealed knowledge is hereby no different from natural knowledge, and claims to the mysterious workings of the supernatural should be understood as priestly attempts to keep the people in ignorance. Section II of *A Tale* provides just such a critique of priestly manipulation. Eager to justify the addition of "Silver Fringe" to the brothers' coats in defiance of their father's express prohibition, Peter speciously argues that "the same Word which in the Will is called *Fringe*, does also signifie a *Broom-stick*; and doubtless ought to have the same Interpretation in this Paragraph" (88). When one of the brothers objects to such opportunistic logic, Peter exhorts that mysteries "ought not to be over-curiously pryed into, or nicely reasoned upon" (88). It is this episode that Wotton cites as evidence for his view that "The Author . . . copies from Mr. *Toland*, who always raises a Laugh at the Word *Mystery*, the Word and Thing whereof he is known to believe to be no more than a *Tale of a Tub*."[49] Wotton is correct to intuit that Swift plays a dangerous game here. By alluding to Toland's linking of Christian mysteries to priestcraft and fraud in religion generally, Swift threatens to broaden the ostensibly limited critique of Peter's imposture.[50]

Adding to the suspicion of heterodoxy in *A Tale* is yet another probable instance of radical allusion and borrowing. In the twenty-second letter of his *Lettres philosophiques* (1734), Voltaire asserts that Swift's *Tale* "is an imitation of the ancient story of three indiscernible rings that a father bequeathed to his three children. The three rings were Judaism, Christianity, and Mahommedanism."[51] Voltaire does not pursue explicitly the implications of this possible source for *A Tale*, but if his hunch is correct, it greatly magnifies our sense of Swift's shadowy links to the Enlightenment critique of religion. Best known from Boccaccio's *Decameron* (1349–52), the parable of the three rings also informed Gotthold Lessing's *Nathan der Weise* (1779), in both instances hinting that Judaism, Christianity, and Mohammedanism were equally suspect religions. What is more, H. B. Nisbet has shown that the parable derives from the ancient theory of imposture, the blasphemous view, dating back to the

Greek Sophist Critias, that all religions began as fraudulent attempts at power and mastery over the multitude. With the birth of Christianity, Nisbet argues, this theory expressed itself in one of the most notorious clandestine treatises of the age, *De tribus impostoribus*, a work whose underground circulation, in varied forms and languages, spanned from the thirteenth to the eighteenth century, becoming "a favourite myth of the Enlightenment."[52]

If, then, like Hobbes, Toland, and the many versions of *De tribus impostoribus*, Swift attacks the heart of Christianity's pretensions to supernatural revelations, whether in the form of divine mysteries, or a belief in spiritual elevation more broadly, his target in section II of *A Tale* is religion's false attribution of spiritual qualities to mere matter. Swift's satire, informed by, not directed against, materialism, thus falls on *revealed religion* and its mistaken belief in spiritual transcendence.[53] Consider the opening passage of *Leviathan*, taken as the model for Swift's outline of the sartorists' system of belief, in which Hobbes describes how man learns to imitate nature's creation through art:

Nature (the art whereby God hath made and governes the World) is by the *Art* of man, as in many other things, so in this also imitated, that it can make an Artificial Animal. For seeing life is but a motion of the Limbs, the beginning whereof is in some principall part within; why may we not say, that all *Automata* (Engines that move themselves by springs and wheeles as doth a watch) have an artificiall life? For what is the *Heart* but a *Spring*; and the *Nerves*, but so many *Strings*; and the *Joynts*, but so many *Wheeles*, giving motion to the whole Body, such as was intended by the Artificer? *Art* goes yet further, imitating that Rationall and most excellent worke of Nature, *Man*. For by Art is created that great Leviathan called a Common-wealth, or State, (in latine Civitas) which is but an Artificiall Man; though of greater stature and strength than the Naturall, for whose protection and defence it was intended; and in which, the *Soveraignty* is an Artificiall *Soul*, as giving life and motion to the whole body.[54]

As Harth suggests, Swift's parallel passage, cited above ("What is that which some call *Land*, but a fine Coat faced with Green?" etc.), echoes the basic structure of Hobbes's paragraph. Both develop an analogy between divine and natural creation through a series of metaphors.[55] Hobbes's version begins by positing nature, described as God's "art," as the divine process of creation to which man's artificial one is compared: man makes automata and machines just as God and nature make life. A closer view, however, reveals that Hobbes subverts the expected hierarchy of God's animate and man's inanimate creation. The hint is that "Life," that which only God seemingly can create, is reduced to a mechanistic "motion of the Limbs." When Hobbes proceeds to compare the human body to an inanimate machine, the distinction between divine and natural creation becomes yet more ambiguous. If Hobbes's aim were to prove that man's creations have an "artificial" anima similar, but in no way commensurate, to the divinely infused life force of a human body, we would expect to see the human elements predominate in the sequence of comparisons between body and machine. In crafting a machine, man would aspire to construct springs that approximated the wondrous beating of the heart, and strings that mimicked the function of nerves, and so forth. Significantly, however, Hobbes inverts this order, reducing God's design to a series of mechanical processes and thereby leveling his creation to the equivalent status of a man-made machine.

The sartorists' comparisons between divinely created nature—land, sea, and trees—and mechanically produced clothes mirror the logic of Hobbes's comparisons between the body and machines. Here, too, the sartorists' confusion between "Land"—God's creation—and "a fine Coat faced with Green"—a man-made article of clothing—levels the traditional hierarchy between God and man, divine and natural creation. In this case, however, the leveling is unwitting. Indeed, Swift's satire depends upon our recognition of an important irony: the sartorists elevate man's creation above God's and yet continue to offer religious worship to objects that are now wholly natural. The key to understanding the relationship between Swift's satire on the sartorists and his reliance on the opening of Hobbes's *Leviathan*, therefore, is to take seriously the sartorists' belief that clothes are divine elements worthy of worship. When they foolishly grant a sublimity to "Perewig" that they deny to "the Head of a Beech," the effect is to recall Hobbes's emphasis on the identity of body and machine as against the more orthodox belief in man's special dispensation.[56]

What is more, behind the reduction of body to machine and universe to a suit of clothes in both Hobbes's and Swift's passages is the yet more radical reduction of God to the workings of nature; for if bodies and machines become equivalent terms, then, like machines, bodies are created through natural and mechanical, rather than divine, processes. According to the logic of Hobbes's analogies, nature thus makes man mechanically, just as man fabricates machines and commonwealths. As we know, Swift ends his Hobbesian parody of the sartorist system with the rhetorical question, cited above, "Is not Religion a Cloak?" As Warren Montag astutely points out, however, crucial to Swift's purpose in this section is our awareness, somewhere along the way, that pure worship, as well as superstition, has no nobler referent than "coat" in the universe of *A Tale*.[57] The sartorist initiate scandalously compares religion to a cloak, but so does the father of primitive Christianity. The metaphor of coats thus subversively encompasses "both true religion and its perversions," thereby linking Christianity generally to pagan error. Whether the plain coat of primitive Christianity or the ornamented coat of paganism and popery, *religion itself* is figured as "artificially fabricated" and "external."[58]

What do we learn, then, from Swift's attack on pagan superstition and its polluting effect on Christianity? Is the lesson gleaned from the sartorists' errors meant to be the superiority of the initial purity of early Christianity, and if so, what if any revealed element abides in this tradition? Section VI of *A Tale* represents the Reformation through Martin's attempt to return the brothers' coats to their original state. Swift's allegory suggests here that the mysteries and superstitions that remain in modern Christianity are true not so much in a spiritual sense as in a practicable one. In Martin's effort to strip the layers of adornment from his coat, he significantly leaves additions whose removal would damage the fabric:

where he observed the Embroidery to be workt so close, as not to be got away without damaging the Cloth, or where it served to hide or strengthen any Flaw in the Body of the Coat, contracted by the perpetual tampering of Workmen upon it; he concluded the wisest Course was to let it remain, resolving in no Case whatsoever, that the Substance of the Stuff should suffer Injury; which he thought the best Method for serving the true Intent and Meaning of his Father's Will. (136–37)[59]

The sartorists' clothes-worship is full of improvident idolatry, but the alternative represented by the father's directions to Peter, Martin, and Jack seems equally rooted in the material as in the sensible necessities of the everyday: "with good wearing, [the coats] will last you fresh and sound as long as you live," and "grow in the same proportion with your Bodies . . . so as to be always fit" (73). The "virtue" of the brothers' coats indeed seems to extend no higher than their exemplary durability. The problem, we come to understand, is thus not the sartorist initiate's audacious claim that religion is a cloak (for the father tells his three sons no better), but rather the brothers' idolatrous attempt to embellish that cloak—to claim a higher transcendence for its material, quotidian uses. We return here to the notion that the best version of Christianity is that which is the least hampered by elaborate claims to revealed truth.

II

This problem persists when the satire turns from Peter's idolatry to Jack's fanaticism in Section VI of *A Tale*. Rejecting the range of papish rites, ceremonies, and superstitions represented by the layers of fringe, lace, and embroidery on his coat, Jack zealously begins to tear and rip away the ornament in a crazed effort to spite Peter's tyranny and make his coat as dissimilar to Peter's as possible (137–42). The frenzy of his alterations, however, leaves the coat torn and ragged, so that at a distance Jack's rags and Peter's finery share "a sort of fluttering Appearance" (200) by which people mistake the one brother for the other. Swift's own note provides the gloss on this episode in the allegory, remarking on the "near Resemblance in many things" (198) between the papists and fanatics. Not coincidentally, then, Jack goes on to found his own version of an idolatrous sect—the aeolists, or wind worshippers—in section VIII. Here Swift abandons the conceit of coats as a vehicle for idolatry, but the error of claiming the spiritual sublimity of matter remains central to his purposes, as does the suggestion that Christianity differs minimally from pagan superstition.

It comes as no surprise to discover Hobbes as the source for Swift's satirical reduction of spirit to wind in his account of the aeolists. Wotton was again the first to see Hobbes's influence on Swift's parody in section VIII, identifying Hobbes's "banter upon in-blowing" in chapter 34 of *Leviathan* as the culprit.[60] Here Hobbes discusses "the Signification of Spirit" among radical Protestants, asserting that a correct understanding of the term depends on a prior understanding of the various senses of "inspiration." Hobbes reminds his readers that inspiration has two usages, one literal, the other figurative. The literal meaning denotes the physical action of blowing on or into something; the more figurative and theological sense refers to the influence of the divine on the human mind. Hobbes contends that when Scripture uses the word "inspire" to describe the action of the Holy Spirit, it, of course, indicates this latter, figurative sense. When God is said to breathe life into man in Genesis 2.7, for example, Scripture means us to understand God's breath as a metaphor for his capacity to give man "vitall motion." Likewise, when Christ offers to breathe the Holy Spirit on his disciples, we are again meant to read breath symbolically, as "a sign of the spirituall graces he gave unto them." And when Christ is said to be "full of the Holy *Spirit*," that fullness is not an actual "*Infusion* of the substance of God" but rather the "accumulation of his gifts."[61]

In stressing the distinction between the literal and figurative meanings of inspiration, Hobbes's aim is to expose a fundamental paradox in radical Protestantism. The enthusiast's excessive spirituality, Hobbes suggests, leads him to read Scripture literally, thereby rendering pious allegories, intended to move men toward faith, absurd and preposterous: to say that God, in fact, blows his spirit on or into us is to construe spirit as a sort of body "to be carryed hither and thither." Hobbes argues, on the contrary, that the spirit of God as related in Scripture is to be understood in a figurative sense only, as the signification of his virtues and their persuasive power over our minds. Such virtues are intangible graces that influence our behavior but cannot in any way be said to be present in us. Behind this assertion is Hobbes's extreme materialism, his conviction that matter is the only substance in the universe. Thus, to the extent that the enthusiast claims an indwelling spirit (defined by Hobbes as literal inspiration), at most such spirit signifies "the blowing into a man some thin and subtile aire, or wind, in such manner as a man filleth a bladder with his breath."[62] Hobbes's strategy in this chapter is especially ingenious, as the reductive and literalizing tendency typically ascribed to materialism is here transferred quite persuasively to the religious enthusiast who deludedly perceives himself to be filled with spirit and inhabited by God. The enthusiast, Hobbes suggests, fails to recognize that the Bible speaks allegorically when it describes the infusion of holy breath, spirit, and inspiration into man.

Swift's aeolists, concluding "the Original Cause of all Things to be *Wind*" (150), represent the logical extreme of Hobbes's account of enthusiasm. Embracing the enthusiastic premise that the spirit is actively present within them, the aeolists fall prey to the very confusion between literal and metaphorical inspiration that Hobbes documents. If something is in the enthusiast, both Hobbes and Swift imply, that something is wholly material. To the extent that the aeolists are nature (wind) worshippers, critics have read their practices as another critique of atheism and materialism in *A Tale*.[63] Such a reading, however, misses Swift's subtlety in selecting wind, itself a bodiless element, as a satiric conceit for spirit. Because the object of the aeolists' worship, though natural, is crucially immaterial, the aeolists reinvoke the superstition of the sartorists with a difference, for whereas the sartorists perceived divine properties in concretely tangible matter—clothes—the aeolists venerate an incorporeal entity as deity. As with the sartorists, then, the in-joke is the aeolists' failure to see that, though wind may resemble spirit in lack of substance, it remains rooted in natural, not supernatural, phenomena. To the extent that they worship wind, the aeolists may be unwitting materialists, but the target of Swift's satire is erroneous *belief*. His mark, once again, is religion.

By transforming the divine principle—spirit—into Hobbes's wind, Swift's satire reminds his readers of the absurdly false pretenses of the aeolists' claims to inspiration. Nodding to Hobbes at his most notorious, Swift constructs an ingenious parody of Hobbes's enthusiast's persuasion that the spirit could somehow be "powred [sic] into men, as into barrels."[64] Having already received an infusion of wind by the aid of "a

Pair of Bellows applied to his . . . Breech" (153), the aeolist priest enters a "Barrel" to experience the crescendo of the inspiration process:

[I]nto this *Barrel*, upon Solemn Days, the Priest enters; where, having before duly prepared himself . . . , a secret Funnel is also convey'd from his Posteriors, to the Bottom of the Barrel, which admits new Supplies of Inspiration from a *Northern* Chink or Crany. Whereupon, you behold him swell immediately to the Shape and Size of his *Vessel*. In this Posture he disembogues whole Tempests upon his Auditory, as the Spirit from beneath gives him Utterance. . . . It is in this Guise, the Sacred *Aeolist* delivers his oracular *Belches* to his panting Disciples; Of whom, some are greedily gaping after the sanctified Breath; others are all the while hymning out the Praises of the *Winds*; and gently wafted to and fro by their own Humming, do thus represent the soft Breezes of their Deities appeased. (156)

In Hobbes's version, the simile of pouring spirit into men "as into barrels" emphasizes the enthusiast's ludicrous conviction that the spirit could be infused into him: if he believes that spirit can be tangibly present in man, he must of necessity conceive spirit to be a kind of substance akin to something one pours into a barrel. Swift takes this material reduction of inspiration one step further here by emphasizing the bodily signification of wind. Whereas Hobbes uses wind synonymously with "subtile aire" or "breath," Swift impishly transmogrifies wind into gas, the emission of which the aeolists cultivate into the sacred arts of belching and farting (153–54).

Swift's brutal insistence upon the body as the natural source of the mistaken belief in divine inspiration returns us to the part *A Tale* plays in seventeenth-century anthropology of religion. For just as Peter's extravagant rites and ceremonies are linked to their pagan equivalent in the sartorists, the aeolists' confusion between bodily wind and divine inspiration has an ancient precursor in the practices of the oracle priestesses at Delphi:

It is from this Custom of the Priests, that some Authors maintain these *Aeolists*, to have been very antient in the World. Because, the Delivery of their Mysteries, which I have just now mention'd, appears exactly the same with that of other antient Oracles, whose Inspirations were owing to certain subterraneous *Effluviums of Wind*, delivered with the *same* Pain to the Priest, and much about the *same* Influence on the People. It is true indeed, that these were frequently managed and directed by *Female* Officers, whose Organs were understood to be better disposed for the Admission of those Oracular *Gusts*, as entring and passing up thro' a Receptacle of greater Capacity, and causing also a Pruriency by the Way, such as with due Management, hath been refined from a Carnal, into a Spiritual Extasie. And to strengthen this profound Conjecture, it is farther insisted, that this Custom of *Female* Priests is kept up still in certain refined Colleges of our *Modern*

Aeolists, who are agreed to receive their Inspiration, derived thro' the Receptacle aforesaid, like their Ancestors, the *Sibyls*. (156–57)[65]

William Kupersmith has identified two probable sources in early patristic writing for Swift's satire on the oracles: Origen and Saint John Chrysostom. According to Origen, the Delphic prophetess "receives a spirit through her womb; after being filled with this she utters oracular sayings, supposed to be sacred and divine." Chrysostom similarly describes how "the evil spirit ascending from beneath, and entering the lower part of her body, fills the woman with madness."[66] As we saw in the previous chapter, the Enlightenment debate over the pagan oracles posited two potential explanations for ancient prophecy, one supernatural, the other material. Christian apologetics were limited to the supernatural, for to suggest a natural derivation for the oracles was seen to threaten Christian claims to authentic prophecy: if pagan prophecy could be explained by natural means, so could Christian revelation. Kupersmith argues that Swift upholds the orthodox Christian view that the pagan oracles were attributable to demon possession. The link between the aeolists and the ancient oracles thus deepens the satire on the former by suggesting that their misguided enthusiasm perpetuates "a species of pagan devil worship whose origins are wholly pagan."[67]

And yet nothing in Swift's parody of the oracle prophetess in any way suggests a supernatural element to her supposed inspiration. On the contrary, Swift's emphasis is exclusively material and physical.[68] In his discussion of the natural origins of the Delphic oracle, Fontenelle explains that the top of Parnassus, the site of the oracle, contained a sort of chasm "out of which an Exhalation came." These exhalations were said to make "Goats dance and caper, by fuming into their Heads." Such evidence indicates that the first (so-called) prophet at Delphi was likely nothing more than an "Enthusiast" made dizzy by the cavern's natural gases. Hobbes, too, had argued that the prognostications of the priests at Delphi were merely "senslesse answers" attributable not to divine revelation, but rather to "the intoxicating vapour of the place, which is very frequent in sulphurous Cavernes."[69] Swift's parodic emphasis in the above passage on the "subterraneous" "Oracular Gusts," which enter the priestess's lower regions, is thus informed by natural rather than supernatural explanations of prophecy. As Kupersmith himself points out, moreover, the Greek word *pneuma*, used in Origen's account of the oracle priestess's inspiration, can signify "breath," "wind," and "vapor," as well as "spirit."[70] It is precisely this ambiguity that Swift exploits in his attempt to document a continuity of error spanning from ancient paganism to modern Christianity: the multiple senses of *pneuma* provide an ancient equivalent to Hobbes's gloss on the physical and spiritual senses of "inspiration." By suggesting, in other words, that modern enthusiasm is merely a repetition of the oracle priestess's wholly natural frenzy, Swift insinuates that religious enthusiasm, like popish superstition, reproduces the false worship of ancient paganism. The aeolists and the ancient oracle prophets unite in the bodily source of their frenzy: "certain subterraneous Effluviums of Wind." As we saw with Swift's satire on the sartorists, such an emphasis on the natural roots of the spirit was a perilous tactic, for its fulfillment is reached only with the rejection of all claims to supernatural inspiration, not just enthusiastic and superstitious ones.

III

If the critique of enthusiasm and superstition aimed to arrive at the source of all the wrong-headed delusions about religion, what was more fundamental and universal than the body and its unavoidable functions and urges? In "A Digression concerning Madness," commonly taken to form the epicenter of *A Tale*, Swift's narrator famously asserts that the "*Madness*" and "*Phrenzy*" (162) characteristic of propagators of new religions can be explained through "Recourse to my *Phoenomenon of Vapours*, ascending from the lower Faculties to over-shadow the Brain" (167). Said "Vapours" are often gas and wind, but as Swift's parody of the Delphic oracle suggests, if they enjoy a slightly more elevated referent, it is nonetheless determinedly bodily. Indeed, throughout *A Tale* Swift's critique of religious inspiration, ancient and modern, relies on the radical notion that "Spiritual Extasie" is merely a "refined" version of the "Carnal" drive. Fontenelle emphasized the role of concupiscence in his rejection of the supernatural workings of the oracles. As he related of the oracle priestesses, "The *Gods* never failed to fall in Love with the *fair Ladies*; for they must come and pass away the Nights in their Temples, tricked up for the purpose by their own Husbands."[71] This reduction of the spirit into sublimated sexual excitement forms the focus of the "Fragment" appended to *A Tale*, entitled "A Discourse concerning the Mechanical Operation of the Spirit." Here the narrator's investigations into "the History of *Fanaticism*, from the most early Ages to the present" (283) unearth a momentous discovery: "The Seed or Principle, which has ever put Men upon *Visions* in Things *Invisible*, is of a Corporeal Nature" (287). The first fanatics in history, Swift's narrator informs us, were the Dionysian and Bacchic cults. And in case "superficial Readers" imagine "that the whole Business was nothing more than a Set of roaring, scouring Companions, over-charg'd with Wine" (283), the narrator provides a "deeper Foundation" for their "Fanatick Rites," namely, "an entire *Mixture and Confusion of Sexes*" in their Bacchanalian celebrations (285). From this origin all subsequent fanatics follow suit, encouraging the narrator to conclude that "the *Thorn in the Flesh* serves for a *Spur to the Spirit*" (287).[72]

Harth has shown the influence of writers like Robert Burton, Meric Casaubon, and Henry More on Swift's account of the physiological basis for enthusiasm.[73] Burton's *Anatomy of Melancholy* (1632), in particular, explicitly linked enthusiasm to the world of sexuality by categorizing "religious melancholy" under the broader rubric of "love melancholy." About the specifics of this relationship, Burton has little to say except that "God himselfe" constitutes the (often mistaken) love object.[74] Interestingly for our purposes, however, Burton has much to say about the Delphic oracle and may well have provided the impetus for Swift's irreverent insinuation that the prophetess's frenzy was not supernaturally inspired but rather sexually generated.[75] Casaubon's *A Treatise concerning Enthusiasme, as it is an Effect of Nature* (1655) also suggests a latent association between enthusiasm and sexuality, defining what Casaubon calls "naturall Enthusiasme" as "a fervency" whose "strange effects" are "apt to be mistaken for supernaturall." When we consider the natural causes of enthusiasm, Casaubon argues, we discover that "it is indeed (in divers kinds of it) a very ardor, and nothing else, whereof all men are naturally capable." More's *Enthusiasmus Triumphatus* (1656) is likewise informed by Burton's linking of religious and love melancholy. More asserts that "the sense of Love at large is eminently comprehended in the temper of the *Melancholist*." This wisdom is indicated by "the fancie of a late new fangled Religionist, when he sat so kindly by a Gipsie under an hedge, and put his hand into her bosome in a fit of devotion, and vaunted afterwards of it as if it had been a very pious and meritorious action."[76]

For Burton, moreover, the prophecies of the pagan oracles "proceed from the same cause" as the supposed inspiration of "Enthusiasts." In defining this cause, Burton attempts to consider both natural and supernatural explanation. One possibility is that the various fanatics in history suffer from "meere melancholy," a psychophysiological pathology that Burton defines early in his treatise as the process by which "*vapours which arise from the other parts, and fume up into the head, alter the animal faculties.*"[77] More's *Enthusiasmus Triumphatus*, seen by Harth as the primary source for Swift's scatological account of inspiration, works off of Burton's claim that melancholics suffer from the deranging effects of vapors ascending from the lower regions of the body. More asserts that the "Spirit" so exalted by enthusiasts "is nothing else but that flatulency which is in the melancholy complexion, & rises out of the *Hypochondriacal* humour upon some occasionall heat, as winde out of an *Aeolipila* applied to the fire." He supports this theory, not coincidentally, by citing the Delphic oracle and the way in which "the *Pythia* of old are conceived to have been inspired through the power of certain exhalations breathed from those caverns they had their recesse in."[78] The links between *A Tale* and contemporary writings on the physiology of enthusiasm are thus readily apparent. In the tradition of Burton, Casaubon, and More, then, Swift aims to disparage and ridicule the pretensions of enthusiasts by emphasizing the bodily source of their raptures. Harth fails to acknowledge, however, that Swift's influences all take pains to preserve the supernatural as an operative force in religious inspiration, making sure that natural modes of explanation remain limited to appropriate targets of religious error.

Even while offering physiological accounts of enthusiasm, Burton stresses that the devil is the corrupting force behind all manifestations of superstition and fanaticism: "The *primum mobile* therefore, and first mover of all superstition, is the Divell, that great enimy of mankinde, the principall agent, who in a thousand severall shapes, after divers fashions, with severall engines, illusions, & by severall names hath deceived the inhabitants of the earth."[79] Though Casaubon stresses the natural grounds of many instances of supposed supernatural enthusiasm, he excepts what he calls "Divinatory Enthusiasme," an instance of which is the pagan oracles. Here, "a concurrence of Naturall Causes," such as melancholy, and hysteria in women, prepares and disposes the body for "the Devil to work upon." When the natural distemper is cured, the Devil, too, is "driven away, and hath no more power over the same bodies." Natural causes thus contribute to the onset of divination, though they are "not wholly sufficient to produce this effect." Like Burton, then, Casaubon is concerned to preserve the supernatural as a sphere of influence against impious attempts, both ancient and modern, to prove that all divination stems from wholly natural causes. More, too, is careful to distinguish between "*Religion* and *Melancholy*," and to declare that "there has not one word all this time been spoken against that true and warrantable Enthusiasme of devout and holy souls."[80] Such necessary caveats, however, proved insufficient, and in the 1662 edition of *Enthusiasmus Triumphatus*, More added further clarification along the lines of Burton and Casaubon: "And further touching the Defectuousness in my *Enumeration* of the *Causes* of Enthusiasm, in that I omitted the Agency of the Devil, I answer, that his *Causality* is more vagrant, more lax and general then to be brought in there, where my aim was to [indicate] the more proper and constant causes of that *Disease*."[81]

Van Dale's and Fontenelle's writings on the oracles make clear that

orthodox Christian apologists were obliged to keep open the possibility
of the devil and demon possession in their accounts of the various false
claims to inspiration throughout history. To do otherwise was inevitably
to suggest that supernatural forces—both good and evil—were merely
fictional. As John Edwards proclaims in his *Thoughts concerning the
Several Causes and Occasions of Atheism*, "the denial of Daemons and
Witches" leads inexorably to atheism: "for Witchcraft and all Diabolick
Transactions are disbeliev'd on the account of the improbability, if not
impossibility of Spirits. So that it is plain the rejecting of the being and
commerce of Daemons or Infernal Spirits opens a door to the denial
of the Deity."[82] In his "Fragment," Swift's narrator nods to orthodoxy
by citing the received wisdom on the causes of enthusiastic inspiration:
prophecy or inspiration, possession or "the immediate Act of the Devil,"
and natural causes. The stated aim of "A Fragment," however, is to describe a fourth and less acknowledged source of enthusiasm, namely,
the mechanical operation of the spirit. This latter source, the narrator
claims, "is purely an Effect of Artifice," and "tho' it is an Art of great
Antiquity," it "has been sparingly handled, or not at all, by any Writer"
(267). Artificial or mechanical enthusiasm, Swift argues, is vitally linked
to natural enthusiasm, as the "Effect[s] of Art" are "inclined to work
upon certain Natures and Constitutions, more than others" (267). Our
natural tendency to mistake lust for spiritual zeal provides the basis for
the following mechanical process:

Then, by frequently moving your Body up and down, you perceive the Vapors to
ascend very fast, till you are perfectly dosed and flustred like one who drinks too
much in a Morning. Mean while, the Preacher is also at work; He begins a loud
Hum, which pierces you quite thro'; This is immediately returned by the Audience, and you find your self prompted to imitate them, by a meer spontaneous
Impulse, without knowing what you do. The *Interstitia* are duly filled up by the
Preacher, to prevent too long a Pause, under which the *Spirit* would soon faint
and grow languid. (273)

Swift's suggestion in this passage that the mechanical operation of
the spirit is encouraged by the clergy, who take advantage of and exploit
the people's natural vulnerability to superstition, anticipates the radical
arguments of John Trenchard and David Hume later in the century.[83] For
Trenchard, the fact that fraud and imposture have prevailed in religion
from its earliest stirrings suggests that "something innate in our Constitutions ma[kes] us easily to be susceptible of wrong Impressions, subject to Pannick Fears, and prone to Superstition and Error."[84] Trenchard
is thus typically credited with broadening the physiological theories of
Burton, Casaubon, and More from a description of religious error to a
characterization of all religion in all ages.[85] *A Tale* suggests, however,

that Swift was a crucial intervening voice in this tradition. As the narrator of "A Fragment" observes, "For I do not remember any other Temper of Body, or Quality of Mind, wherein all Nations and Ages of the World have so unanimously agreed, as That of a *Fanatick* Strain, or Tincture of *Enthusiasm*" (266). It is characteristic of "A Fragment" thus to magnify the incidence of enthusiasm, historically and geographically, to the point that all religious expression threatens to fall under its aegis. This was Wotton's suspicion from the start; his *Observations* complained that, though Swift appeared to attack Protestant dissent, "all extraordinary Inspirations are the Subjects of his Scorn and Mockery" (325).

Later in "A Fragment," the narrator returns to the question of supernatural inspiration, remarking that "it hath continued these hundred Years an even Debate, whether the Deportment and the Cant of our *English* Enthusiastick Preachers, were *Possession*, or *Inspiration*" (275). His contribution to the debate is to include a footnote citing Horace's caution in *Ars poetica* on the infelicitous use of a deus ex machina in drama: "Nec Deus intersit, nisi dignus vindice nodus Inciderit" (275n5) (And let no god intervene, unless a knot come worthy of such a deliverer).[86] The narrator applies Horace's remarks on tragedy to "Life," for in both, "it is held, a Conviction of great Defect, both in Order and Invention, to interpose the Assistance of preternatural Power, without an absolute and last Necessity" (275). Though Horace allows for prudent recourse to the divine, the narrator's following comments make clear that Swift's emphasis falls on the absurdity of such pretenses:

However, it is a Sketch of Human Vanity, for every Individual, to imagine the whole Universe is interess'd in his meanest Concern. If he hath got cleanly over a Kennel, some Angel, unseen, descended on purpose to help him by the Hand; if he hath knockt his Head against a Post, it was the Devil, for his Sins, let loose from Hell, on purpose to buffet him. Who, that sees a little paultry Mortal, droning, and dreaming, and drivelling to a Multitude, can think it agreeable to common good Sense, that either Heaven or Hell should be put to the Trouble of Influence or Inspection upon what he is about? Therefore, I am resolved immediately, to weed this Error out of Mankind, by making it clear, that this Mystery, of venting spiritual Gifts, is nothing but a *Trade*. (275–76)

The voice in this passage, skeptical and haughtily contemptuous, is Swift's own.[87] Reminiscent of Rochester's "Satyre" and Montaigne's *Apology*, the freethinking position Swift articulates begins with the remoteness of the Epicurean gods and reaches its fruition in Spinoza's rejection of miracles. "What could the blessed, the immortal," asks Lucretius, "gain / From any such munificence as ours / To tackle anything for our sweet sake?"[88] As Montaigne contends with like disdain, "The hand with which [God] governs lends itself to all things with the same tenor, the same power, and the same order; the effect on us adds nothing to it; our movements and our measures do not touch him."[89] This recognition of divine indifference to human concerns renders supernatural intervention an absurdity, for God does not single man out from the rest of his creation. "I laugh aloud," says Swift, "to see these Reasoners, at the same time, engaged in wise Dispute, about certain Walks and Purlieus, whether they are in the Verge of God or the Devil, seriously debating, whether such and such Influences come into Mens Minds, from above or below" (275).

By dismissing the possibility of an authentic instance of supernatural possession, whether divine or demonic, and by offering only natural and political explanations for both ancient and modern enthusiasm in its stead, Swift's "Fragment" hearkens back to Hobbes's suggestion that Scripture refers to the spirit in a figurative sense only. Once spirit is merely an allegory marshaled for the purposes of instilling belief, we are forced to grant, along with Lucretius and Spinoza, that the universe operates according to natural laws. For the Epicurean tradition—the locus classicus for the anthropology of religion, according to Strauss—it is precisely our ignorance of natural laws that encourages our susceptibility to superstition. Man fears what he cannot understand, and in a state of emotional excitement, he ascribes supernatural power to what appears awesome and perplexing.[90] The Epicurean campaign against religion, as Strauss explains, was thus fought "in the name of human peace of mind." This motive became freshly topical, Strauss suggests, in the seventeenth century, when the wars of religion provoked a renewed animus against the destabilizing function of religion in society. Though the original Epicurean incentive was the quest for peace of mind, the seventeenth-century critics of religion transformed this individual emphasis into a social one: concern for peace of mind became concern for peace within society.[91] It was this very desire for social peace that motivated Herbert's search for a set of common religious notions in ancient religion, discussed in the previous chapter. And the same desire galvanized the critique of fanaticism and superstition in *A Tale*; for the madness of false inspiration, defined by Swift as "*Vapours* issuing up from the lower Faculties," has been "the Parent of all those mighty Revolutions, that have happened in *Empire*, in *Philosophy*, and in *Religion*" (171).

Though skeptical about the truth of the spirit, Swift's solution to the instability provoked by warring beliefs, as we know, was not to reject religion. His discussion of miracles in his sermon "On the Trinity" provides an instructive example of his peculiar method of concession. As Michael DePorte has argued, the orthodox position on the truth of the Gospels in the period attested that miracles provided empirical proof of the authenticity of the apostles' inspiration.[92] Swift rejects this view, arguing alternatively that "there is no Miracle mentioned in Holy Writ, which, if it were strictly examined, is not as much contrary to common Reason, and as much a Mystery as this Doctrine of the Trinity; and therefore we may with equal Justice deny the Truth of them all" (9:165). This statement dismisses the rational possibility of supernatural truth, yet Swift defends belief on different ground. We believe the miracles related in Scripture, Swift continues tautologically, precisely because Scripture affirms their truth; to do otherwise is to "give up our Holy Religion to Atheists and Infidels" (9:166). We return here to Swift's pragmatic preference of Christianity over the moral teachings of the classical philosophical tradition. As we remember, Christianity, unlike ancient philosophy, provides the ballast of official theological principles, without which most men fail to embrace a moral life. To intimates like Stella, Swift can offer the wisdom of the best of the pagan philosophers that virtue is its own reward, thereby acknowledging the likelihood that future rewards and punishments are indeed merely "an entertainment to poets," and "a terror of children" (9:245).[93] For most, however, only revealed religion imparts the requisite encouragement to right action. The specifics of this compromise will form the subject of the following chapter.

CHAPTER FOUR

Suspending Disbelief

Swift, Credulity, and the Pious Fraud

> A religionist may . . . know his narrative to be false, and yet persevere in it, with the best intentions in the world, for the sake of promoting so holy a cause.
> —David Hume, "Of Miracles" (1748)

If Wotton and other contemporaries were correct to intuit that Swift's *Tale of a Tub* absorbed all of revealed Christianity in its ostensible ridicule of the corruptions of popery and Protestant fanaticism, they were nonetheless wrong to read Swift's satire as a paean to unbelief. Although *A Tale* looks askance at the transcendence of the spirit, most critics agree that it supports the necessity of religion as an institution. How *A Tale* succeeds in upholding the teachings of the Anglican Church while making clear that the spirit is a fiction will be the concern of this chapter. Swift begins the preface to *A Tale* by suggesting just such a double character to his design. Establishing the motives for his writing, Swift's narrator describes the threat to Church and State posed by "the Wits of the present Age," who enjoy "pick[ing] Holes in the weak sides of Religion and Government" (39). Selected to protect the nation from their destructive sallies, the narrator distracts the wits with what he calls "*A Tale of a Tub*" (41). As the narrator defines it, "a tale of a tub" refers to a strategy among seamen for beguiling aggressive whales. According to legend, the seamen "fling [the whale] out an empty *Tub*, by way of Amusement, to divert him from laying violent Hands upon the Ship" (40). For the narrator, the legend serves as an instructive parable for his contemporary moment: the whale is interpreted as Hobbes's *Leviathan*, the source "from whence the terrible Wits of our Age . . . borrow their Weapons," and the Ship "is easily understood to be . . . the *Commonwealth*." Only the

"Tub" is taken literally as something "hollow, and dry, and empty, and noisy, and wooden, and given to Rotation" (40).

The custom of throwing a tub to a whale as a diversionary tactic was familiar to seventeenth-century readers. And Swift was not the first writer to employ the phrase "a tale of a tub" as a metaphor for creating diversion and amusement with the aim of neutralizing a present danger. The success of Swift's parable, however, depends crucially upon the reader's recognition that the proverbial phrase, "a tale of a tub," also and relatedly signifies an apocryphal story, a deceptive fiction.[1] Indeed, the narrator's emphasis in his parable on the tub's "hollow" and "empty" qualities implies a sly allusion to this commonplace understanding of the phrase. That the narrator plays innocent, so to speak, regarding this second usage of "a tale of a tub" is significant, for freethinkers applied the term to indicate the falsehoods of religion, as the anonymous poem "The Deist: A Satyr on the Parsons" attests:

> Religion's a Politick Law,
> Devis'd by the Priggs of the Schools;
> To keep the Rabble in awe
> And amuse poor Bigotted Fools.
>
> . . .
>
> And they, for good victualls and Bubb,
> Will bellow their Nonsense aloud,
> And rant out a Tale of A Tub,
> To fright the ignorant Croude.
>
> $(1-8)^2$

As we know, religion and its manifold corruptions form the subject of Swift's work, itself entitled *A Tale of a Tub*. Is Swift's latent purpose to insinuate, as I suggested in the previous chapter, that the supposed truths of Christian religion are "a tale of a tub"—mere flimflam and nonsense? His choice of title and subject matter demands, at least, that readers ask this question. Contemporaries certainly did. As the Duchess of Marlborough reminisced, Swift "turned all religion into a Tale of a Tub, and sold it for a jest." Wotton likewise complained about "the Ludicrous Allegory" of *A Tale*, and the way in which "God and Religion, Truth and Moral Honesty, Learning and Industry are made a May-Game, and the most serious Things in the World . . . described as so many several Scenes in a *Tale of a Tub*."[3] And yet it is equally important to acknowledge that in Swift's parable it is precisely "a tale of a tub" that promises to *prevent* the wits from subverting Church and State. Here, too, the referent is still religion, for what else will keep the wits in check but a right respect for religious orthodoxy? In this instance, then, rather than suggesting radical critique, "a tale of a tub" appears to serve the ends of civil and religious stability.

While these two usages may seem to be mutually exclusive, they, in fact, inform one another. An anonymous contribution to *Fog's Weekly Journal* declares, for example, that "it is highly necessary to *throw out the Tub*; that is to say, to amuse the Publick by some well-concerned Plot," as a way to keep the State's "Enemies in Awe." The author here makes explicit what is only suggested in Swift: that the actual content of the "tub" or "plot" is lies and fabrications, merely "an Enquiry about Nothing." Indeed, to the extent that the author stresses the need to take "Care" in "contriving, projecting, and framing the said Plot, that it may look plausible to the People," he assumes its necessarily fictional status. The essential feature of "a tale of a tub," in other words, is not its relationship to truth but rather its ability to charm and activate the people's imaginations: "It is a Dish for the Publick, and therefore should be made palatable, that it may go down the better."[4] This privileging of utility over truth is central to the phrase "a tale of a tub" and represents the key to Swift's distinctive attitude toward religion: the tub (religion) may indeed be empty, hollow, and utterly contrived, but it controls the encroachments of whales and wits quite handily. To put it another way, though strictly speaking the teachings of Christianity might be tales and flimflam (a thesis Swift will only put forward under the protection of a disavowed persona), such fictions are still vitally useful, even indispensable, to the health and stability of the Commonwealth.

This reading returns us to the organizing conceit of the allegory of the three brothers in *A Tale*, the notion that religion is a "cloak." As discussed in the previous chapter, Swift's use of clothes as a satiric trope through which to condemn the idolatrous practices of the sartorist sect implodes when we realize that virtually the same metaphor is used to represent true religion. As Warren Montag persuasively argues, when Swift's narrator impiously asks, "Is not religion a cloak?" his question cannot but evacuate Christianity (figured in Swift's allegory by the brothers' coats) of any positive or normative value:

The reader is thereby conducted to the proposition immanent in the effects of Swift's satire, a proposition no less true for being disavowed in the Apology: religion in a world of matter without spirit is *artificial*, a purely human practice, and it is *material*; it is nothing more than the rituals, practices and institutions that compose it. . . . It is thus not the truth of the Holy Spirit that is the foundation of religious rituals, practices and institutions and that is expressed in them. Quite the contrary: it is the rituals, practices and institutions in their materiality that *produce* the 'spiritual' truths that appear to be their foundation but which are in fact their excrescence, a cover and a camouflage that conceal their merely

material nature. . . . At this point the political stakes of *A Tale of a Tub*, its relation to Swift's stated positions, become clear. The problematization of spirit, the
disappearance of transcendentality, the abolition of immutable essences, all render
imperative the defense of the rituals, practices and institutions of the Church, its
visible and actual manifestations, as something like necessary fictions, beautiful
lies that conceal an abominable truth. . . . The absence of transcendental and immutable truths must itself be concealed by the cloak of religion.[5]

The notion that, for good and for bad, religion is a cloak/coat that con-
ceals the absence of spirit, is itself a version of "throwing out the tub,"
of using, in Montag's words, "necessary fictions" and "beautiful lies" to
preserve the institution of the Church against the challenges posed by its
various enemies.

The necessity of maintaining the cloak of religion and "throwing out
the tub" to the foes of the Church serves as the informing principle of
"A Digression concerning Madness," the heart of Swift's *Tale*, where the
narrator switches his focus from wits and freethinkers to the seditious
impulses of Protestant fanatics.[6] The argument of this most famous of
the digressions has been rehearsed many times by critics. The authors of
new empires, new religions, and new schemes of philosophy, the narrator claims, suffer uniformly from a species of madness, the bodily causes
of which were discussed in the last chapter. This madness exhibits itself
in a variety of ways, but the common thread that unites its different expressions is the extreme vainglory of the respective madman. Religious
enthusiasts, political tyrants, and innovators in philosophy unite in their
inflated attempts to "reduce the Notions of all Mankind, exactly to the
same Length, and Breadth, and Height of [their] own" (166). What has
not been addressed is the way in which "A Digression concerning Madness" supports the assertion of section II of *A Tale* that "Religion [is] a
Cloak," or as Harold Kelling puts it, "that the best religion is that which
deceives best."[7] Swift gestures back to this earlier claim by linking individual enthusiasm—the process by which "a Man's Fancy gets *astride* on
his Reason . . . and common Understanding, as well as common Sense, is
Kickt out of Doors" (171)—to imposture. In one of the most frequently
cited passages of "A Digression," Swift suggests that all imposture begins
with a single mad enthusiast who soon attempts to generate disciples by
proselytizing his (false) beliefs:

The first Proselyte he makes, is Himself, and when that is once compass'd, the
Difficulty is not so great in bringing over others; A strong Delusion always operating from *without*, as vigorously as from *within*. For Cant and Vision are to the
Ear and the Eye, the same that Tickling is to the Touch. Those Entertainments
and Pleasures we most value in Life, are such as *Dupe* and play the Wag with
the Senses. For, if we take an Examination of what is generally understood by

Happiness, as it has Respect, either to the Understanding or the Senses, we shall find all its Properties and Adjuncts will herd under this short Definition: That, *it is a perpetual Possession of being well Deceived*. And first, with Relation to the Mind or Understanding; 'tis manifest, what mighty Advantages Fiction has over Truth; and the Reason is just at our Elbow; because Imagination can build nobler Scenes, and produce more wonderful Revolutions than Fortune or Nature will be at Expence to furnish. Nor is Mankind so much to blame in his Choice. . . . How fade and insipid do all Objects accost us that are not convey'd in the Vehicle of *Delusion*? How shrunk is every Thing, as it appears in the Glass of Nature? So, that if it were not for the Assistance of Artificial *Mediums*, false Lights, refracted Angles, Varnish, and Tinsel; there would be a mighty Level in the Felicity and Enjoyments of Mortal Men. (171–72)

This famous passage moves almost imperceptibly from a focus on the deceiver—the deluded enthusiast seeking converts to his visions—to the deceived—the rest of us who are equally prone to delusion, if not to establishing religious sects. As the narrator reminds us, "A strong Delusion always operate[s] from *without*, as vigorously as from *within*." From this point on, the passage describes a seemingly universal human tendency to be duped and, further, to enjoy the *"Possession of being well Deceived."* It would seem fairly obvious, as critics have long claimed, that Swift is critical of this process, and that we are meant to read the narrator's praise of the pleasures of delusion as wholly ironic. For one, Swift's condemnation of enthusiasm as a radically destabilizing force is unambiguous; thus it would make no sense for him to condone any particular enthusiast's deluded followers, however innocently gulled they may be. As Ricardo Quintana has argued, "There is never any question as to the speciousness of everything that is here being advanced in favor of the happiness derived from superficial appearances. All our moral feelings run counter to this dismissal of the real condition of things and to such a form of self-deception."[8] Quintana's reading, along with others like it, relies on the common and not incorrect assumption in Swift criticism that Swift's satiric strategy is to blame through ironic praise, or to say one thing and mean another. Interpretive problems arise, however, if we attempt to apply a static critical formula—this or any other—to Swift's satire. Indeed, the distinctive brilliance (and persistent difficulty) of his artistry has long been seen to derive from his tendency to defy expectations and challenge our assumptions.

When the narrator remarks on the "mighty Advantages Fiction has over Truth," lauding the "noble Scenes" constructed by the "Imagination," it is thus quite possible that Swift turns the screw on the reader by meaning just what he says. Indeed, as we continue reading, what began as a satire of those foolish enough to be hoodwinked by religious cant no longer seems so straightforwardly satiric.[9] Somewhere along the way, the critique of fanaticism and its followers transforms into a broad-based account of the psychology of belief. As an account of the human condition more generally, Swift's mockery is, if not gentler, perforce more accepting. If we are *all* equally vulnerable to the imposture of others, then "Mankind" cannot be "blamed" for preferring "Cant and Vision" to "the Glass of Nature." The condemnation of fanaticism as a form of madness and delusion becomes, in other words, a covert reflection on the fundamental nature of belief itself. The narrator's heralding of the universal pleasures of delusion thus refigures in only slightly different terms the claim that religion is a cloak, for as we remember, the metaphor of the cloak refers to all of religion, not just to the idolatrous practices of the sartorists. While, strictly speaking, delusion, like the false clothes-worship of the sartorists, is a negative condition of belief, linked to superstition and enthusiasm, Swift implies that it is also all we have. Indeed, Swift ends his extended discussion of delusion in "A Digression concerning Madness" by defining *"the Possession of being well deceived"* as "The Serene Peaceful State of being a Fool among Knaves" (174), thereby indicating that there is no pure position outside of deception.[10] Just as clothes (the brothers' coats) figure the right worship of primitive Christianity as well as the sartorists' misguided belief, so too does delusion necessarily characterize the full spectrum of religious positions, from enthusiasm to orthodox worship.

I

The phrase "Fool among Knaves" comes from Sir William Temple's own treatment of imposture. In his essay "Of Popular Discontents," Temple describes the process by which depraved and licentious men, masking their own private ends under the pretense of serving the public good, impose upon well-meaning citizens: "The practice begins of knaves upon fools, of artificial and crafty men upon the simple and the good; these easily follow, and are caught, while the others lay trains, and pursue a game."[11] As I have suggested, Swift's analysis of imposture switches the focus from the depravity of the corrupt knave to the genuine pleasures of the simple fool, thereby implying that imposture might have a brighter side than is typically acknowledged. In their notes to *A Tale*, A. C. Guthkelch and D. Nichol Smith identify Horace as a possible source for Swift's discussion of the pleasures of delusion. In his *Epistles* Horace declares, "I should prefer to be thought a foolish and clumsy scribbler, if only my failings please, or at least escape me, rather than be wise and unhappy." Horace then tells the story of a Greek who lived under the illusion that he was at the theater, watching and listening to actors. Importantly, Horace emphasizes that despite this delusion, or perhaps because of it, the Greek "correctly perform[ed] all other duties of life" and was exemplary as a neighbor, host, husband, and master. When the man was cured of his madness by his kinsmen's help, he was said to cry, "Egad! You have killed me, my friends, not saved me; for thus you have robbed me of a pleasure and taken away perforce the dearest illusion of my heart."[12] Horace's example, itself not ironic, suggests that there was a tradition of thought that took the possibility of pleasant and useful delusions quite seriously. Swift's narrator's delight in the possession of being well deceived thus provides another instance where Swift confounds our expectations (and protects himself) by using his absurd speaker to articulate what were likely his own beliefs.

Horace's anecdote about the Greek's pleasant delusions reappears, moreover, in two additional influences on Swift: Erasmus and Montaigne.[13] In *The Praise of Folly* (1511), long acknowledged as an important model for Swift's satiric strategies in *A Tale* generally and in "A Digression concerning Madness" particularly, Erasmus's Folly declares that there was nothing wrong with "the judgment of the Greek" who believed that "wonderful tragedies" were being acted before him, particularly since "in the other duties of life he conducted himself very well."[14] Montaigne, too, whom Bolingbroke refers to in a letter to Swift as "your old prating friend," argues in his *Apology* that "many philosophers" would agree with the man who "by some alteration of his senses had stamped in his imagination this hallucination: he thought he was perpetually at the amphitheaters watching entertainments." Like Horace and Erasmus, Montaigne is sympathetic to the Greek's conviction that the men who "cured" him in fact took away "the pleasure of these fancies."[15] Wisdom, on this view, is tantamount to unhappiness. Both Erasmus and Montaigne revere Socrates for refusing to accept the title of wise man and insisting that the wisest man is he who admits that he knows nothing. The simple people of the golden age were happy, both also contend, because they had no formal learning and knew better "than to pry into the secrets of Nature with irreligious curiosity . . . [and] seek the causes of mysterious phenomena."[16] The happy man is thus he who "recognizes human limitations and does not strive to leap beyond them," understanding that "there is great advantage in not being so wise."[17]

If, as Erasmus and Montaigne teach, knowledge and wisdom produce unhappiness, then delusion, simplicity, and even imposture can indeed become positive goods. As Erasmus contends, "But to be deceived, they say, is miserable. Quite the contrary—not to be deceived is most miserable of all. For nothing could be further from the truth than the notion that man's happiness resides in things as they actually are." Erasmus makes explicit that such a view finds its roots in the skeptical tradition: "For human affairs are so manifold and obscure that nothing can be clearly known, as is rightly taught by my friends the Academics, the least arrogant of the philosophers. Or, if anything can be known, it often detracts from the pleasures of life."[18] Once we accept, with the Skeptics, that certain knowledge is, in fact, impossible to attain, then delusion not only increases our happiness, it also defines our fundamental condition in even the best of circumstances. Delusion, indeed, is equivalent to the ideal state of quietude that the ancient sects called *ataraxia*, "a peaceful and sedate condition of life, exempt from the agitations we receive through the impression of the opinion and knowledge we think we have of things."[19] Erasmus refers to this quietude as a kind of desirable madness occurring "whenever a certain pleasant mental distraction relieves the heart from its anxieties and cares and at the same time soothes it with the balm of manifold pleasures."[20] *Ataraxia*, in other words, is crucially linked to the pleasures of Horace's mad Greek, to the happiness that results from accepting delusion and resigning oneself to one's essential ignorance and state of misunderstanding.

Swift's borrowings from Erasmus and Montaigne on the pleasures of delusion suggest his attraction to the skeptical heritage.[21] Like his predecessors, Swift refers, in his "Tritical Essay" (1707), to the intelligence of Socrates' remark that he knew nothing, as well as to the skeptical dictum that "Truth . . . lives in the Bottom of a Well." Philosophers, he urges, should not attempt to "account for every Phaenomenon in Nature," and their various opinions, far from contributing to our felicity and hope, "have scattered through the World as many Plagues of the Mind, as *Pandora's* Box did those of the Body" (1:247, 248). When Swift's narrator discusses the wits who threaten Church and State in the introduction to *A Tale*, he emphasizes that his task in writing is to prevent "those formidable Enquirers, from canvasing and *reasoning* upon such delicate Points" (39). It is Skepticism, moreover, that informs Swift's animus in "A Digression concerning Madness" against "Innovators in the Empire of Reason" (167), not to mention innovators in religion.[22] The narrator explains that reason's efforts to dissect nature only expose her flaws and imperfections to no identifiable purpose (173–74). When it is not plagued by the officious promptings of vain reason, "the Brain," he suggests, "disposeth its Owner to pass his Life in the common Forms." These common forms, aided by "the Pattern of Human Learning," warn man against the folly of "particular Notions" and "instruct him in his private

Infirmities" (171).[23] The view that the insufficiency of man's reason leads to the necessity of conforming to the laws and conventions of his time is itself canonically skeptical, dating back to Pyrrho himself. And yet this conformity, though socially and politically conservative, is crucially evacuated of any trace of recognizable belief. As Terence Penelhum argues, it is because life requires action that the skeptic chooses to adhere to appearances, consenting to obey local law and opinion with a kind of "aloof conformity" and "surface piety":[24] "Although the Skeptic's practice may not differ outwardly from that of his unphilosophical fellows, he is someone who *returns* to a common practice that is disinfected of those underpinnings of belief and valuation that have given it meaning and helped to establish it for those with whose behavior he allows himself to conform. He is *in* their world, but not *of* it."[25]

When applied to Christianity, philosophical skepticism results in a kind of fideism, itself a highly ambiguous religious stance with regard to conventional orthodoxy. Because reason establishes no adequate knowledge or truth, the argument went, we must abide by the dictates of faith in matters of religion. That this was Swift's position is evident from his argument in "On the Trinity" that "Rules of Philosophy" (9:160) have no place in theology, and that whatever cavils our reason might raise about the Holy Trinity, we must accept the doctrine as it is affirmed in Scripture and taught by the Church of England. Swift defines faith as "a Virtue by which any Thing commanded us by God to believe, appears evident and certain to us, although we do not see, nor can conceive it" (9:164). As the Anglican rationalists intuited, however, the trouble with the injunction to believe in what we cannot see or conceive is that such belief cannot help but hover on the borders of unbelief. Rochester's example is instructive: if we remove reason from theology, do we not threaten to make faith, at best, the Skeptic's suspension of disbelief?

If religious faith becomes suspended disbelief, then Christianity itself must be embraced as yet another profitable delusion, one whose promises of rewards and infinite bliss carry unique powers to increase our comfort. As Erasmus argued:

Now who could be more foolish—rather, who could be happier—than those who assure themselves they will have the very ultimate felicity because they have recited daily those seven little verses from the holy psalms? . . . So rife, so teeming with such delusions is the entire life of all Christians everywhere. And yet priests are not unwilling to allow and even foster such delusions because they are not unaware of how many emoluments accumulate from this source. In the midst of all this, if some odious wiseman should stand up and sing out the true state of affairs . . . , look how much happiness he would immediately take away from the minds of mortals, look at the confusion he would throw them into![26]

The Church itself, Erasmus scandalously implies, practices a version of the ancient twofold philosophy in perpetuating delusions among the people that "wisemen" know to be philosophically false. The "Apology" to *A Tale*, in which Swift comments several times that "judicious" readers of "tast and candor" (7, 12, 3, 8) have read the book correctly, invokes this strategy, suggesting that these like-minded men of discernment understand that the institutional function of religion must be preserved despite their unbelief.[27] Skeptical fideism indeed allowed the form of twofold philosophy known as the double truth—the theory that what may be "true" for philosophy cannot be admitted for theology.[28] As we know from Behn's translator's preface to *A Discovery of New Worlds*, the doctrine of the double truth is rooted in a fundamental split between philosophy and theology, and like fideism generally, it taught a suspension of disbelief in religion that always threatened to expose Christian revelation as fiction. Though there were sincere practitioners of the double truth who separated reason and faith for the benefit of the latter, particularly by the seventeenth century, the same separation was put to more ambiguous purpose.[29] The Church, not surprisingly, condemned fideism in 1348 and banned the double truth doctrine as early as 1277.[30] Erasmus' suggestion that Christianity is a pious fraud fostered by (well-meaning) priests to perpetuate man's happy delusions invited attacks on his piety not dissimilar from the controversy surrounding Swift's *Tale*. Thus, despite Skepticism's essentially conservative tendencies, beginning with Erasmus' and Montaigne's later links to aristocratic libertinism, Skepticism and even fideism took on an increasingly antireligious tone, one that reached its fruition in the infamous example of Hume.[31] It is this peculiar combination of conservative conformity and unbelief that has long perplexed Swift's readers, and Skepticism provides a useful context through which to decipher what have appeared to be long-standing contradictions in his writing.

II

Swift's fascination with the skeptical notion that religion functioned through the ages as a series of pious frauds, useful for maintaining happiness, morality, political obedience, and social stability, is indicated by the number of times the view appears in his writings. To the extent, as I have argued, that the phrase "a tale of a tub" is itself a synonym for a pious or useful fraud, religion's status as a productive deception forms the operating principle of Swift's major satire of that name. It is also central to his darkly satiric "Argument against Abolishing Christianity

(1711), which like *A Tale* suggests that the perpetuation of certain kinds of religious fictions can serve the interests of the State. Here Swift once again distances himself from the irreverent implications of this view by adopting yet another bold and impertinent persona.[32] We know we are listening to an ironic voice when the narrator expresses his earnest hope that "no Reader imagines [him] so weak to stand in the Defence of *real* Christianity." To do so, he continues, "would be to dig up Foundations; to destroy at one Blow *all* the Wit, and *half* the Learning of the Kingdom; to break the entire Frame and Constitution of Things" (2:27). That Swift means us to reject his persona's praise of nominal Christianity would thus seem fairly obvious, and yet, as is always the case with Swift, the matter is somewhat more complicated.

As Ehrenpreis points out, the occasion of the "Argument" was the sectarians' agitation for the repeal of the Test Act, the legislation that required all those who would hold government office to receive the Sacrament and participate in the rituals of the Anglican Church. Behind the "Argument," then, is Swift's conviction that repealing the Test Act was tantamount to abolishing Christianity. What is more, by Christianity, Ehrenpreis argues, Swift means not so much Christian religion generally, but rather "the Episcopal Protestant faith as distinguished from Presbyterianism, Roman Catholicism, all non-Christian creeds, and any form of irreligiosity."[33] It is this narrower definition of Christianity as the Church of England that informs the narrator's argument that the Church should be preserved as a kind of "tub" for the fanatics to sport with: "There is a Portion of Enthusiasm assigned to every Nation, which if it hath not proper Objects to work on, will burst out, and set all in a Flame. If the Quiet of a State can be bought by only *flinging Men a few Ceremonies to devour*, it is a Purchase no wise Man would refuse. Let the Mastiffs amuse themselves about a Sheep-skin stuffed with Hay, provided it will keep them from worrying the Flock" (2:35; italics mine).

Encouraging sectarian agitation against the rituals and discipline of the Church—"flinging Men a few Ceremonies to devour"—would seem outrageous and patently indefensible, evidently the object of Swift's satiric scorn: even a sincere defender of nominal Christianity would pull up before advocating that the ceremonies of the Church be laid open for attack. And yet Swift's logic ingeniously implies that as long as "Ceremonies" endure to be attacked, a Church necessarily lives and breathes behind them. On the contrary, without a Church upon which to expend their aggression, the fanatics' unruly energy would be forced to find yet more destructive outlets: "If Christianity did not lend its Name, to stand in the Gap, and to employ or divert these Humours, they must of Necessity be spent in . . . Disturbance to the publick Peace" (2:35). On the one hand, Swift's irony seems to demand that we recoil from this grossly cynical vision of the Church's function. Yet on the other hand it challenges us by suggesting, quite seriously, that if faced with the prospect of no Church at all, we ought to fight tooth and nail for a Church as "a tale of a tub"—"a Sheep-skin stuffed with Hay."[34]

Later in "An Argument," the libertine narrator provides another instance in which religion serves as "a tale of a tub." However one feels about sectarianism's threat to the State, most readers would agree to preserve Christianity, he casually remarks, if only because "it may perhaps admit a Controversy, whether the Banishing all Notions of Religion whatsoever, would be convenient for the Vulgar." He continues,

Not that I am in the least of Opinion with those, who hold Religion to have been the Invention of Politicians, to keep the lower Parts of the World in Awe, by the Fear of invisible Powers; unless Mankind were then very different from what it is now: For I look upon the Mass, or Body of our People here in *England*, to be as Free-Thinkers, that is to say, as stanch Unbelievers, as any of the highest Rank. But I conceive some scattered Notions about a superior Power to be of singular Use for the common People, as furnishing excellent Materials to keep Children quiet, when they grow peevish; and providing Topicks of Amusement in a tedious Winter Night. (2:34)

As Claude Rawson argues, Swift's irony in this passage "has many coils," and the narrator's position on the use of religion as "a tale of a tub" is symptomatically difficult to pin down.[35] Though the narrator begins by acknowledging the persuasive power of the age-old view that religion is "convenient for the vulgar," he then goes on to reject the frequently related idea that religion was invented by politicians "to keep the lower Parts of the World in Awe." His reason for rejecting this theory is telling, as it rests on a crucial distinction between the masses of today and those of an earlier and simpler time. Contrary to the masses of former ages, the masses of today are "as stanch Unbelievers, as any of the highest Rank" and are thus too enlightened to be hoodwinked by pious frauds.[36] Buried in the layers of Swift's irony is a nostalgia for a day when freethinking was less rampant and religion successfully kept the bulk of society well deceived and therefore willing to defer to existing social structures and traditions. Such a reading is supported by the fact that the passage ends with the narrator articulating this same theory of religion yet a third time, now in a watered-down, trivialized form. As is frequent with Swift, his final parody of the argument that religion functions as a useful form of social control—providing diversion for "peevish" children and "Amusement" of an evening—belies his actual attraction to the basic spirit of such a view.[37]

Swift had several models for this radically conservative position on the role of religion in society, all deriving ultimately from classical antiquity. Montaigne had praised Plato for supporting "fabulous fictions" and "profitable lies" in his capacity as "lawgiver," acknowledging that such "inventions" and "phantasms" are "as useful for persuading the common herd as they are ridiculous for persuading himself."[38] In his *Letter to Martin Dorp*, Erasmus' response to criticisms from Dorp and other theologians that his writing was impious and irreverent, Erasmus, too, had extolled "the wisest men of ancient times" for "deliver[ing] the most wholesome rules of conduct in humorous and (to all appearances) childish fables." These fables, he explains, function like the sweetening properties of honey, "penetrat[ing]" men's minds through "the allurement of pleasure."[39] Erasmus identifies this reference to honey as an allusion to Lucretius, whose *De rerum natura* describes how doctors use honey to trick children into taking bitter medicine.

Swift alludes to this same moment in Lucretius at the end of section VI of *A Tale*: "Mellaeo contingens cucta Lepore" (Touching all things with honeyed charm) (142).[40] The relevant lines in Lucretius appear twice, first at the end of book 1 and again in the beginning of book 4:

> . . . I teach great things,
> I try to loose men's spirit from the ties,
> Tight-knotted, which religion binds around them.
> The Muses' grace is on me, as I write
> Clear verse about dark matters. This is not
> A senseless affectation; there's reason to it.
> Just as when doctors try to give to children
> A bitter medicine, they rim the cup
> With honey's sweetness, honey's golden flavor,
> To fool the silly little things, as far
> As the lips at least, so that they'll take the bitter
> Dosage, and swallow it down, fooled but not swindled,
> But brought to health again through double-dealing,
> So now do I, because this doctrine seems
> Too grim for those who never yet have tried it,
> So grim that people shrink from it, I've meant
> To explain the system in a sweeter music,
> To rim the lesson, as it were, with honey,
> Hoping, this way, to hold your mind with verses
> While you are learning all that form, that pattern
> Of the way things are.[41]

Lucretius' stratagem in these lines is to use the sweetness of his verse as a "trick" by which his readers are encouraged, despite themselves, to abandon religion and the fear that it inspires.[42] Swift and Erasmus, though likely as skeptical about the truths of religion as Lucretius, instead suggest that religion can *itself* function as a kind of deluding honey by which men are "fooled but not swindled" and "brought to health . . . through double-dealing." The fables and fictions of divine superintendence, in other words, provide soothing comfort and happiness to those who are able to suspend their disbelief. As it turns out, even Lucretius, so infamous for his insistence that all religion is base superstition, acknowledges (however begrudgingly) the persuasive power of its fictions. Conceding that the stories of the Gods, though "far / From the real Truth," are "wonderfully told, / A marvel of tradition," he permits men to enjoy them ("Let a man / Call upon Neptune, if he likes, say Ceres / When he means corn or wheat") as long as the investment in religion is knowing and self-conscious. "Let him," Lucretius explains, "keep on repeating that our globe / Is the gods' mother—but let him, all this while, / Be careful, really, not to let religion / Infect, pollute, corrupt him."[43]

As Swift's narrator argues in "A Digression concerning Madness," "In the Proportion that Credulity is a more peaceful Possession of the Mind, than Curiosity, so far preferable is that Wisdom, which converses about the Surface, to that pretended Philosophy which enters into the Depth of Things, and then comes gravely back with Informations and Discoveries, that in the inside they are good for nothing" (173). When read in the context of religion, this skeptical passage suggests, like many others in Swift's corpus, that while the orthodox teachings of the church may be equivalent to "Surface" fictions, they are laudable in their promotion of peace, piety, and stability. Penetrating and dissecting these surface fictions will succeed only in producing great misery and unhappiness. "Men should consider," Swift advises in his essay "On the Trinity," "that raising Difficulties concerning the Mysteries in Religion, cannot make them more wise, learned, or virtuous; better Neighbours, or Friends, or more serviceable to their Country" (9:166–67).

Once again, the inspiration for Swift's preference for credulity over curiosity and delusion over knowledge came from Lucretius himself, whose account of sensation in book 4 of *De rerum natura* unexpectedly admits the limits of our knowledge and the necessity of accepting deception as the best we can do. As Lucretius explains, according to Epicurean doctrine, all of our knowledge begins with the "images" and "film" that are "sent forth from every surface" and "fly / This way and that across the air."[44] In certain cases, however, the images that flow from an object are misconceived by our minds, as when a ship we sail in seems to stand still or the square towers of a city appear to be round when perceived from far away. Lucretius insists that, in such instances, the fault lies not with the senses, for nothing can tell the truth more clearly, but rather with the mind's powers of reason. And yet since knowledge can never break from the senses (given that all truth is derived from them), when we find ourselves unable to explain why our ship appears to stand still, we must acquiesce to the inescapable truth that the process of life involves being deceived:

> Even so, it might be better for a man
> Who lacks the power of reason, to give out
> Some idiotic theory, than to drop
> All hold of basic principles, break down
> Every foundation, tear apart the frame
> That holds our lives, our welfare.[45]

It is this wisdom to which Swift refers when, in his "Digression concerning Madness," the surface fictions of religion are presented to us through the lens of Epicurean philosophy: "He that can with *Epicurus* content his Ideas with the *Films* and *Images* that fly off upon his Senses from the *Superficies* of Things; Such a Man truly wise, creams off Nature, leaving the Sower and the Dregs, for Philosophy and Reason to lap up" (174).

Because "A Digression" satirizes Epicurean atomism as an instance of enthusiastic innovation "in the Empire of Reason" (167), critics have assumed that *A Tale* censures all aspects of Epicurean theory.[46] It is indeed the case that Swift rejects much of Epicurean natural philosophy on the grounds that it arrogantly, and thus mistakenly, presumes to penetrate the mysterious operations of the natural world. Yet as his influences suggest, it was possible to distinguish between science and ethics in traditions of philosophy, rejecting the one while embracing the other. While clearly advancing the premium placed on happiness in both Epicurean and Skeptical ethics, Erasmus disdains all philosophical attempts, of any school, to explain causes "and other unfathomable phenomena" in Nature. In his *Apology*, Montaigne, like Swift, ridicules the Epicureans' confidence that atoms built the world, but he also includes them among the ancient sects who laudably define "the sovereign good" as the condition of *ataraxia*, or tranquillity of soul and body.[47] In his essay "Upon the Gardens of Epicurus" (1685), Temple similarly argues that knowledge of the natural world "in its originals or operations . . . is not our game"; the various theories of nature put forward from Plato and Aristotle to Hobbes and Descartes are so contradictory that all appear equally improbable. Following Montaigne, Temple argues that in moral philosophy, however, the ancients seemed largely to agree that the end "desirable by every man" is "the ease and happiness of life."[48] For Swift, then, it was no contradiction to satirize the arrogance of Epicurean natural philosophy while promoting Epicurus' more modest appreciation of *ataraxia*, or what Swift renames for modernity as "*the Possession of being well deceived*" (174).[49]

How, then, does the possession of being well deceived function as a basis for right religious mentality? Since all belief is based on a form of delusion, the trick, the narrator explains in "A Digression concerning Madness," is to know how to turn this delusion to good use. What is important, Swift repeatedly implies, is not the truth content fueling religious behaviors and practices but, rather, whether particular practices serve laudable ends. As he opines early in "A Digression," under the right circumstances, "the Fumes issuing from a Jakes, will furnish as comely and useful a Vapor, as Incense from an Altar" (163). The same point is made a few pages later when the narrator again remarks that it is "Of such mighty Consequence . . . where those Exhalations fix; and of so little, from whence they proceed" (166). Or again, "It is of no Import from what Originals this *Vapour* proceeds, but either in what *Angles* it strikes and spreads over the Understanding, or upon what *Species* of Brain it ascends" (169).[50]

As the proverbial phrase "a tale of a tub" indicates, delusion can indeed be productively channeled for the improvement of the State. This task, then (in Swift's view, the primary mission of the Anglican Church), is the central preoccupation of the "Digression," particularly in the final six pages. Here the narrator asserts "that the main Point of Skill and Address, is to furnish Employment for this Redundancy of Vapour [Spirit], and prudently to adjust the Seasons of it; by which means it may certainly become of Cardinal and Catholick Emolument in a Commonwealth" (175). He then goes on to describe a program through which the various inmates of bedlam might be rehabilitated, their capacities adapted to "produce admirable Instruments for the several Offices in a State" (176). What we define as madness, Swift suggests, is actually "Talents and Acquirements . . . now buried, or at least misapplied" (179). When given the proper direction, a foaming lunatic can be transformed into a worthy general, a chattering idiot into a fine courtier, and so forth (176–8). It is in the sphere of religion, of course, that this program for rehabilitating madness and delusion is most urgently necessary. Since, as I have suggested, delusion is definitive of that sphere, the solution is not so much to replace delusion with a truer apprehension of the spirit but, rather, to defuse the spiritual element of belief entirely, making it, on the contrary, a cooler matter of suspending doubt and embracing religion's uses on pragmatic grounds.

III

If the question of Tory Anglicans like Swift was how to counter both atheism's and enthusiasm's inherent threat to public peace, the answer was to make politics a part of religion, minimize the distinction between the spiritual and temporal powers, and elevate the civic over the spiritual realm.[51] Whereas the lessons of superstition and enthusiasm were tyranny and revolution, under the proper conditions Swift believed that the pious frauds of religion, as the ancients' example taught, could generate social and political peace and stability. As I have argued, Swift's ancient bias was based on his esteem for the eminent virtue and moral rectitude of the pagan philosophers as well as his admiration for their skeptical tendency to uphold religion as a civil strategy rather than as a body of spiritual truths. In his "Sentiments of a Church-of-England Man," Swift tellingly considers schism as a "Temporal" rather than a "Spiritual Evil," citing Plato's maxim "that Men ought to worship the Gods, according to the Laws of the Country" (2:11–12). While our private opinions on the truths of religion might be free, our religious behavior, "how far [we] shall publicly act in pursuance of those opinions," should be regulated by the magistrate (9:263).

Temple argued that the peculiar plague of modernity was precisely "our different opinions in religion and the factions they have raised or animated." And yet, to assert that the great end of religion is not one's inward relationship with God but rather "the peace, order, and safety of all civil societies and governments among men" is to confront the inescapable problem of belief.[52] When Swift discusses the need for the civil power to proscribe the infractions of sectarians and atheists, he comes close to admitting that the realm of the spirit is merely a contrivance, its existence and influence dependent on how the State chooses to oversee the institutions created to perpetuate its fictions: "I wish I could not say," he writes in "On the Testimony of Conscience," "that the Majesty of the living God may be offended with more Security than the Memory of a dead Prince. But the Wisdom of the World at present seems to agree with that of the Heathen Emperor, who said, If the Gods were offended, it was their own Concern, and they were able to vindicate themselves" (9:151). The point is made again in "Some Thoughts on Free-Thinking": "They leave it to God Almighty to vindicate the injuries done to himself, who is no doubt sufficiently able, by perpetual miracles, to revenge the affronts of impious men. And it should seem, that this is what princes expect from him, though I cannot readily conceive the grounds they go upon" (4:50).[53] Behind Swift's suggestion in these passages that "the Gods" do not "vindicate themselves," or perform miraculous acts of revenge against the impious, is the skeptical notion, embraced by Montaigne, Hobbes, Blount, and Rochester, that we can say and know nothing about the substance of supernatural power; for as Rochester's example has shown, the logical corollary of the skeptical position that God is an incomprehensible, inexpressible power is a humble rejection of divine Providence on the grounds that this unknowable divinity would not concern itself with man's affairs.[54]

In his critique of the skeptical position that the deity is incomprehensible, Thomas Tenison warns that if we are denied any knowledge of God, "Then will all Religion dye away; for if we know not that God is True, we cannot believe his Revelations."[55] It is notable, moreover, that neither *A Tale* nor Swift's other writings attempt to defend the authenticity of the teachings of Christianity. As I have argued, though the semblance of belief in Christian religion is everywhere commended as necessary and worthy, that belief is nowhere honored as true. The best of the clergy, Swift suggests in his "Letter to a Young Gentleman," "deliver the Doctrine as the Church holds it" (9:77) and avoid asking too many questions. His informal "Thoughts on Various Subjects," described by Kathleen Williams as "good indications of the subjects which Swift turned over in his mind," warns readers against inquiring too deeply into the motives of even "the best Actions," including religion.[56] It is wrong, he urges, to destroy men's belief in "imaginary Goods," even when "it requires but little Philosophy to discover and observe that there is no intrinsick Value in all this" (4:243).

It is important to acknowledge, then, that however much Swift advocated the tradition of the pious fraud for the ends of political and religious stability, the idea that religion was invented to regulate civic life is a fundamental feature of what Strauss has called "the critique of religion."[57] To contemporaries, in other words, the view that religion rested upon human authority could not help but suggest, as Charles Wolesley objected, that "all things beyond this world are merely fabulous, and such phantasms, as men have fondly conceived and created within themselves."[58] To the extent that Swift appears to hover on the fringes of belief, suggesting, with Behn and Rochester, that Christian revelation and the supernatural itself are largely tales and fiction, he must be seen in the tradition of freethinking. That he himself acknowledged his shadowy links to this otherwise-detested movement is indicated in his "Some Thoughts on Free-thinking." Here Swift cites an Irish prelate on the distinction between the mad and the wise:

He said, that the difference betwixt a mad-man and one in his wits, in what related to speech, consisted in this: That the former spoke out whatever came into his mind, and just in the confused manner as his imagination presented the ideas. The latter only expressed such thoughts, as his judgment directed him to chuse, leaving the rest to die away in his memory. And that if the wisest man would at any time utter his thoughts, in the crude indigested manner, as they come into his head, he would be looked upon as raving mad. . . . So that I cannot imagine what is meant by the mighty zeal in some people, for asserting the freedom of thinking:

Because, if such thinkers keep their thoughts within their own breasts, they can be of no consequence, further than to themselves. (4:49)

Implicit in these remarks is Swift's conviction, suggested in "A Digression concerning Madness," that the actual content and character of thought in the wise man and the madman (or freethinker) are the same. The difference between them lies, then, not in their respective belief or unbelief, but rather in how they choose to conduct their lives. Strictly speaking, we are all freethinkers "within [our] own breasts," but only some decide (wrongly) to "publish" such thoughts "to the world" (4:49). As Rawson astutely points out, the passage relies on a pun on freethinking, which "slid[es] tacitly between a general meaning of 'unrestricted flow of thought' and the more usual technical sense of 'free exercise of reason in matters of religious belief.'" In this way, Swift emphasizes the degree to which freethinking "is the product of elementary mental instincts common to us all" and thus "must be regulated: by concealment, discretion, discipline, . . . [and] political restrictions."[59]

Paradoxically, perhaps, it is Swift's skeptical recognition of man's tendency towards doubt, unbelief, and corruption more generally that fuels his passionate commitment to maintaining the structures and institutions of religion; it is these pious frauds that keep us virtuous. For the skeptic, then, conformity follows from a self-conscious suspension of disbelief that itself grows out of the double pressures of uncertainty and practical need. We must and ought to reject disbelief, Swift suggests in his "Project for the Advancement of Religion," because "the Livery of Religion" is preferable to "open Infidelity and Vice" (2:57). Indeed, with the "Project" and its recommendation that religious virtue be encouraged and rewarded in worldly terms by the civil power, Swift brings the tradition of the pious fraud full circle.

The ancient lawgivers, as the story goes, invented deities as a corrective to civil law's failure to prevent deeds of secret perfidy. The earliest known version of the pious fraud is attributed by Sextus Empiricus to Critias of Athens, whom he quotes at length:

> A time there was when anarchy did rule
> The lives of men which then were like the beasts',
> Enslaved to force; nor was there then reward
> For good men, nor for wicked punishment.
> Next, as I deem, did men establish laws
> For punishment, that Justice might be lord
> Of all mankind, and Insolence enchain'd;
> And whosoe'er did sin was penalized.
> Next, as the laws did hold men back from deeds
> Of open violence, but still such deeds

Were done in secret,—then, as I maintain,
Some shrewd man first, a man in counsel wise,
Discovered unto men the fear of Gods,
Thereby to frighten sinners should they sin
E'en secretly in deed, or word, or thought.
Hence was it that he brought in Deity,
Telling how God enjoys an endless life,
Hears with his mind and sees, and taketh thought
And heeds things, and his nature is divine,
So that he hearkens to men's every word
And has the power to see men's every act.

. . .

So, with reasonings like these,
A most clever doctrine did he introduce,
Hiding the truth beneath a speech untrue.[60]

Critias here maintains that the legislators of old fabricated the idea of God—a "clever doctrine"—for the purposes of social control. Whereas secular law provided a deterrent to public violations of various sorts, something else was needed to prevent men from transgressing in private. Hence a supernatural and all-knowing power was created so that men would be intimidated into a more far-reaching obedience.

The modern age, Swift suggests, requires a slight adjustment in strategy. In full agreement that a religious conscience (ideally) "determines us where the Laws of the Land can lay no hold" (9:153), Swift also acknowledges that this same conscience has proven of late to be largely ineffective: we live, lamentably, in an age of reprobate libertinism and irreligion, in which religious morality and its promises of other-worldly rewards and punishments no longer holds any motivating (or deterring) power. Though religious conscience with its "Hopes of everlasting Happiness, and the Fears of everlasting Misery" *should* move us to live rightly, as the canny narrator of "An Argument" has already intuited, the current age is too knowing for such primitive duplicity. Swift thus asks us to confront religion's conspicuous failure to prevent an ever-growing culture of infidelity and vice (9:155). Christianity, he regretfully concedes in "A Sermon upon the Excellency of Christianity," "doth not . . . still produce the same effects" as it did in the days of its infant purity (9:249).

On the other side, secular law has shown itself to be equally incapable of promoting virtue. As Swift bemoans in "On the Testimony of Conscience," "the World is so corrupted, that no Man can reasonably hope to be rewarded in it, merely upon account of his Virtue. And consequently, the Fear of Punishment in this Life will preserve Men from very few Vices, since some of the blackest and basest do often prove the surest

Steps to Favour; such as Ingratitude, Hypocrisy, Treachery, Malice, Sub-ornation, Atheism, and many more which human Laws do little concern themselves with" (9:155). The consequence of this dismal truth is thus a begrudging yet firm conviction that the civil power, also insufficient without the influence of religion, must fill the breach and offer all ranks of society, from servants and tradesmen to courtiers and men of public office, tangible, worldly incentives to appear to believe and embrace the moral teachings of religion.

Referring once again to the heterodox tradition that sees religion as a cloak, a device, and thus a human, not a supernatural, phenomenon, Swift thus advocates a beliefless orthodoxy in religion that forms the distinctive core of the literature of English freethinking and its contradictory radical conservatism. As I have suggested, the implications for Swift's orthodoxy of this absence of belief are complex to say the least. Even Herbert's and Blount's more radical examples indicate that in the right hands, the imposture thesis could circle back to a defense of religion and the appearance of belief on the grounds that religion is man's shrewdest political invention and thus not to be dispensed with lightly.[61] Yet over the long haul, as we know, this tendency to evacuate the spiritual content of religion fueled the secularization of Enlightenment Europe, for whom the pious fraud became a stepping stone towards a fuller and more fearless embrace of natural religion. In conclusion, I will examine Alexander Pope's participation in this next phase of the freethinking initiative.

Pope's *Essay on Man* and the Afterlife of English Freethinking

I've ever thought the best piece of service one could do to our religion was openly to expose our detestation and scorn of all those
artifices and *piae fraudes* which it stands so little in need of, and
which have laid it under so great a scandal among the enemies.
  —Alexander Pope to John Caryll, 19 July 1711

☾

In a letter of 1 November 1734, Swift offers Alexander Pope some initial
impressions of the first three epistles of *An Essay on Man*, published
anonymously in 1733. Though Pope's letters to Swift had referred to his
work on "a system of Ethics in the Horatian way" as early as November
1729, Pope had kept his authorship of *An Essay on Man* a secret from
his good friend.[1] Swift writes that though he "never doubted about your
Essay on Man," he also "never imagine[d] you were so deep in Morals,
or that so many new & excellent Rules could be produced so advanta-
geously & agreeably in that Science from any one head."[2] Swift's description of the treatment of "Morals" in *An Essay on Man* as a "Science"
insinuates rightly that Pope has dared to move the study of morality even
further out of the purview of traditional theological teaching, a state of
affairs about which Swift likely had some mixed feelings.

As it turns out, Bolingbroke had been preparing Swift for what he
later termed Pope's "noble work" for several years.[3] In a letter of August
1729, he discourses on philosophy's improvement on theology, encouraging the dean to "part with your broad brimmed Beaver, your Gown,
your Scarf, or even that emblematical vestment your Surplice." In March
of 1731 Bolingbroke again exhorts Swift, this time in a joint letter with

Pope that alludes to Pope's work in progress, to "fence against moral Evil by Philosophy" and not "work up imagination against [nature's] plainest Dictates."[4] An explicit discussion of the content of Pope's *Essay on Man* comes finally in a letter of early August 1731, in which Bolingbroke provides a summary of the broad strokes of Pope's poem, explaining that it "pleads the cause of God . . . against that famous charge which atheists in all ages have brought, the supposed unequal Dispensations of Providence." Bolingbroke goes on to oppose the way in which this imagined inequity has been admitted by "you Divines" as an essential foundation for belief in a future state of rewards and punishments. "What if you should find," he objects, "that this future state will not account for Gods justice, in the present state, which you give up, in opposition to the atheist? Would it not have been better to defend God's justice in this world against these daring men by irrefragable Reasons, and to have rested the proof of the other point on Revelation?"[5] Bolingbroke hereby indicates that in choosing to defend the justice of God's dispensations on earth, Pope's *Essay on Man* refutes the atheist, on the one hand, and, perhaps even more significantly, the religious establishment and its investment in the deliverance of a future state, on the other.[6]

For Bolingbroke, to defer to revelation on the existence of a future state is to adopt a posture of respectful agnosticism that hovers on the borders of unbelief.[7] "The Philosophia prima is above my reach," he writes to Swift in the same letter. "I dare not pronounce why things are made as they are, state the ends of infinite wisdom, & shew the proportion of the means."[8] At the same time, however, like Swift, Bolingbroke recognizes that religion is a powerful expedient to enforce obedience and that men, ancient and modern, have not always been wrong to instill belief in revelations they know to be false. On Bolingbroke's view, the doctrine of future rewards and punishments, indeed, stands as the most salient example of the logic of these pious frauds, as "the dread of superior power, maintained and cultivated by superstition, and applied by policy," had a uniquely civilizing effect among the multitude, particularly given men's natural disposition to be "flattered with immortality in any shape, . . . though the consequence of it might be their own damnation."[9] Indeed, as we remember from the introductory chapter, Bolingbroke's *Letters, or Essays, Addressed to Alexander Pope*, described as communications of conversations between the three friends in Pope's garden, acknowledges throughout the public dangers of shaking the foundations of belief and the call, therefore, to impose fictions and conceal certain truths. The following example, cited previously in the introductory chapter, is one among many: "Truth and falsehood, knowledge and ignorance, revelations of the Creator, inventions of the creature, dictates of reason, sallies of enthusiasm, have been blended so long together in our systems of theology, that it may be thought dangerous to separate them; lest, by attacking some parts of these systems, we should shake the whole. It may be thought, that errour itself deserves to be respected on this account, and that men who are deluded for their good, should be deluded on."[10]

Though the passage encourages us to respect error and delusion in the interests of the stability of the whole, Bolingbroke's repeated use of the potential verb construction "it may be thought" invites us to view his defense of the theological lying so definitive of Swift's defense of Christianity and the Anglican Church with a degree of skepticism. A more careful examination of Bolingbroke's writings on philosophy and religion supports this uncertainty. While Bolingbroke's "Esprits forts" will "think it their duty not to disturb the peace of the world," they may also, he makes clear to Swift, "express their sorrow, as I have done, to see Religion perverted to purposes so contrary to her true intention, & first design."[11] Bolingbroke's meaning here is illuminated more fully in his discussion of pious frauds in the *Fragments, or Minutes of Essays* appended to his *Letters to Pope*:

If the fathers of the church, and modern divines, had made no other use of this method of reasoning, than to strengthen a sense of our moral obligations, and to raise in the minds of men a greater veneration for the Scriptures, after they had proved the authenticity of them by eternal proofs, it had been well both for natural and revealed religion. But they have made a very different use of it. They have shook the former down to it's very foundation, and, under pretence of explaining and defending the other, they have laid it more open to the attack of unbelievers.[12]

The ancient tradition of imposing falsehoods and concealing truths in matters of religion developed, Bolingbroke here reminds us, as a way to promote and "strengthen" morality and discourage and curb vice. When it performs that job successfully, then, the pious fraud is to be accepted as an honorable practice. However, when the means no longer serve these noble ends, when theological lying corrupts "union, peace, and charity" more than it prevents them, on Bolingbroke's view, it should be practiced no longer.[13] As suggested in Bolingbroke's summary letter to Swift on *An Essay on Man*, the Christian doctrine of a future state serves as a case in point.

As we know, Swift was adamant that full endorsement of the Church of England's stance on belief in a future state of rewards and punishments was a moral absolute, and if religious fictions and civil machinations, both, were needed to enforce this belief, then so be it. The interests of morality would be served. As I have proposed, Bolingbroke held similarly that the doctrine had a special capacity to restrain vice and promote virtue. Though reason "cannot decide" for a future state on "principles of natural theology," it "will not decide against it on principles of good policy." And yet, Bolingbroke continues, reason will be forced to deny a future state when the theological tradition refuses to rest its proof humbly and modestly on revelation, attempting, rather, through vain hubris and "artificial theology," to prove that which is impossible to be proven.[14] In order to maintain themselves at "imaginary heights," Bolingbroke complains, divines have invented one false hypothesis after another until they have "deviated at last so far from natural theology, and raised so much confusion in their notions about it, that they [have] no means left of returning to the first principle."[15] Vitiated beyond recognition, the moral impetus behind the concept of a future state is lost amidst "precarious suppositions" and "problematical and futile reasonings." As Bolingbroke writes to Swift regarding Pope's *Essay on Man*, the final irony of these accretions is that they "betray the cause of God to the atheist":

If there is not a future state, God is neither good nor just, according to our ideas of goodness and justice, in his dispensations. If he is not good and just, according to our ideas of these moral attributes, neither can the physical attributes, such as infinite wisdom and power, belong to him; and a Being, who has none of these, is not God. But there is a future state. Thus divines have dared to argue.[16]

With Bolingbroke in the role of "guide, philosopher, and friend," Pope's *Essay on Man* thus defends the cause of God by also defending man's place in the present world.[17] The poem argues that "Whatever IS, is RIGHT," a refrain made infamous by its insistence that God's justice manifests itself in the here and now and thereby needs no later opportunities.[18] With this conspicuous and unprecedented silence on matters of revelation, Pope's poem takes English freethinking into new territory and, for this reason, represents a particularly useful end point for this study. This chapter will argue, then, that *An Essay on Man* marks a crucial transition in the history of English literary freethinking outlined in this book. With little interest in Swift's suspension of disbelief, the poem's promotion of natural religion serves as a bridge between the earlier and more conservative Enlightenment tradition in England and the later more radical movement in France.[19] Whereas Swift's works, on Voltaire's view, will never be well understood in France ("to understand him, one must visit his country"), Pope's themes had an immediate international appeal and accessibility: "One can translate him, because . . . his subjects, for the most part, are general and of relevance to all nations."[20] The story of Voltaire's later apostasy from the creed of Pope's *Essay on*

Man serves as the final episode in my examination of the afterlife of English freethinking. For though "Whatever is, is right" was laudable in its staunch silence on revelation, it also could not escape a quietism that reinvoked, inescapably, the conservatism of the English tradition. Voltaire's more decisive break with a traditional religious worldview, one that left man a productive agent in a world devoid of supernatural order, was negotiated, however, with Pope's poem as crucial fodder. Both inspiration and disappointment, *An Essay on Man* opened the door to a secular modernity that owes a debt, heretofore underacknowledged, to English freethinking.

I

Pope's interest in natural religion predates his friendship with Bolingbroke as well as his *Essay on Man*. As early as 1711, his *Essay on Criticism* expresses a veiled critique of Christianity in a metaphor that likens provincialism in wit to sectarian faith:

> (Thus *Wit*, like *Faith*, by each Man is apply'd
> To *one small Sect*, and All are *damn'd beside*.)
> Meanly they seek the Blessing to confine,
> And force *that Sun* but on a *Part* to Shine.
>
> (394–97)

True wit, like true faith, Pope suggests, should have a universal validity, a position informed by deism's insistence that salvation be available to all. Pope elaborates on this view in a letter to John Caryll that same year. Responding to Caryll's reports that several passages in *An Essay on Criticism* had offended his Catholic brethren, Pope defends his position on universal salvation in the above lines in much the same terms as Bolingbroke's. It is precisely "artifices and *piae fraudes*" such as Christianity's exclusive promise of salvation, Pope argues, that open the door to atheism by making religion "a scandal among the enemies."[21] In a letter of November 1717 to Bishop Atterbury, Pope again affirms his allegiance to a universal, antisectarian notion of religious worship, answering the bishop's attempt to convert him to Anglicanism by admitting that his reading in Church controversies left him "a Papist and a Protestant by turns, according to the last book I read." Indeed, Pope affirms, "all honest and reasonable Christians" would find themselves to be "of the same religion, if . . . they did but talk enough together every day; and had nothing to do together, but to serve God and live in peace with their neighbour."[22] In this statement and in his exchange with Caryll, Pope reveals the implicit influence of natural religion as well as the reigning deist conviction that any valid system of belief must rise above the particular spiritual claims of various sects, Christian ones not excepted.[23] Pope's "Universal Prayer," composed, according to Pope, in 1715 but first published in June of 1738, similarly omits all mention of specifically Christian doctrine, addressing instead a deity whom all rational minds may worship:

> Father of All! in every Age,
>   In every Clime ador'd,
> By Saint, by Savage, and by Sage,
>   Jehovah, Jove, or Lord!
>
>   (1–4)

And in another conspicuous rejection of the use of Christian revelation, the poem posits conscience as our guide to moral virtue, rather than the promise of a future state:

> What Conscience dictates to be done,
>   Or warns me not to doe,
> This, teach me more than Hell to shun,
>   That, more than Heav'n pursue.[24]
>
>   (13–16)

Needless to say, the sympathy for natural religion implied in these early works culminates in *An Essay on Man*. In the poem's introductory description, "The Design," Pope reiterates the antisectarian sentiment from *An Essay on Criticism*, commenting that the study and practice of morality have been hampered by *"disputes"* over questions that will "ever escape our observation" and that have "sharpened . . . the *hearts* of men against each other." His solution to this impasse is to attempt to "steer betwixt extremes of doctrines seemingly opposite."[25] Though Pope does not specify the content of these opposite doctrines, his reference to "disputes" suggests that his subject is religious disagreement over what we can and cannot know of God and his dispensations. Importantly, Pope's project is not only to find a peaceful middle ground between conflicting camps but also to show that these camps are indeed not so opposed to one another: the doctrines in question are only *seemingly* opposite. If the poem's aim, as Pope and Bolingbroke explain it, is "to vindicate the ways of God to Man" in this world (1.16), then it is likely that Pope's intent here is to show that natural and revealed religion are not as at odds as they appear to be. Natural religion, in other words, contains all that is true in revealed religion, rendering the latter largely superfluous—useful as reinforcement, perhaps, though not as supplementation.[26]

The poem's defense of natural religion leans heavily on several features of freethought familiar to us through Rochester, Behn, and Swift. Indeed, the refrain "Whatever is, is right" is crucially linked to the related views that (1) God does not privilege man above beasts and other parts of his creation with any particular attention or care; (2) that the universe is not organized around man's happiness and fulfillment; and (3) that man is vain and presumptuous in his reason to think that he enjoys a special status in the natural order.[27] "Has God, thou fool! work'd solely for thy good," Pope's speaker asks?

> Know, Nature's children all divide her care;
> The fur that warms a monarch, warm'd a bear.
> While Man exclaims, "See all things for my use!"
> "See man for mine!" replies a pamper'd goose;
> And just as short of Reason he must fall,
> Who thinks all made for one, not one for all.
>
> (3.27, 43–48)

As Bolingbroke observes to Swift, this hard truth leads vain fools to atheism: for upon looking at what appears to be divine indifference to man, the atheist fatuously concludes that "Heav'n [is] in fault" (1.69). Pope answers this grievance by showing how it rests on a fundamental misconception about man's relationship to the divine order. What can appear to us to be imperfections and evils in man's realm in fact constitute a necessary part of the general system. Man forms one small part of this system, and its logic is beyond our comprehension. The lesson, as above, is one in humility:

> Respecting Man, whatever wrong we call,
> May, must be right, as relative to all.
>
> . . .
>
> So Man, who here seems principal alone,
> Perhaps acts second to some sphere unknown,
> Touches some wheel, or verges to some goal;
> 'Tis but a part we see, and not a whole.
>
> (1.51–52, 57–60)

Humbling man's pride and its investment in the idea of special providence is vital to the task of reconciling man to the perceived deficiencies of his existing state and showing him his proper place in the larger whole. Man pompously thinks he deserves perfection, with which Christianity promises to reward him for living virtuously. Pope argues that once we concede our fallibility, our weakness, and our limited knowledge, we are ready to allow that, in fact, man is "as perfect as he ought" (1.70), currently, in his worldly condition. And, "If to be perfect in a certain

sphere, / What matter, soon or late, or here or there" (1.73–74)? Coming
to grips with the fitness of our present state, in other words, negates our
need for the compensation of perfection in a future one.

Pope admits to Caryll that the poem's use of the word *if* instead of
since in the above lines from epistle one equivocates deciding on a future
state by at once implying and evading its existence.[28] In a later passage
strongly reminiscent of the virtuous heathens of Blount's *Anima Mundi*,
Pope does admit, however, the moral rectitude of hoping, modestly, for
God to provide for us after death:

> Hope humbly then; with trembling pinions soar;
> Wait the great teacher Death, and God adore!
> What future bliss, he gives not thee to know,
> But gives that Hope to be thy blessing now.
> Hope springs eternal in the human breast:
> Man never Is, but always To be blest:
> The soul, uneasy and confin'd from home,
> Rests and expatiates in a life to come.
>
> (1.91–98)

Like the heathens' unbelieving faith, the "Hope" of a future blessing has
meaning, Pope suggests, only insofar as it becomes our "blessing now."
It is our desire for an always future bliss, about which we know nothing,
that keeps us virtuous in the present moment. The question, then, is not
whether there is, in fact, a future state but rather what the anticipation
of one can do for us in this life.[29] As does Blount, Pope offers a "poor
Indian" (1.99) as an example of this logic. Once again, Pope's heathen
follows "simple Nature" (1.103), rather than "proud Science" (1.101),
which "to his hope has giv'n, / Behind the cloud-topt hill, an humbler
heav'n" (1.103–4). It is important to Pope's purpose that the Indian's
belief is not only humble but also, strictly speaking, false. His "untutor'd
mind / Sees God in clouds, or hears him in the wind" (1.99–100) and
his great comfort is the prospect that "admitted to that equal sky, / His
faithful dog shall bear him company" (1.111–12). The Indian's superstition is benign, even morally efficacious, however, because characterized
by humility and simple piety: "To Be, contents his natural desire, / He
asks no Angel's wing, no Seraph's fire" (1.109–10).

This humility and piety is not visible, by contrast, in most of Pope's
history of religion in epistle three, which is notably vague about the
role of Christianity. Beginning with the origin of simple monotheism
among the best of the ancients, Pope explains how "simple Reason never
sought but one: / Ere Wit oblique had broke that steddy light, / Man,
like his Maker, saw that all was right" (3.230–32). Though his relation
of the introduction of superstition into the simple and virtuous worship

of early religion suggests a critique of pagan idolatry (and possibly its popish afterlife), as we remember from Hobbes's and Toland's infamous examples in Chapter Three, Pope's account could just as well apply to Christianity itself:

> Who first taught souls enslav'd, and realms undone,
> Th' enormous faith of many made for one;
> That proud exception to all Nature's laws,
> T'invert the world, and counter-work its Cause?
>
> (3.241–44)

That Pope's statement is formed as an open (and unanswered) question reinforces the surreptitious inclusion of Christianity in the indictment of these lines, as does the censure of "Th' enormous faith of many made for one" (3.242), a critique that hearkens back to the denunciation of Christianity's exclusive salvation in *An Essay on Criticism*.[30] The corruption of true religion by superstition reaches its culmination when "Zeal, . . . not charity, became the guide, / And hell was built on spite, and heav'n on pride" (3.261–62). It is here that Pope sets down, similarly to Bolingbroke, the limit case for belief in a revealed future state as a kind of morally useful pious fraud. Though itself an instance of superstition, the Indian's unassuming faith in "an humbler heav'n" for him and his "faithful dog" fortifies and bolsters his exemplary piety. For this reason, his false belief is morally beneficial and thus not to be contradicted. Yet the current state of Christianity, Pope suggests, has strayed far from this model. "In Faith and Hope the world will disagree," the speaker reminds us, "But all Mankind's concern is Charity: / All must be false that thwart this One great End, / And all of God, that bless Mankind or mend" (3.307–9). The question comes down, once again, to the problem of Christianity's exclusive and thus fundamentally uncharitable salvation, a prejudice that for Pope destroys the moral efficacy of our faith in salvation in the first place. Defending this conviction against sectarian parsimony, he writes to Caryll, "There may be errors [in others' doctrine and belief], I grant, but I can't think 'em of such consequence as to destroy utterly the charity of mankind, the very greatest bond in which we are engaged by God to one another [as Christians]" (1.126).[31] In matters of revealed religion, *An Essay on Man* proposes, the "Vanity" and "defects of mind" upon which so much of our belief rests must fulfill "Virtue's ends," contributing to "The Joy, the peace, the glory of Mankind" (2.245, 247–48). With virtue thus served, revealed religion and natural religion work to each other's mutual benefit. Yet if virtue's ends are not served, if "Charity," religion's greatest virtue, is undermined, the pious fraud should be exploded, for it no longer performs the job for which it was intended.

II

In England, many early readers of *An Essay on Man* applauded Pope's poetic accomplishment, intuiting little to nothing of its more heterodox implications. Bolingbroke had written in his *Letters, or Essays, Addressed to Alexander Pope* that his friend would have "less to apprehend . . . than a writer in prose on the same subjects would have:" "You will be safer in the generalities of poetry, and I know your precaution enough to know, that you will screen yourself in them against any direct charge of heterodoxy."[32] Johnson later reiterated this view, observing that "the essay abounded in splendid amplifications and sparkling sentences, which were read and admired with no great attention to their ultimate purpose; its flowers caught the eye, which did not see what the gay foliage concealed." Pope, it seems, had depended on poetry's unique capacity to provide a screen against heterodoxy, particularly when coupled with the poem's anonymous publication and his own devious attempt to insinuate that it had been written by a divine.[33] His conviction turned out to be only partly right. Two anonymous critiques of the poem in the *Weekly Miscellany* in 1733 and 1734 took issue with Pope's theriophilia. The first, a satiric poem entitled "On Some Authors Leveling the Rational Nature with the Brutal," associated Pope with Rochester and Swift, while the second pointed out the irreligious implications of Pope's denial of man's superiority to the rest of creation, asserting that "this way of arguing" reproaches Scripture and "the Infinite Wisdom of God," as well as "our *Redemption* by *Jesus Christ*." In December 1735, the *Prompter* published another attack on the heterodoxy of Pope's poetry, this time censuring *An Essay on Man* for its implied denial of "*discrete* Providence," a position whose impiety the writer traces to Lucretius. A year later, another response to the poem contended that "the Atheist might be more reasonably argued with on the contrary Hypothesis" to Pope's view that the natural and moral world are as perfect as God originally designed, particularly since revealed religion "is entirely built on a Supposition of the Degeneracy and Corruption of Man."[34] The storm was beginning to brew.

That same year, the *London Evening-Post* reported that Pope's *Essay on Man*, recently translated into French, was "in great Esteem at Paris, and in the Hands of all the polite People there."[35] This first translation, a prose work by Étienne de Silhouette, remarkably went through four editions in 1736, and the preface, though referring to accusations of Spinozism in the poem, asserted poetry's separate status from theology, maintaining that "one doesn't have to interpret the sallies of poetry rigorously and theologically."[36] In 1737, a verse translation of the poem appeared at the hands of the Abbé Du Resnel, a friend of Voltaire's, in whose production the *philosophe* may well have played a role.[37] Popular throughout the century, this rendering, entitled *Principes de la morale*, was condemned by the Jesuit journal *Mémoires de Trévoux* shortly after its publication as a deist work destructive of morality and religion.[38] Now, it seems, the French religious establishment had begun to appreciate how the ornaments of verse could disguise radical views. Indeed, that same year, Jean-Pierre de Crousaz, a Swiss professor and theologian at Lausanne, published his legendary attacks on *An Essay on Man*: first, *Examen de l'Essai de M. Pope sur l'homme*, based on Silhouette's translation, and the next year, a *Commentaire sur la traduction en vers de Mr. L'Abbé du Resnel, de l'Essai de M. Pope sur l'homme*, a paragraph-by-paragraph censure of Du Resnel's version.[39] In 1739, both the *Examen* and the *Commentaire* were translated and published in England, the latter by Samuel Johnson. By this time, Warburton had already begun publishing letters in defense of Pope's orthodoxy in *The History of the Works of the Learned* (1738–39). These letters were later collected and reissued in 1739 and then again in 1742, with two additional letters, as the *Critical and Philosophical Commentary on Mr. Pope's "Essay on Man."* Their influence over how *An Essay on Man* was read was secured and consolidated when the commentary was appended to the 1740 edition of the poem and later to Pope's *Works*, both edited by Warburton in 1743–44.[40] The controversy continued on both sides of the Channel well into the 1740s and even after Pope's death in 1744. In 1742, Louis Racine published his poem *La religion*, the second canto of which represents Pope's mantra, translated as *Tout est bien*, as characteristic of the infidel's threat to orthodoxy.[41] Then in 1746, the Jansenist theologian Jean-Baptiste Gaultier published *Le poème de Pope intitulé Essai sur l'homme convaincu d'impiété*, an elaborate refutation of Pope's freethinking. According to Gaultier, *An Essay on Man* relies on the atheistic philosophy of Spinoza, impiously celebrating the basic principles of natural religion, including theriophilia and the dismissal of divine providence, the immortality of the soul, and a future state, all at the expense of Christian faith.[42]

Gaultier's attack also was the first to point to the strong resemblances between *An Essay on Man* and the notorious twenty-fifth letter of Voltaire's *Lettres philosophiques*, "Sur les pensées de M. Pascal," which was seen to fuel the banning and burning of the *Lettres* upon their publication in 1734.[43] Voltaire himself famously commented on these resemblances in a variant of the twenty-second letter of *Lettres philosophiques*, "Sur M. Pope et quelques autres poëtes fameux," from 1756. Though earlier editions of this letter had praised Pope as "the most elegant, the most correct, and what is even more, the most harmonious poet that England has produced," they did not mention *An Essay on Man*. [44] The added remarks on Pope's philosophical poem strongly praise Pope's accomplishment, asserting that "Pope's *Essay on Man* seems to me the most beautiful, the most useful, and the most sublime didactic poem that has ever been written in any language." Yet more significant for our purposes, however, is the following much-cited statement on the confluence of ideas between the two poets: "I have been flattered, I confess, to see that [Pope] agrees with me in one thing that I said many years ago. 'You are surprised that God made man so limited, so ignorant, so little happy. Does it not surprise you that He did not make man more limited, more ignorant, and more unhappy?' When a Frenchman and an Englishman think the same, they have to be right."

Voltaire states his pleasure in discovering in Pope's *Essay on Man* a satire on man's frustrated vanity akin to "one thing that I said many years ago." He refers here to remarks in the twenty-fifth letter on Pascal in *Lettres philosophiques* whose similarity to Pope is indeed striking:

Is not the present state of man a gift of the Creator? Who told you that God owed you more than that? Who told you that your existence warranted more knowledge and more happiness? . . . You are surprised that God made man so limited, so ignorant, so little happy. Why are you not surprised that He did not make him more limited, more ignorant, and more unhappy? You complain that life is so short and miserable; thank God that it is not more short and more miserable. [45]

Voltaire indicates that this harmony of thought between the two writers on man's misguided belief that he deserves benefits and considerations from God was a happy accident, but as George Havens pointed out long ago, the above passage was added to the commentary on Pascal in a variant of 1739, when Pope's poem had been in Voltaire's hands for close to six years. Though Voltaire's indebtedness to Pope in this instance continues to be denied, the evidence strongly suggests otherwise. [46] On the Enlightenment refusal of special providence, at least, Pope's presence had been strongly registered.

The heterodox intellectual influence of *An Essay on Man* was felt beyond the works of Voltaire alone. In 1748, La Mettrie lauded the poem in the dedication to his *L'homme machine*, the most radical text to come out of the French Enlightenment to that point. That same year, Montesquieu published *L'esprit de lois*, another radical text that supported the cause of natural religion. In a review of the text in 1749, the Abbé de La Roche invoked Gaultier's attack on Pope of 1746, arguing that the notion of laws as "necessary relations," itself derived from Spinoza's determinism, merely rearticulated Pope's blasphemous insistence in *An Essay on Man* that "Whatever is, is right."[47] Here again, Pope's work was seen as emblematic of the dangerous new thought circulating among the first generation of France's *parti philosophique*. As is well known, however, after the disastrous Lisbon earthquake of 1755, Voltaire abandoned his espousal of the combination of optimism and philosophical fatalism implied by the phrase, "Whatever is, is right," now seen as both naïve and socially irresponsible.[48] Beginning with his *Poème sur le désastre de Lisbonne* (1756) and culminating in the bitter mockery of optimism in *Candide* (1759), Voltaire honed the French freethinking platform, distinguishing it powerfully from the English tradition of which Pope was the most radical literary exemplar.

This last piece of our story is noteworthy on several fronts. For one, in his insistence against Pope that evil does indeed exist on earth, Voltaire makes natural religion, concurrently, more amenable to morality and less Christian. In doing so, he throws into relief the central criticisms of Pope's creed articulated so prominently by Crousaz, yet with an important difference. Both theologian and *philosophe* express concern that the fatalism inherent in "Whatever is, is right" casts a cold eye on the corruption and vice everywhere visible around us. Yet Voltaire's *Candide* insists that ethical responsibility becomes possible only when morality is understood as a secular initiative in a world that man must at least attempt to determine and create for himself. In this sense, we see through Voltaire the way in which Pope's natural religion remains tied to the conservatism of the freethinking literary tradition that preceded him.

III

Upon discovering the Jesuits' condemnation of *An Essay on Man*, precipitated by Du Resnel's translation, Voltaire expresses his outrage that Pope's poem had been marked as "a devilish book against the Christian religion."[49] Curiously enough, however, as Voltaire comes later to appreciate, the heterodoxy of Pope's *Essay on Man* grew out of its sustained dependence on a vastly amplified notion of general Providence. As we know, the poem's central argument that "Whatever is, is right" depends on the notion that the universe is governed by a few general and necessary principles that are not overthrown for the advantage of any one piece of the whole. Appearances of natural and moral evil are to be understood, then, as unavoidable parts of the larger plan: "God sends not ill; if rightly understood, / Or partial Ill is universal Good" (4.113–14).

Anticipating objections to this idea in the moral realm, Pope asserts that God acts by general laws as much in this as in the natural order:

> If plagues or earthquakes break not Heav'n's design,
> Why then a Borgia, or a Catiline?
>
>   . . .
>
> From pride, from pride, our very reas'ning springs,
> Account for moral as for nat'ral things:
> Why charge we Heav'n in those, in these acquit?
> In both, to reason right is to submit.
>
>   (1.155–56, 161–64)

Crousaz's *Commentaire* emphasizes repeatedly that this parallel between the processes of moral and physical actions creates irresolvable difficulties around the question of free will.[50] Since every event in Pope's universe—good and evil—is part of God's plan, Pope, on Crousaz's view, cannot help but imply that man is not accountable for his vicious conduct, and even, most blasphemously, that God is. Far from banishing God, Pope's system makes him so present that God becomes the agent of sin, our power of action indistinct from his. Vital to the Christian mission of the *Commentaire*, then, is Crousaz's success in convincing his readers, against Pope, that morality is an active choice, that God grants man liberty to exercise his will and determine his own actions, and, thus, that moral turpitude is a consequence of man's misuse of this freedom, rather than an unseen advantage in the ultimate plan of a First Cause:

But let us beware of reckoning among those events, which the order of the world requires, the bad actions, or wicked customs of men. God indeed may sometimes display his power by producing good from them. He that could call beings out of *nothing* into existence, can make the most beautiful regularity arise from confusion, but he does not cause that confusion that he may have an opportunity of reforming it. It is the consequence of human blindness and depravity.[51]

When stripped of poetic flourishes, Pope's injunction in epistle one that we "submit" to the necessary decrees of divine power, for Crousaz, "consists in looking undisturb'd and careless upon every thing that passes, in an indolent and supine unconcern about our actions and those of others." To conquer this tendency, he exhorts his reader to remember that "intelligent beings have received from [God] a real power of action distinct from his." Without this power to determine our actions, the "submission required by Mr. Pope" leads to the "overthrow of morality and religion," replacing vigilance and "careful and circumspect conduct" with passivity and "a fatal calm."[52]

Recalling the English attacks on libertine infidelity from the 1670s, Crousaz also emphasizes how Pope's fatalism grossly seeks to justify indulgence of the appetites, as his connection between "morality and the course of natural things" discourages all vigilance "by flattering the inclination so prevalent in most men, to live without constraint, without remorse, and without apprehension of future punishment."[53] *Candide*, unexpectedly, echoes this critique, while from a secular perspective.[54] Though Candide is indeed motivated primarily by his lust for Cunégonde, a lust in no way censured in the novel, to say with Pope that "The surest Virtues thus from Passions shoot, / Wild Nature's vigor working at the root" (2.183–84) refuses to acknowledge that not all instinctive desires are necessarily good. At the start of *Candide*, for example, the hero passes through a village recently burned by the Bulgars and watches while "girls, disemboweled after having satisfied the natural instincts of some hero, breathed their last."[55] And yet, though rape and sexual exploitation loom large in the litany of atrocities experienced in "the best of all possible worlds," Voltaire also makes clear against Crousaz that it is nonsense to imagine that a reprobate excuses himself by way of philosophical systems. A brutal sailor takes advantage of the Lisbon earthquake to find money, get drunk, and buy "the favours of the first willing woman that he met among the ruins of the shattered houses," yet the novel's satire here falls on the philosopher, Pangloss (the spokesman for optimism in the novel), and his absurd effort to upbraid the sailor for "falling short of the standard set by universal reason."[56]

Candide serves as a reminder, finally, that Crousaz's preoccupation with the possibility of philosophical sexual immorality blinds us to a far more worrisome failure of Pope's fatalist system. Just before the earthquake, the debauched sailor had caused the drowning of two good men in a shipwreck off the coast of Lisbon, yet Pangloss watches these deaths with equanimity, explaining to Candide that "the Bay of Lisbon had been especially made" for such a purpose.[57] Voltaire's aim here is to show the insidious way in which philosophical optimism neutralizes and excuses *all* iniquitous acts, not merely libertine ones. He hereby suggests in a corrective to Crousaz that the problem with the mixture of libertinism and determinism underpinning English freethinking is its uneasy ties to a politics of protest and emancipation.[58] Pope, on this view, can look a lot like the Rochester who pronounces from the country on his indifference to the "giddy" world and all affairs of state. Through the lens provided by *Candide*, we come to see, indeed, that optimism in particular is a system exceptionally well suited to keeping things as they are.[59] Despite strong evidence that "everywhere the weak loathe the powerful, while cringing before them, and the powerful treat them like sheep whose wool and meat go to market," one cannot resist tyranny, slavery, and other social and political injustices because all is always well. In the concluding chapter of the novel, Candide and his friends ask a renowned dervish "what should one do" in the face of "a terrible amount of evil on earth"? Advising that they "keep quiet," the dervish promptly "closed his door in their faces."[60] It is here that Voltaire finds himself again in shadowy agreement with Crousaz, equally troubled, though for different reasons, by the moral and ethical straitjacket imposed by fatalism.

And yet whereas Crousaz emphasizes the importance of free will for its Christian insistence on the lapsed state of man, for Voltaire, Pope's conviction that "Whatever is, is right," though commendable in its implicit refusal of special providence, remains excessively reliant on the notion of a general providential will that by force curtails any project of Enlightenment change; for if all events are determined and controlled by a higher intelligence, to whose larger plan we must quietly submit, in what way can we shape our world? "We are on the threshold of a great revolution in human thinking," Voltaire wrote to Diderot as he began work on *Candide*.[61] This revolution depends vitally on the assumption, against Pope and the dervish, that we not keep quiet and that we act, as much as possible in a world determined largely by chance, out of our own initiative and volition. In such a world, though physical evil is admittedly unavoidable, moral evil can and should be weeded out.[62] And rather than reminding us of a divine logic hidden from view, its existence serves to confirm, on the contrary, the lack of a supernatural presence guiding the universe. Though this conclusion may appear to replace optimism with pessimism, as Jean Starobinski has argued, it is the very absence of a providential dispensation in the world that motivates man to action: "Against a metaphysics that postulates the eternal presence of a global meaning of the universe (a meaning that we only inadequately perceive), Voltaire erects a reason that sees the requisite clarity lacking everywhere and that finds in this very defect, this scandalous deficit of meaning, the spur to its own militancy." At the close of *Candide*, the farm community outside Constantinople has learned to replace submission to the divine order with human work and productivity: "Il faut cultiver notre jardin"—we must work our land—says Candide, thus providing us, at last, with a constructive guide to survival in a world that is cruel and inhospitable, yet also dynamically in process.[63]

Returning to *An Essay on Man* with this in view, the poem's repeated injunction to "Submit" to God's order takes on a newly familiar meaning. That Pope had no mission to change the world, despite his evident distaste for much of institutional religion, is indicated as early as *An Essay on Criticism*. In response to Caryll's warnings that divines had objected to hints of heterodoxy in the poem, Pope expresses his willingness, in letters of June and July 1711, to revise the offensive elements in the interests of "the quiet of mankind."[64] And though Pope went on again to eschew revealed in favor of natural religion in *An Essay on Man*, the fraught reception of the poem motivated his abandonment, on prudential grounds, of the larger, more ambitious, and more radical "Ethic Epistles," of which *An Essay on Man* was to form a part. Discussing this project with Joseph Spence before his death, Pope describes how the third of his four anticipated "Ethic Epistles," on ecclesiastical and civil government, became the impetus behind jettisoning the whole: "I could not have said what I would have said, without provoking every church on the face of the earth: and I did not care for living always in boiling water."[65] This same weariness of controversy, compounded perhaps by failure of nerve, is the most likely explanation of Pope's acceptance of Warburton's reinvention of *An Essay on Man* as a Christian poem whose aim was "to intimate the Necessity of a more sublime Dispensation to Mankind."[66] On the subject of Warburton's "absurd refinement" of the poem, Jonathan Richardson indeed attests that Pope "never dreamed of the scheme he afterwards adopted, perhaps for good reasons," adding that Pope had "taken terror about the clergy, and Warburton himself, at the general alarm of its fatalism, and deistical tendency."[67]

That his nerve had not completely failed, however, is suggested by a letter to Warburton from April 1739, which presumably thanks him for his reclamation of *An Essay on Man* for the cause of orthodoxy. In the letter, Pope thanks Warburton, "in greatest hurry imaginable," for making "my System as clear as I ought to have done & could not":

It is indeed the Same System as mine, but illustrated with a Ray of your own, as they say our Natural Body is the same still, when it is Glorifyed. I am sure I like it better than I did before, & so will every man else. I know I meant just what you explain, but I did not explain my own meaning so well as you: You understand me as well as I do myself, but you express me better than I could express myself.[68]

In his *Lives of the Poets*, Johnson aptly observes that one of Pope's "favourite topicks" is "contempt of his own poetry," and that "in this he was certainly not sincere." As Johnson rightly asks, "His high value of himself was sufficiently observed; and of what could he be proud but of his poetry?"[69] When applied back to Pope's letter to Warburton, Johnson's remarks alert us to be on guard. For perhaps even more difficult to buy than Pope's denigration of his writing is that he would write what is in fact a strikingly bad letter. Not only is the letter hurried, as Pope himself admits, its language is also stilted, awkward, and rudimentary and repetitive, hardly the premeditated and artful production we would expect from Pope on such an occasion. Playing with the twofold philosophy of his predecessors, Pope, I would like to suggest, intends for the philosopher class to understand that his letter is not in earnest, that he does not "like [the poem] better than I did before," and Warburton does not "express me better than I could express myself."[70] Even Pope's metaphoric reference to Warburton's Christianization of the poem is double-edged: the glorification of Pope's "System," figured as the "Natural Body," though ostensibly improved by Warburton's or God's "Ray," is nonetheless "the same still," just as revelation, on Pope's view, adds little of value to natural religion that was not already there.

When Pope concedes to amend his *Essay on Criticism*, it is with the conviction that his expurgations will "gratify" men "of sound faith tho' of weak understanding" as well as show his deference "to the determinations of the Church."[71] Such was his sanguine justification, it seems, of Warburton's bowdlerization of *An Essay on Man*. Like Rochester, Behn, and Swift, Pope did not believe in the Christian providentialism with which Warburton ever after infused his poem. Yet also like them, he was still enough the product of the freethinking of his homeland to remain invested in submission, however informed by skeptical disenchantment.[72] As we have seen, it is precisely the tenacity of this skeptical disenchantment, paradoxically, that motivates one's public deference to the laws of one's country. Yet, if Pope, in the final estimation, looks more like his predecessors than we initially thought, we do well also to remember his unprecedented ability to speak to the intellectual and religious sympathies of the next generation of the Enlightenment.

Indeed, the radical antiprovidentialism of *An Essay on Man* that so stimulated Voltaire's imagination in *Lettres philosophiques* continues to make its mark in *Candide*. Though the dervish of the final chapter tells the friends to "keep quiet" about the evil in the world, he also reminds us, in a distinctly Popeian fashion, that the universe could not be more indifferent toward the human predicament: "When His Highness sends a vessel to Egypt, does he worry whether the rats who are on the ship are comfortable or not?"[73] Though Pope's blind spots as a freethinker became more prominent in Voltaire's mind by the mid-1750s, those same blind spots also stirred the *philosophe* to respond to the deep-seated prejudices of the French civil and ecclesiastical establishment with the peculiar force and energy that distinguish *Candide*. As Crousaz maintained, free will and its implications for morality were critically at stake in deism's determined universe, but the answer was not to shore up the church's doctrinal adherence to man's fallen status and his consequent need for divine grace. Rather, the limits of Pope's vision in *An Essay on Man* invigorated the question of man's agency in his world with a fresh and newly vital urgency, paving the way for a secular humanism of which English freethinking in its various manifestations represents an early and important chapter.

What is more, Pope's move away from the strategy of the pious fraud in *An Essay on Man* also asks us to acknowledge that as a ploy designed to preserve the authority of the religious realm, the pious fraud was finally a failed strategy and that its practitioners on some level knew this to be the case. Over the long haul, as we know, such tactics formed part and parcel of the decline of the very forms of authority they appeared to attempt to bolster. More than anything, perhaps, the case studies this book examines thus point to the deeply fraught and ambivalent nature of belief in the Enlightenment period. Unable to sustain the kinds of religious investments characteristic of tradition, contemporaries were nonetheless loath to tear down an edifice that had provided a bedrock for community and political structure, as well as for identity and self-understanding. David Berman suggests indeed that the "art" of the pious fraud—what he calls "theological lying"—involved a highly complex, even contradictory, set of motivations and allegiances and is not to be reduced to a simple desire to keep the masses ignorant and obedient. As he explains, those writers who made use of this art were, in truth, well aware that their writing carried an always-potential power to spread irreligion. The point, to be sure, of encoding a hidden radical message in a text was precisely the ever-present possibility that previously uninitiated readers might succeed in apprehending its latent meaning. In this sense, he argues, the twofold philosophy is more accurately threefold: containing an exoteric orthodoxy aimed at the censor, an esoteric unbelief decipherable to the intelligentsia, and, lastly, a covert *insinuation* of the latter put forward for whomever in the reading public might be receptive to it.[74]

Once again, the literary is central to this third element of the pious fraud, a recognition dating back to its first adherents in classical antiquity. As Lucretius taught, since a godless universe may seem "Harsh" to those not accustomed to the rigors of a materialist system, he strives to "hold [the] mind with poetry," while at the same time instructing the hesitant reader in what he calls "the nature of things." And since spirit is absent from the nature of things, a lesson both frightening and dangerous to many, casting unbelief in the form of poetry—"Turning the taste of honey into sound"—plays an instrumental part in helping the right readers to see, finally, that his system is "useful" rather than merely destructive.[75] As we remember, Swift alludes to this same moment in Lucretius at the end of section VI of *A Tale of a Tub*: "Mellaeo contingens cucta Lepore." Indeed, though Swift complains that Anglican clergymen, whom he describes as "the Sour, the Envious, the Stupid, and the Tastless" (4), deplored what they saw to be clandestine "ill Meanings" (8) couched throughout *A Tale*, it is hardly plausible that detection of such meanings by at least some was not part of his overall plan. Such a view helps us better to understand not only the religious dimensions of Swift's radical conservatism but also the political ones that have so occupied critics in recent years, particularly around his status as an Irish patriot. Swift was a deeply patrician anticolonialist critic; his Irish writings condescend to the natives, and despair of their capacity for reason, yet they also betray an irrepressible hope that the desire to fight for liberty might be ignited in even a few readers.[76]

Notes

Notes to Introduction

1. Henry St. John, Viscount Bolingbroke, *The Works of the Late Right Honourable Henry St. John, Lord Viscount Bolingbroke*, 8 vols. (London, 1809), 5:97, 98, 99.

2. Ibid., 5:101.

3. See Lori Branch, *Rituals of Spontaneity: Sentiment and Secularism from Free Prayer to Wordsworth* (Waco, TX: Baylor University Press, 2006); Jonathan Sheehan, *The Enlightenment Bible: Translation, Scholarship, Culture* (Princeton, NJ: Princeton University Press, 2005); Pippa Norris and Ronald Inglehart, *Sacred and Secular: Religion and Politics Worldwide* (New York: Cambridge University Press, 2004); S. J. Barnett, *The Enlightenment and Religion: The Myths of Modernity* (New York: Palgrave, 2003); Rodney Stark and Roger Finke, eds., *Acts of Faith* (Berkeley: University of California Press, 2000); Steve Bruce, ed., *Religion and Modernization* (Oxford: Clarendon Press, 1992).

4. J. A. I. Champion, *The Pillars of Priestcraft Shaken: The Church of England and Its Enemies, 1660–1730* (New York: Cambridge University Press, 1992); Champion, "Legislators, Impostors, and the Politic Origins of Religion: English Theories of 'Imposture' from Stubbe to Toland," in *Heterodoxy, Spinozism, and Free Thought in Early-Eighteenth-Century Europe*, ed. Silvia Berti, Françoise Charles-Daubert, and Richard H. Popkin (Boston: Kluwer Academic Publishers, 1996), 333–56; Champion, " 'May the last king be strangled in the bowels of the last priest': Irreligion and the English Enlightenment, 1649–1789," in *Radicalism in British Literary Culture, 1650–1830*, ed. Timothy Morton and Nigel Smith (New York: Cambridge University Press, 2002), 29–44; Champion, " 'Religion's Safe, with Priestcraft is the War': Augustan Anticlericalism and the Legacy of the English Revolution, 1660–1720," *The European Legacy* 5 (2000): 547–61; Mark Goldie, "Priestcraft and the Birth of Whiggism," in *Political Discourse in Early Modern Britain*, ed. Nicholas Phillipson and Quentin Skinner (Cambridge: Cambridge University Press, 1993), 211–12; J. G. A. Pocock, "Post-Puritan England and the Problem of the

Enlightenment," in *Culture and Politics from Puritanism to the Enlightenment*, ed. Perez Zagorin (Berkeley: University of California Press, 1980), 91–111; and J. C. D. Clark, *English Society, 1688–1832: Religion, Ideology, and Politics during the Ancien Regime* (Cambridge: Cambridge University Press, 2000), 10, 318–20.

5. Jonathan Israel, *Radical Enlightenment: Philosophy and the Making of Modernity, 1650–1750* (Oxford: Oxford University Press, 2001); Margaret C. Jacob, *The Radical Enlightenment: Pantheists, Freemasons and Republicans* (London: George Allen & Unwin, 1981).

6. Israel, *Radical Enlightenment*, v. On the question of the Enlightenment in England, see esp. Roy Porter, *The Creation of the Modern World: The Untold Story of the British Enlightenment* (New York: W. W. Norton, 2000); and also Arthur M. Wilson, "The Enlightenment Came First to England," in *England's Rise to Greatness, 1660–1763*, ed. Stephen Baxter (Berkeley: University of California Press, 1983), 1–28; E. P. Thompson, "The Peculiarities of the English," in *The Poverty of Theory* (New York: Monthly Review Press, 1978), 245–301; and Perry Anderson, "Origins of the Present Crisis," in *English Questions* (New York: Verso, 1992), 15–47.

7. Pocock, "Post-Puritan England," 91–111; Pocock, "Conservative Enlightenment and Democratic Revolutions: The American and French Cases in British Perspective," *Government and Opposition* 24 (1989): 81–105; Pocock, "Clergy and Commerce: the Conservative Enlightenment in England," in *L'età dei lumi: Studi storici sul Settecento europeo in onore di Franco Venturi*, ed. L. G. Crocker (Naples: Jovene, 1985): 2:523–68.

8. See Champion, *The Pillars of Priestcraft Shaken*, esp. 170–222; Goldie, "Priestcraft and the Birth of Whiggism," 211–12; and Roger Lund, ed., *The Margins of Orthodoxy: Heterodox Writing and Cultural Response, 1660–1750* (New York: Cambridge University Press, 1995).

9. Peter Gay, *The Enlightenment: An Interpretation*, 2 vols. (New York: A. Knopf, 1966), 1:44. In vol. 1, subtitled "The Rise of Modern Paganism," Gay demonstrates that the *philosophes'* revolutionary doctrine was informed by a dialectical interplay between their appeal to antiquity and their pursuit of modernity (1:8). Though clearly indebted to Gay's discovery of the crucial ways in which the Enlightenment critique of religion relied on aspects of ancient paganism, my study differs from his both in its concern with literary culture and in its emphasis on the curious conservatism of the earlier, British incarnation of this tradition.

10. See Clement Hawes, *Mania and Literary Style: The Rhetoric of Enthusiasm from the Ranters to Christopher Smart* (New York: Cambridge University Press, 1996); Shaun Irlam, *Elations: The Poetics of Enthusiasm in Eighteenth-Century Britain* (Stanford, CA: Stanford University Press, 1999). For many critics, still, the period from 1660 to 1780 is devoid of skeptical religious thought (see, for example, Morton and Smith, *Radicalism in British Literary Culture*).

11. See Ronald Paulson, *The Beautiful, Novel, and Strange: Aesthetics and Heterodoxy* (Baltimore: Johns Hopkins University Press, 1996); Michael McKeon, "Tacit Knowledge: Tradition and Its Aftermath," in *Questions of Tra-*

dition, ed. Mark Salber Phillips and Gordon Schochet (Toronto: University of Toronto Press, 2004), 188–96; and McKeon, "Politics of Discourses and the Rise of the Aesthetic in Seventeenth-Century England," in *Politics of Discourse*, ed. Kevin Sharpe and Steven N. Zwicker (Berkeley: University of California Press, 1987), 36–37, 49–50.

12. J. P. Crousaz, *A Commentary on Mr. Pope's Principles of Morality, or Essay on Man* [1739], trans. Samuel Johnson, in *The Yale Edition of the Works of Samuel Johnson*, ed. J. H. Middendorf, 18 vols. (New Haven, CT: Yale University Press, 1958–), 17:187; *Weekly Miscellany*, 28 September 1734; Swift to Viscount Bolingbroke, May 1719, in *The Correspondence of Jonathan Swift*, ed. Harold Williams, 5 vols. (Oxford: Clarendon Press, 1965–72), 2:321. See also Thomas Brown's satiric rebuke of Aphra Behn's heterodox "Paraphrase on the Lords Prayer" (1685), in which Brown argues for the incompatibility of the "Muse" and "Devotion" (*The Late Converts Exposed, or, the Reasons of Mr. Bays's Changing His Religion: Part the Second* [London, 1690], 3).

13. Annabel Patterson, *Censorship and Interpretation: The Conditions of Writing and Reading in Early Modern England* (Madison: University of Wisconsin Press, 1984), 10, quoted in McKeon, "Politics of Discourses," 43.

14. John Rooke, trans., preface to *A True Ecclesiastical History from Moses to the Time of Martin Luther, by Thomas Hobbes* (London, 1722). Rooke's comment is an extension of Hobbes's original remarks in the Latin preface.

15. Jonathan Swift, "An Apology," in *A Tale of a Tub*, ed. A. C. Guthkelch and D. Nichol Smith, 2nd ed. (Oxford: Clarendon Press, 1958), 7. Subsequent references to *A Tale* will be noted by page number in the body of the text.

16. Viscount Bolingbroke to Swift, 12 September 1724, in Swift, *Correspondence*, 3:27; 3:27–28.

17. Richard Steele, no. 135 in *The Tatler*, ed. Donald F. Bond, 3 vols. (Oxford: Clarendon Press, 1987), 2:280–81; 2:279.

18. See also Joseph Addison's reference to Cicero in no. 588 of *The Spectator*, ed. Donald F. Bond, 5 vols. (Oxford: Clarendon Press, 1965). If he was mistaken that generosity exists in the world, Addison remarks that "I should say, as *Cicero* in Relation to the Immortality of the Soul, I willingly err, and should believe it very much for the Interest of Mankind to lie under the same Delusion" (4:13).

19. Bolingbroke, *Works*, 5:96, 97.

20. Viscount Bolingbroke to Swift, 1 January 1721–22, in Swift, *Correspondence*, 2:413.

21. William Warburton, *The Divine Legation of Moses Demonstrated: On the Principles of a Religious Deist, from the Omission of the Doctrine of a Future State of Reward and Punishment in the Jewish Dispensation* (London, 1738), 309–10, 302–3, 320, 364. On the concept of twofold philosophy in antiquity, see H. D. Jocelyn, "The Roman Nobility and the Religion of the Republican State," *Journal of Religious History* 4 (1966): 89–104; and Denis Feeney, *Literature and Religion at Rome: Cultures, Contexts, and Beliefs* (Cambridge: Cambridge University Press, 1998), 12–46. On the resurrection of this practice in the eighteenth century see, most famously, Leo Strauss, *Persecution and the*

Art of Writing (Glencoe, IL: Free Press, 1952); and also David Berman, "Deism, Immortality, and the Art of Theological Lying," in *Deism, Masonry, and the Enlightenment*, ed. J. A. Leo Lemay (Newark: University of Delaware Press, 1987), 61–78; Frank Manuel, *The Eighteenth Century Confronts the Gods* (Cambridge, MA: Harvard University Press, 1959), 65–69; and Peter Harrison, *"Religion" and the Religions in the English Enlightenment* (Cambridge: Cambridge University Press, 1990), 85–91.

22. Warburton, *Divine Legation*, 297, 299. In his *Treatise concerning Enthusiasme*, Meric Casaubon explains similarly that the political simulation of divine inspiration "hath ever been one of the main crafts & mysteries of government, which the best of heathens sometimes (as well as the worst, more frequently,) . . . have been glad to use." This strategy, he continues, derives from the ancients' conviction that "the nature of the common people [is] such, that neither force, nor reason, nor any other means, or considerations whatsoever, have that power with them to make them plyable and obedient, as holy pretensions and interests, though grounded (to more discerning eyes) upon very little probability" (*A Treatise concerning Enthusiasme*, 2nd ed. [1656], ed. Paul J. Korshin [Gainesville, FL: Scholars' Facsimiles & Reprints, 1970], 4).

23. On the semantics of the term "free thinker" in Steele's essays, see Peter N. Miller, "'Freethinking' and 'Freedom of Thought' in Eighteenth-Century Britain," *Historical Journal* 36 (1993): 602.

24. Anthony Ashley Cooper, 3rd Earl of Shaftesbury, "Miscellany III," in *Characteristics of Men, Manners, Opinions, Times*, ed. Lawrence E. Klein (New York: Cambridge University Press, 1999), 413–14.

25. Richard Steele, no. 55 in *The Guardian*, 2 vols. (London, 1767), 1:237; Parker, *A Discourse of Ecclesiastical Politie* (London, 1670), 138.

26. [Clement Ellis], *The Vanity of Scoffing* (London, 1674), 17, 16, 17; see also Richard Allestree, "Sermon X," in *Eighteen Sermons* (London, 1669), 179. For the orthodox, however, such a division in the nation's religious life was impossible to maintain. Samuel Parker warns that atheism "spreads and . . . creeps out of Cities into Villages" (*Ecclesiastical Politie*, xlii). Ellis cautions similarly that the multitude will inevitably catch on to their superiors' view that Scripture and the mysteries of religion are mere fables and fictions. What, then, is to stop them from "tak[ing] arms to redeem their liberty" (*Vanity of Scoffing*, 14)?

27. On Charles Blount's plagiarism of Cherbury's *Dialogue*, see Harold Hutcheson, "Lord Herbert and His Religious Philosophy," in *Lord Herbert of Cherbury's "De Religione Laici,"* (New Haven, CT: Yale University Press, 1944), 72–74. Passages from *A Dialogue* appear in Blount's *The Two First Books of Philostratus* (1680) and *The Oracles of Reason* (1693), as well as in *Great Is Diana of the Ephesians, or, the Original of Idolatry* (1680, 1695, 1700), the last of whose borrowings have yet to be commented on by scholars. For the argument that *A Dialogue* was in fact written by Blount and not by Herbert, see Champion, *Pillars of Priestcraft Shaken*, 143–48.

28. See [Edward, Lord Herbert of Chirbury], *A Dialogue between a Tutor*

and His Pupil (London, 1768), 116, 129, 184. See also Charles Blount's similar comment that "the Soothsayings of the Ancients are the fables and illusions of Priests, to get money and praise, as also the figments of heathen Priests, to keep the people in awe with the fear of a supream Deity" (*The Two First Books of Philostratus, concerning the Life of Apollonius Tyaneus* [London, 1680], 82).

29. Herbert, *Dialogue*, 94.

30. There is a more radical side to the twofold philosophy. As John Goodman describes, those who consider themselves "privy to the plot" also manage to "keep out of the bondage" of religion, dismissing it to be "a politick trick to catch silly persons with" (*The Old Religion, Demonstrated in Its Principles, and Described in the Life and Practice Thereof* [London, 1684], 311).

31. Herbert, *Dialogue*, 47.

32. Ibid., 271.

33. Thomas Hobbes, *Leviathan*, ed. C. B. Macpherson (New York: Penguin Books, 1968), 1.6.124. Samuel Parker, *Ecclesiastical Politie*, 138. The importance of Hobbes's thought to Restoration and eighteenth-century freethinking, particularly among the upper classes, is long established. See especially Samuel I. Mintz, *The Hunting of Leviathan* (Bristol: Thoemmes Press, 1996), 134–46; and David Berman, *A History of Atheism in Britain: From Hobbes to Russell* (New York: Croom Helm, 1988), 48–69.

34. Hobbes, *Leviathan*, 1.11.168; see especially Hobbes's warning that "men had need to be very circumspect, and wary, in obeying the voice of man, that pretending himself to be a Prophet, requires us to obey God in that way, which he in Gods name telleth us to be the way to happinesse. For he that pretends to teach men the way of so great felicity, pretends to govern them; that is to say, to rule, and reign over them; . . . and is therefore worthy to be suspected of Ambition and Imposture" (*Leviathan*, 3.36.466).

35. Hobbes, *Leviathan*, 1.12.173. On Hobbes's attitude toward religious imposture, see Kinch Hoekstra, "Disarming the Prophets: Thomas Hobbes and Predictive Power," in *New Critical Perspectives on Hobbes's "Leviathan,"* ed. Luc Foisneau and George Wright (Milan: FrancoAngeli, 2004), 126–27.

36. Hobbes, *Leviathan*, 1.12.177; 3.32.410; Hobbes, *De Cive*, in *The Collected Works of Thomas Hobbes*, ed. Sir William Molesworth, 12 vols. (London: Thoemmes, 1994), 2:xii.

37. Charles Blount, *Great is Diana of the Ephesians* (1680), in *The Miscellaneous Works of Charles Blount* (London, 1695), 7. See also 41–44 in the same text. Charles Blount was the author of six heterodox works on religion published between 1679 and 1693, most of which went through several editions each. In 1695 the majority of his writings were collected and published in two editions as *The Miscellaneous Works of Charles Blount*. Despite his notoriety in the period, Blount remains an under-studied figure. For his influence on English freethinking, see J. A. Redwood, "Charles Blount, Deism, and English Freethought," *Journal of the History of Ideas*, 35 (1974): 490–98.

38. Baruch Spinoza, *Theological-Political Treatise*, trans. Samuel Shirley (Indianapolis, IN: Hackett, 1998), 3. For a parody of Spinoza's association of revealed religion with the tyranny of monarchical government, see Matthias

Earbery, *Deism Examin'd and Confuted, in an Answer to a Book Intitled, "Tractatus Theologico Politicus"* (London, 1697): "[Revealed religion] is that Grand Cheat that the Priests in all Ages have dress'd up in Various Habits to please the Vulgar, who are always of a mutable Temper, and to keep them in subjection to those Monarchs who want a Bridle to restrain unruly Subjects. . . . And truly, this . . . makes me very much wish we could see a Commonwealth in England, that we might enjoy the liberty of thinking and speaking of Religion as we pleas'd, which now is too much restrain'd" (10). On the links between English freethinking and republicanism in the late seventeenth century, see Israel, *Radical Enlightenment*, 604–5.

39. Charles Blount, *Great Is Diana*, 22–23; Charles Blount, *The Oracles of Reason* (London, 1693), 18, 2, A4. Even Spinoza is forced to admit religion's use to the state, recognizing that justice and charity, and thus civil peace and harmony, are often absent without the demands of faith. When a state's citizens are motivated by the pious teachings of non-superstitious religion, he notes, "many important causes of disturbance and crime are . . . aborted at source" (*Theological-Political Treatise*, 168). If all men were guided by reason, religion would not be a necessary evil, but since experience teaches that most are motivated by their passions, pleasures, greed, and personal ambition, Scripture's teachings do a good job of discouraging us from living by the laws of appetite only. While superstition has functioned as the tool of despotic government, the basic common notions of natural religion provide a justifiable support for a democratic state. Even if the multitude lacks reason, they "are equally required by God's command to love their neighbour as themselves" (*Theological-Political Treatise*, 188; see also 177–78).

40. Nigel Smith, "The Charge of Atheism and the Language of Radical Speculation, 1640–1660," in *Atheism from the Reformation to the Enlightenment*, ed. Michael Hunter and David Wootton (Oxford: Clarendon Press, 1992), 143.

41. See C. B. Schmitt, "The Rediscovery of Ancient Skepticism in Modern Times," in *The Skeptical Tradition*, ed. Myles Burnyeat (Berkeley: University of California Press, 1983), 225–51. The first Latin translations of Sextus Empiricus appeared in 1562 and 1569, culminating in the *Opera Omnia* of 1621. As Schmitt argues, "Once the translations were in print we see a direct development of skepticism as a more potent force in European life" (237).

42. Daniel Whitby, *A Discourse of the Necessity and Usefulness of the Christian Revelation* (London, 1705), 70–71. For a more sympathetic account of the same view, see Michel de Montaigne, *Apology for Raymond Sebond*, in *The Complete Works of Montaigne*, trans. Donald M. Frame (Stanford, CA: Stanford University Press, 1957), 2.12.370–71.

43. See Louis I. Bredvold, *The Intellectual Milieu of John Dryden* (Ann Arbor: University of Michigan Press, 1956), 21–22, 18. It is useful to note the conservative bent inherent in skepticism's critique of reason. As Montaigne argues in his *Apology*, it is because the common people are unable to judge things for themselves that we should be wary of elevating reason above traditional authorities (*Complete Works*, 2.12.320).

44. Whitby, *Necessity and Usefulness*, 72–73.

45. See, for example, Francis Gastrell, *The Principles of Deism Truly Represented and Set in a Clear Light, in Two Dialogues between a Sceptick and a Deist* (London: J. Morphew, 1708). Here Gastrell's skeptic, like Bolingbroke and Steele, supports the "Infidels of Old" over their modern counterparts and defends the coupling of Christian morality with faith in Christ's divinity. Whether or not it is actually true, he argues, we must believe that Christ is the son of God and that he descended from Heaven if we expect the rules and precepts of Christian morality to have any authority (60–61). On skepticism's complex and shifting religious alliances, see Schmitt, "Rediscovery of Ancient Skepticism," 240; and Richard H. Popkin, *The History of Scepticism from Erasmus to Spinoza* (Berkeley: University of California Press, 1979), 54–55.

46. Thomas Sprat, *History of the Royal Society* (1667), ed. Jackson I. Cope and Harold Whitmore Jones (Saint Louis, MO: Washington University Studies, 1958), 376.

47. Robert Boyle, *A Free Enquiry into the Vulgarly Received Notion of Nature* [1686], ed. Edward B. Davis and Michael Hunter (New York: Cambridge University Press, 1996), 47; Richard Bentley, "Sermon IX: Of Revelation and the Messias," in *Eight Sermons*, 6th ed. (Cambridge, 1735), 306; and Daniel Waterland, *Christianity Vindicated against Infidelity: A Second Charge Deliver'd to the Clergy of the Archdeaconry of Middlesex* (London, 1732), 29.

48. Warburton, *The Divine Legation of Moses Demonstrated*, 2 vols. (London, 1837), 1:531.

49. As Peter Gay argues, to the extent that classical literature was "the common possession of educated men," much of eighteenth-century classicism was politically innocent, indeed part and parcel of the established orthodoxy of the age. And yet at the same time, as early as the seventeenth century, radicals like Harrington and Milton were also beginning to invoke the classical past in their efforts to reform the corruption of present-day institutions (*The Enlightenment*, 39, 44–45n6). The ancient heritage, in other words, had an important volatility for its modern inheritors.

50. For the view that Temple was a deist, see J. M. Robertson, *A History of Freethought, Ancient and Modern, to the Period of the French Revolution*, 4th ed., 2 vols. (London: Watts & Co., 1936), 2:667–68; Israel, *Radical Enlightenment*, 606.

51. Sir William Temple, "Essay upon the Ancient and Modern Learning" [1690], in *Five Miscellaneous Essays*, ed. Samuel Holt Monk (Ann Arbor: University of Michigan Press, 1963), 66.

52. Temple, "Observations upon the United Provinces of the Netherlands" [1673], in *The Works of Sir William Temple*, ed. Jonathan Swift, 4 vols. (London, 1757), 1:171, 174.

53. Temple, "Of Heroic Virtue," in *Five Miscellaneous Essays*, 100.

54. Ibid., 123, 133.

55. See Joseph M. Levine, *Between the Ancients and the Moderns: Baroque Culture in Restoration England* (New Haven, CT: Yale University Press, 1999); Levine, *The Battle of the Books: History and Literature in the Augustan Age* (Ithaca, NY: Cornell University Press, 1991); Richard Kroll, *The Material Word:*

Literate Culture in the Restoration and Early Eighteenth Century (Baltimore: Johns Hopkins University Press, 1991); William Dowling, *The Epistolary Moment: The Poetics of the Eighteenth-Century Verse Epistle* (Princeton, NJ: Princeton University Press, 1991); Howard D. Weinbrot, *Augustus Caesar in 'Augustan' England: The Decline of a Classical Norm* (Princeton, NJ: Princeton University Press, 1978); and Isaac Kramnick, *Bolingbroke and His Circle: The Politics of Nostalgia in the Age of Walpole* (Ithaca, NY: Cornell University Press, 1968), esp. 205–35. Some critics continue to associate the appeal to the authority of the "ancients" in the early modern period with a "conservative" support for tradition as opposed to the more "radical" spirit of modernity (see Douglas Lane Patey, "Ancients and Moderns," in *The Cambridge History of Literary Criticism*, vol. 4, *The Eighteenth Century*, ed. H. B. Nisbet and Claude Rawson [New York and Cambridge: Cambridge University Press, 1997], 32).

56. For the traditional view of the religious orthodoxy of literary "neoclassicism," see, for example, James William Johnson's remark that "the Christian bias of writers from Dryden to Johnson, with a few exceptions, is indisputable, prima facie" (*The Formation of English Neo-Classical Thought* [Princeton, NJ: Princeton University Press, 1967], xi; also 106–21; and also Harry Levin, *The Myth of the Golden Age in the Renaissance* [Bloomington: Indiana University Press, 1969], xv); and Gay, *The Enlightenment*, 1:39–41). On the recourse to ancient theology among the eighteenth-century British freethinkers, see Champion, *Pillars of Priestcraft Shaken*, 170–95. For an earlier articulation of this argument, see John Orr, *English Deism: Its Roots and Its Fruits* (Grand Rapids, MI: Eerdmans, 1934), 47; and Manuel, *The Eighteenth Century Confronts the Gods*. For an exception to the neglect of literature in studies of freethinking and the classical heritage, see Philip Ayres, *Classical Culture and the Idea of Rome in Eighteenth-Century England* (New York: Cambridge University Press, 1997), 152–64.

57. Many years ago, Arthur Lovejoy maintained in his seminal essay, "The Parallel of Deism and Classicism" (1932), that the aesthetic neoclassicism so pervasive in the seventeenth and eighteenth centuries involved the same fundamental preconceptions as deism in religion. Both are committed to principles of transhistorical uniformity, to the idea that all individuals are equally rational, to the importance of the *consensus gentium*, to the critique of enthusiasm and particularity, to the celebration of the primitive as purest and best, and, finally, to the rejection of theories of progress. Though Lovejoy demonstrates that a consistent set of intellectual inclinations characterizes the deism of Voltaire and the poetry of Pope, he nowhere suggests that the latter was also a neoclassicist in religion or a deist. As he points out, we are accustomed to seeing deism as a form of religious radicalism involving a rejection of authority and tradition and neoclassicism as a return to authoritarianism in matters of taste. Although Lovejoy points out the error in both of these assumptions, he nonetheless fails to see his argument through to its logical endpoint (*Essays in the History of Ideas* [Baltimore: Johns Hopkins University Press, 1948], 78–98).

58. Swift to Alexander Pope, 20 September 1723, in Swift, *Correspondence*, 2:465.

59. Alexander Pope to Swift, 28 November 1729, in Swift, *Correspondence*, 3:365. On Pope's frequent allusions to classical figures in *An Essay on Man*, see Martin Kallich, *Heav'n's First Law: Rhetoric and Order in Pope's Essay on Man* (DeKalb: Northern Illinois University Press, 1967), 134.

60. Joseph Warton links the poem's doctrine to Plato and the Stoics (*An Essay on the Genius and Writings of Pope*, 5th ed., 2 vols. [London, 1806], 2:58), and he charges Pope with imagining "that the goodness and justice of the Deity might be defended, *without* having recourse to the doctrine of a future state, and of the depraved state of man" (2:60).

61. *An Essay on Man*, in *The Poems of Alexander Pope*, ed. John Butt (New Haven, CT: Yale University Press, 1963), 3.305–10. Subsequent references to Pope's poetry will refer to this edition and be noted by line number in the text and notes.

62. Bredvold, *The Intellectual Milieu of John Dryden*, 114. On Dryden's links to deism, see John Spurr, "The Piety of John Dryden," in *The Cambridge Companion to John Dryden*, ed. Steven N. Zwicker (Cambridge: Cambridge University Press, 2004), 253–54; Bredvold, *Intellectual Milieu of John Dryden*, 107–8; Sanford Budick, *Dryden and the Abyss of Light* (New Haven, CT: Yale University Press, 1970), 28–33; A. W. Verrall, *Lectures on Dryden*, ed. Margaret De G. Verrall (Cambridge: Cambridge University Press, 1914), 147–56, 217–37; Sir Walter Scott, *The Life of John Dryden*, ed. Bernard Kreissman (Lincoln: University of Nebraska Press, 1963), 264–68; William Empson, "Dryden's Apparent Scepticism," *Essays in Criticism* 20 (1970): 172–81; Oscar Kenshur, "Scriptural Deism and the Politics of Dryden's *Religio Laici*," *ELH* 54 (1987): 869–92; and Leon M. Guilhamet, "Dryden's Debasement of Scripture in *Absalom and Achitophel*," *SEL* 9 (1969): 395–413. For the opposing view on Dryden's Anglican orthodoxy, see Philip Harth, *Contexts of Dryden's Thought* (Chicago: University of Chicago Press, 1968), 56–225; Thomas H. Fujimura, "Dryden's *Religio Laici*: An Anglican Poem," *PMLA* 76 (1961): 205–17.

63. See John Dryden, *Tyrannick Love* [1670], in *The Works of John Dryden*, ed. Edward Niles Hooker H. T. Swedenberg, Jr., and Vinton A. Dearing, 20 vols. (Berkeley: University of California Press, 1956–2000), 10:2.1.181–84.

64. Dryden, Preface to *Tyrannick Love*, in *Works*, 10:111.

65. Steven Zwicker, *Politics and Language in Dryden's Poetry* (Princeton, NJ: Princeton University Press, 1984), 104. On politics as the motivating force behind Dryden's religious commitments, see 103–22.

66. For the definition of libertinism, see the *Oxford English Dictionary*, 2nd ed., 1989. On the semantic history of "libertinism," see Miller, " 'Freethinking' and 'Freedom of Thought,' " 601; and J. S. Spink, *French Free-Thought from Gassendi to Voltaire* (New York: Athlone Press, 1960), 4.

67. M. L. Stapleton, "Aphra Behn, Libertine," *Restoration* 24 (2000): 78. In his *Lettres philosophiques*, Voltaire takes issue with St. Evremont's portrait of Rochester as "the man of pleasure," describing him instead as "the man of genius, the great poet" whose "satire sur l'homme" stands as an exemplar of the "impetuous freedom" that characterizes the best of English poetry (*Oeuvres complètes*, ed. Louis Moland, 52 vols. [Paris: Garnier Frères, 1877–85],

22:164, 165), translation mine. For some notable exceptions to recent scholarship's propensity to overlook the religious aspects of libertinism, see Peter Cryle and Lisa O'Connell, eds., *Libertine Enlightenment: Sex, Liberty and License in the Eighteenth Century* (New York: Palgrave, 2004); Turner, "Properties of Libertinism," 75–87; Christopher Hill, "Freethinking and Libertinism: The Legacy of the English Revolution," in Lund, *The Margins of Orthodoxy*, 54–70; Margaret C. Jacob, "The Materialist World of Pornography," in *The Invention of Pornography*, ed. Lynn Hunt (New York: Zone Books, 1993), 157–202.

68. On Rochester's sexual libertinism, see, for example, Jonathan Brody Kramnick, "Rochester and the History of Sexuality," *ELH* 69 (2002): 277–301; Paul Hammond, "Rochester's Homoeroticism," in *That Second Bottle: Essays on John Wilmot, Earl of Rochester*, ed. Nicholas Fisher (Manchester: Manchester University Press, 2000), 47–62; Duane Coltharp, "Rivall Fops, Rambling Rakes, Wild Women: Homosocial Desire and Courtly Crisis in Rochester's Poetry," *The Eighteenth Century* 38 (1997): 23–42; Warren Chernaik, *Sexual Freedom in Restoration Literature* (Cambridge: Cambridge University Press, 1995); Stephen Clark, " 'Something Genrous in Meer Lust'? Rochester and Misogyny," in *Reading Rochester*, ed. Edward Burns (Liverpool: Liverpool University Press, 1995), 21–41; Harold Weber, "Drudging in Fair Aurelia's Womb: Constructing Homosexual Economies in Rochester's Poetry," *The Eighteenth Century* 33 (1992): 99–117; Sarah Wintle, "Libertinism and Sexual Politics," in *Spirit of Wit: Reconsiderations of Rochester*, ed. Jeremy Treglown (Hamden, CT: Archon Books, 1982), 133–65; and Reba Wilcoxon, "Rochester's Sexual Politics," *Studies in Eighteenth-Century Culture* 8 (1979): 137–49. On the religious aspects of Restoration libertinism, see James G. Turner, *Libertines and Radicals in Early Modern London: Sexuality, Politics, and Literary Culture, 1630–1685* (Cambridge: Cambridge University Press, 2002), x; Turner, "The Properties of Libertinism," *Eighteenth-Century Life*, 9 (1985): 75–87.

69. David M. Vieth, *Attribution in Restoration Poetry: A Study of Rochester's 'Poems' of 1680* (New Haven, CT: Yale University Press, 1963), 272. On neoclassical formal verse satire, see Howard D. Weinbrot, "The Swelling Volume: The Apocalyptic Satire of Rochester's *Letter from Artemisia in the Town to Chloe in the Country*," *Studies in the Literary Imagination* 5 (1972): 19–21; and Weinbrot, "The Pattern of Formal Verse Satire in the Restoration and the Eighteenth Century," *PMLA* 80 (1965): 394–401.

70. John Tillotson, "The Folly of Scoffing at Religion," in *The works of the Most Reverend Dr. John Tillotson, Late Lord Archbishop of Canterbury, containing Fifty Four Sermons and Discourses, on Several Occasions* (London, 1696), 36; see also Ellis, *The Vanity of Scoffing*, 30–31; Edwards, *Some Thoughts*, 38–42; and Philip Skelton, *Ophiomaches: or Deism Revealed* [1749], 2 vols. (Bristol: Thoemmes, 1990), 2:284–85.

71. David Vieth argues that Rochester is an early neoclassicist whose "innermost values were as conservative as Pope's," without acknowledging that such conservatism is complicated in both instances by a keen religious doubt (*Attribution in Restoration Poetry*, 1963], 221).

72. Criticism on Aphra Behn has been primarily concerned with questions of sex and sexuality. See Ann Marie Stewart, "Rape, Patriarchy, and the Libertine Ethos: The Function of Sexual Violence in Aphra Behn's 'The Golden Age' and *The Rover, Part I*," *Restoration* 12 (1997): 26–39; Anthony Kaufman, " 'The Perils of Florinda': Aphra Behn, Rape, and the Subversion of Libertinism in *The Rover, Part I*," *Restoration* 11 (1996): 1–21; Robert Markley and Molly Rothenberg, "Contestations of Nature: Aphra Behn's 'The Golden Age' and the Sexualizing of Politics," in *Rereading Aphra Behn*, ed. Heidi Hutner (Charlottesville: University Press of Virginia, 1993), 301–24; Markley, " 'Be impudent, be saucy, forward, bold, touzing, and leud": The Politics of Masculine Sexuality and Feminine Desire in Behn's Tory Comedies," in *Cultural Readings of Restoration and Eighteenth-Century English Theater*, ed. J. Douglas Canfield and Deborah C. Payne (Athens: University of Georgia Press, 1995), 114–40; Jessica Munns, " 'But to the touch were soft': Pleasure, Power, and Impotence in 'The Disappointment' and 'The Golden Age,' " in *Aphra Behn Studies*, ed. Janet Todd (Cambridge: Cambridge University Press, 1996), 178–98; and Stapleton, "Aphra Behn, Libertine," 75–97.

73. On Behn's Tory feminism and its contradictory support of freedom for women and order for the state, see Susan J. Owen, " 'Suspect My Loyalty When I Lose My Virtue': Sexual Politics and Party in Aphra Behn's Plays of the Exclusion Crisis, 1678–83," *Restoration* 18 (1994): 37–47; Owen, "Sexual Politics and Party Politics in Behn's Drama, 1678–83," in Todd, *Aphra Behn Studies*, 15–29; Elizabeth Bennett Kubek, " 'Night Mares of the Commonwealth': Royalist Passion and Female Ambition in Aphra Behn's *The Roundheads*," *Restoration* 17 (1993): 88–103; Donald R. Wehrs, "*Eros*, Ethics, Identity: Royalist Feminism and the Politics of Desire in Aphra Behn's *Love-Letters*," *SEL* 32 (1992): 461–78; and Arlen Feldwick, "Whigs, Wits and Women: Domestic Politics as Anti-Whig Rhetoric in Aphra Behn's Town Comedies," in *Political Rhetoric, Power, and Renaissance Women*, ed. C. Levin and P. A. Sullivan (Albany: SUNY Press, 1995), 223–40.

74. Janet Todd, *The Secret Life of Aphra Behn* (New Brunswick, NJ: Rutgers University Press, 1996), 292.

75. Melinda Zook argues that Tory ideology has received less scholarly attention than its Whig alternative, and that most characterizations of Toryism are overly broad and general ("Contextualizing Aphra Behn: Plays, Politics, and Party, 1679–1689," in *Women Writers and the Early Modern British Political Tradition*, ed. Hilda L. Smith [Cambridge: Cambridge University Press, 1998], 77). My reading of Behn's royalism aims to provide a more nuanced picture of one particular facet of Tory-royalism in the period.

76. *The Works of Aphra Behn*, ed. Janet Todd, 7 vols. (London: William Pickering, 1992–96), 4:77. All future references to Behn's works will refer to Todd's edition and be cited by volume and page number in the body of the text and notes (plays will be cited by act, scene, and line number).

77. Warburton, *Divine Legation*, 416; Howard, *History of Religion*, iv.

78. Jonathan Swift, *The Prose Works of Jonathan Swift*, ed. Herbert Davis, 14 vols. (Oxford: Basil Blackwell, 1939–68), 4:27. With the exception of *A Tale*

of a Tub, all subsequent references to Swift's prose writings will cite the Davis standard edition and be noted by volume and page number in the body of the text and notes.

79. In his essay "On the Trinity," Swift includes the doctrine in a list of "false and detestable" opinions attributed to the unbelieving critics of the Trinity (*Prose Works*, 9:167).

80. Bolingbroke, *Works*, 5:97. Swift may well have influenced Bolingbroke on the subject of twofold philosophy and pious frauds. As Bolingbroke remarks in a letter of 1722 to Swift, "Take it as you will, I . . . will undertake to find, in two pages of yr Bagatelles, more good sence, useful knowledge, and true Religion, than you can shew me in the works of nineteen in twenty of the profound Divines & Philosophers of the age" (Viscount Bolingbroke to Swift, 1 January 1721/2, in Swift, *Correspondence*, 2:415–16).

81. This same stress on the distinction between belief and action informs the "Apology" to Swift's *Tale of a Tub*. Whatever ambiguities his *Tale* might contain relating to matters of belief, he cannot be accused of "impious Assertions" that are "openly intended against all Religion" and supportive of "immoral Lives" (*Tale of a Tub*, 5). On Swift's comparison of his active defense of the Church to the debauched lives of the freethinkers, see Frank T. Boyle, "Profane and Debauched Deist: Swift in the Contemporary Response to *A Tale of a Tub*," *Eighteenth-Century Ireland* 3 (1988): 36.

82. See John Traugott, "*A Tale of a Tub*," in *The Character of Swift's Satire*, ed. Claude Rawson (Newark: University of Delaware Press, 1983), 83–126; C. J. Rawson, "The Character of Swift's Satire," in *Swift* (London: Sphere Books, 1971), 17–75. The most recent accounts of Swift's religion seem to reaffirm his orthodoxy. See for example, Marcus Walsh, "Swift and Religion," in *The Cambridge Companion to Jonathan Swift*, ed. Christopher Fox (New York: Cambridge University Press, 2003), 161–76.

83. Rawson, "Character of Swift's Satire," 17, 20.

84. Traugott, "*Tale of a Tub*," 84.

85. Ibid., 87.

86. William King complains that Swift "searches his antient Authors for their lewdest images" (*Some Remarks on the "Tale of a Tub"* [1704], in *The Original Works of William King*, 3 vols. [London, 1776], 1:216). On Swift's parody of the narrator's reliance on ancient sources in *A Tale*, see Kenneth Craven, "*A Tale of a Tub* and the 1697 Dublin Controversy," *Eighteenth-Century Ireland* 1 (1986): 102; and Robert H. Hopkins, "The Personation of Hobbism in Swift's *Tale of a Tub* and *Mechanical Operation of the Spirit*," *Philological Quarterly* 45 (1966): 378.

87. On Restoration freethought as a reaction to religious enthusiasm and sectarianism, see Michael Hunter, *Science and Society in Restoration England* (Cambridge: Cambridge University Press, 1981), 167; Hunter, "The Problem of 'Atheism' in Early Modern England," *Transactions of the Royal Historical Society* 35 (1985): 154; J. M. Robertson, *The Dynamics of Religion* (London: Watts, 1926), 65–69; and Robertson, *A History of Freethought*, 2:630, 634.

88. Clement Ellis, *The Gentile Sinner, Or England's Brave Gentleman*, 2nd

ed. (Oxford, 1661), 183. See also Edward Stillingfleet, *A Letter to a Deist, in Answer to Several Objections against the Truth and Authority of the Scriptures* (London, 1677), A3–A3ᵛ; Stillingfleet, epistle dedicatory to *Origines Sacraes* (London, 1662); William Assheton, *An Admonition to a Deist, Occasioned by Some Passages in Discourse with the Same Person* (London, 1685); Isaac Barrow, "Against Rash and Vain Swearing," in *The Works of the Learned Isaac Barrow*, ed. John Tillotson and Abraham Hill, 2nd ed., 4 vols. (London: M. Flesher, 1687), 1:221–22; [Anon.], *The Character of a Town-Gallant, Exposing the Extravagant Fopperies of Som[e] Vain Self-Conceited Pretenders to Gentility and Good Breeding* (London, 1675), 2, 8; and Skelton, *Ophiomaches*, 2:287. On the elite character of Restoration irreligion, see Hunter, "Science and Heterodoxy: An Early Modern Problem Reconsidered," in *Reappraisals of the Scientific Revolution*, ed. David C. Lindberg and Robert S. Westman (Cambridge: Cambridge University Press, 1990), 442, 445, 448–49; Berman, *History of Atheism in Britain*, 48–69; Richard H. Popkin, "The Deist Challenge," in *From Persecution to Toleration: The Glorious Revolution and Religion in England*, ed. Ole Peter Grell, Jonathan I. Israel, and Nicholas Tyacke (Oxford: Clarendon Press, 1991), 209; Thomas Franklin Mayo, *Epicurus in England, 1650–1725* (Dallas, TX: Southwest Press, 1934), 200; and Lawrence Stone, *The Crisis of the Aristocracy, 1558–1641* (Oxford: Oxford University Press, 1965), 332–34. In the seventeenth century, the term "atheism" typically denoted a broader form of doubt and irreligion than its current sense of a denial of the existence of God (see Hunter, "The Problem of 'Atheism' in Early Modern England," 135–36, 138–42; David Wooton, "Unbelief in Early Modern Europe," *History Workshop Journal* 20 [1985]: 86; and G. E. Aylmer, "Unbelief in Seventeenth–Century England," in *Puritans and Revolutionaries*, ed. Donald Pennington and Keith Thomas [Oxford: Clarendon Press, 1978], 24–26).

89. John Edwards, *Some Thoughts concerning the Several Causes and Occasions of Atheism, Especially in the Present Age* (London, 1695), 80, 2. Though "deism" as opposed to "atheism" was meant to indicate a rejection of revealed religion rather than disbelief in God, many contemporaries used the terms interchangeably. As John Edwards argues, "At this day Atheism it self is slily call'd Deism by those that indeed are Atheists. Though they retain the thing, yet they would disguise it by a false Name, and thereby hide the Heinousness of it" (*Some Thoughts*, 136; see also Richard Bentley, *The Folly of Atheism, and (What Is Now Called) Deism*, 2nd ed. [London, 1692], 5–6; and William Stephens, *An Account of the Growth of Deism in England* [London, 1696], 5). More than deism, however, "freethinking" denoted a refusal to submit to religious authority and a related reliance on one's own reason in matters of belief. While some deists, therefore, were also freethinkers, others promoted natural religion. On libertinism as a synonym for religious freethinking, see Skelton, *Ophiomaches*, 2:280–83; and Turner, "The Properties of Libertinism," 75, 77–78. For a useful account of the range of terminology used to describe religious doubt in the early modern period, see Robertson, *History of Freethought*, 1:1–26.

90. On the links between Restoration freethought and wit and education, see

Hunter, "Problem of 'Atheism,'" 141–42; Wooton, "Unbelief in Early Modern Europe," 92–93. For the view that Restoration freethinking was a product of the French cosmopolitanism of Charles II's court, see Dryden, "Defence of the Epilogue," in *Essays of John Dryden*, ed. W. P. Ker, 2 vols. (Oxford: Clarendon Press, 1900), 1:176.

91. Thomas Sprat, *History of the Royal Society*, 374, 375–76.

92. Joseph Addison, no. 458 in *The Spectator*, 4:117. For similar accounts, see also Edwards, *Some Thoughts*, 42–43; Charles Wolseley, *The Unreasonableness of Atheism Made Manifest* (London, 1669), 18–19; and Gilbert Burnet, *Bishop Burnet's History of His Own Time*, 6 vols. (Oxford, 1833), 1:168.

93. Skelton, *Ophiomaches*, 2:288.

94. This view has been put forward most famously by Hill. See especially "Freethinking and Libertinism," 54–70; Hill, "Irreligion in the 'Puritan' Revolution," in *Radical Religion in the English Revolution*, ed. J. F. McGregor and B. Reay (New York: Oxford University Press, 1984), 191–211. In this latter article Hill does mention upper-class religious skepticism briefly (see 194–95, 200).

95. Jonathan Scott, "Review Essay: Radicalism and Restoration: The Shape of the Stuart Experience," *Historical Journal* 31 (1988): 453; Robert Zaller, "The Continuity of British Radicalism in the Seventeenth and Eighteenth Centuries," *Eighteenth-Century Life* 6 (1981): 20–22.

96. Hill, "Irreligion in the 'Puritan' Revolution," 206; George H. Sabine, ed., *The Works of Gerrard Winstanley* (New York: Russell & Russell, 1965), 451.

97. J. Scott, "Review Essay: Radicalism and Restoration," 454. For the view that sectarian radicalism is distinct from strict unbelief, see also Hunter, "Problem of 'Atheism,'" 136; Smith, "Charge of Atheism," 131–58; Israel, *Radical Enlightenment*, 601.

98. Smith, "Charge of Atheism," 140. On the distinction between heresy and unbelief, see Smith, "Charge of Atheism," 131; Wooton, "Unbelief in Early Modern Europe," 93–98; and Wayland Young, *Eros Denied* (London: Weidenfeld & Nicolson, 1964), 212, 219.

99. Wooton, "Unbelief in Early Modern Europe," 90.

100. In a discussion of religion in *The Spectator* (1712), Addison speaks to the important distinction in the period between religious belief and religious practice. Faith, he contends, "comprehends what we are to believe," and morality "what we are to practice." While "the perfect Man" fuses both, Addison nonetheless gives preeminence to morality over faith for several reasons. Not only does faith derive its "excellency" from "the influence it has upon Morality"; infidelity is clearly a more benign offense than immorality: a virtuous infidel may be saved, but there is no hope for "a vicious Believer" (no. 459 in *The Spectator*, 4:118, 119).

101. Wooton, "Unbelief in Early Modern Europe," 90, 98. John Locke famously gives voice to the view that a religious conformist was, strictly speaking, still a heretic if his practice was not rooted in actual belief: "All the Life and Power of true Religion consists in the inward and full perswasion of the mind; and Faith is not Faith without believing. Whatever Profession we make, to what-

ever outward Worship we conform, if we are not fully satisfied in our own mind that the one is true, and the other well pleasing unto God, such Profession and such Practice, far from being any furtherance, are indeed great Obstacles to our Salvation" (*A Letter concerning Toleration*, ed. James H. Tully [Indianapolis, IN: Hackett, 1983], 26–27).

102. Wooton, "Unbelief in Early Modern Europe," 98–99.

103. See Rachel Weil, "Sometimes a Scepter Is Only a Scepter: Pornography and Politics in Restoration England," in Hunt, *The Invention of Pornography*, 132; Mayo, *Epicurus in England*, 200; Hunter, "Science and Heterodoxy," 449; and David Wooton, "New Histories of Atheism," in *Atheism from the Reformation to the Enlightenment*, ed. Michael Hunter and David Wooton (Oxford: Clarendon Press, 1992), 46.

104. Anon., *Eilon Basilike Deutera* (London, 1694), 2–3; quoted in Weil, "Sometimes a Scepter," 132–33.

105. On the links between Catholicism and the "atheistical" doctrine of state authority in religion, see Bredvold, *Intellectual Milieu*, 86n23; and Burnet, *History of His Own Time*, 1:342–43; 168–69.

106. On the continued commitment to religion in English radicalism, see n. 4 above.

107. Pocock, "Post-Puritan England," 97–98.

108. Ibid., 96.

109. Ibid., 95. Interestingly, as Pocock attests, Hobbes's positions were on many fronts indistinguishable from Harrington's. Despite the fact that the two men read the political legacy from the Israelites to the Romans to the Christian apostles very differently—the one saw the history of republics where the other saw the history of kingship and empire—both agreed that in all good government civic authority was (rightly) privileged. On Hobbes and civil religion, see Richard Tuck, "The Civil Religion of Thomas Hobbes," in Philipson and Skinner, *Political Discourse*, 120–38; and Tuck, "The 'Christian Atheism' of Thomas Hobbes," in *Atheism from the Reformation*, 111–38.

110. Skelton, *Ophiomaches*, 2:274; Alymer, "Unbelief in Seventeenth-Century England," 36. See the comment in *The Character of a Coffee-House* (London, 1673) that the genteel unbeliever appears in town with "three or four wilde Companions, half a dozen bottles of Burgundy, [and] two leaves of *Leviathan*" (4).

111. Robertson, *History of Freethought*, 2:617.

112. Hobbes, *De Cive*, in *Collected Works*, 2:xii. For the relationship between Harrington and Hobbes on the ancient model of civil religion, see also Champion, *Pillars of Priestcraft Shaken*, 180. On Hobbes's reliance on ancient sources for his notion of civil religion, see Tuck, " 'Christian Atheism' of Thomas Hobbes," 116, 125.

113. Hobbes, *De Copore Politico*, in *Collected Works*, 4:171.

114. Hobbes, *Leviathan*, 3.36.567–68. On the absence of a Christian notion of "belief" in ancient religion, see Jocelyn, "Roman Nobility," 92; Feeney, *Literature and Religion*, 12–46; and Glenn W. Most, "Philosophy and Religion," in *The Cambridge Companion to Greek and Roman Philosophy*, ed. David

Sedley (Cambridge: Cambridge University Press, 2003), 303. Feeney emphasizes rightly that "belief" as we tend to understand it "is a concept entirely specific to European Christian culture" (12).

115. Hobbes, *Leviathan*, 2.21.267, 266. It is important to note that elsewhere in *Leviathan* Hobbes very explicitly associates rebellion with "the Reading of the books of Policy, and Histories of the antient Greeks, and Romans," going so far as to suggest that such books should not be allowed in a monarchy (2.29.369). He suggests, however, that those who find a license to kill kings from reading the ancients are in need of a correcting view.

116. Warburton, *Divine Legation*, 307–8. Champion acknowledges the reliance of eighteenth-century freethinking on Hobbes's anticlericalism but does not pursue the implications of the relationship between the two (see *Pillars of Priestcraft Shaken*, 174–75, 180).

117. John Toland, *Pantheisticon* [1751] (New York: Garland, 1976), 99, 100. Pocock notes the paradoxical way in which Toland is both the heir of the Puritans and the deistical foe of the prophetic tradition (*The Machiavellian Moment* [Princeton, NJ: Princeton University Press, 1975], 403). On Toland's disdain for the politics of the Civil War radicals, see Kramnick, *Bolingbroke and His Circle*, 258.

118. Pocock, "Post-Puritan England," 109; Pocock, *The Machiavellian Moment*, 401–61; Issac Kramnick, *Bolingbroke and His Circle*, 236–60; Christopher Hill, *Reformation to Industrial Revolution: A Social and Economic History of Britain, 1530–1780* (London: Weidenfeld & Nicolson, 1967), 174; Jacob, *The Radical Enlightenment*, 95.

119. Kramnick, *Bolingbroke and His Circle*, 205–35, 260.

120. Ibid., 243–44, 249–50.

121. Although Jacob's discussion of Tory radicalism includes religion, she argues that the Tory opposition is "piously Anglican" and therefore separate from "the freethinking and radical Whigs" (*The Radical Enlightenment*, 95).

122. See Wilson, "The Enlightenment Came First to England," 1–28; and Porter, *The Creation of the Modern World: The Untold Story of the British Enlightenment*.

123. Thompson, "Peculiarities of the English," 267. For recent efforts to link the republican heritage of the English 1640s to the radical critiques of religion in eighteenth-century France, see esp. Champion, " 'May the last king be strangled in the bowels of the last priest': Irreligion and the English Enlightenment, 1649–1789," in Morton and Smith, *Radicalism in British Literary Culture*, 29–44.

Notes to Chapter One

1. Turner, "Properties of Libertinism," 76. Larry Carver notes that the debate over Rochester's faith "began the day [he] died and . . . has continued on into criticism" ("Rascal before the Lord: Rochester's Religious Rhetoric," in *John Wilmot, Earl of Rochester: Critical Essays*, ed. David M. Vieth [New York:

Garland, 1988], 108n2). For the view that Rochester was more conventionally Christian than has typically been thought, see also Vivian deSola Pinto, *Enthusiast in Wit* (Lincoln: University of Nebraska Press, 1962), 185–226; Kenneth Murdock, "A Very Profane Wit," in *The Sun at Noon: Three Biographical Sketches* (New York: Macmillan, 1939), 269–306; and George Williamson, *The Proper Wit of Poetry* (Chicago: University of Chicago Press, 1961), 126.

2. Jonathan Kramnick, "Rochester and the History of Sexuality," 283.

3. See especially Marianne Thormählen, "Dissolver of Reason: Rochester and the Nature of Love," in Fisher, *That Second Bottle*, 21–34.

4. Gillian Manning, "Rochester's *Satyr against Reason and Mankind* and Contemporary Religious Debate," *The Seventeenth Century* 8 (1993): 107. For the poem's immediate context of religious debate, see also David Trotter, "Wanton Expressions," in *Spirit of Wit*, ed. Jeremy Treglown (Hamden, CT: Archon Books, 1982), 111–32; Kristoffer F. Paulson, "The Reverend Edward Stillingfleet and the 'Epilogue' to Rochester's *A Satyr against Reason and Mankind*," *Philological Quarterly* 50 (1971): 657–63; Marianne Thormählen, *Rochester: The Poems in Context* (New York: Cambridge University Press, 1993), 167–74; and Dustin Griffin, *Satires Against Man* (Berkeley: University of California Press, 1973), 183–88. On the poem's reception in the period more generally, see Nicholas Fisher, "The Contemporary Reception of Rochester's *A Satyr Against Mankind*," *RES* 57 (2006): 185–205.

5. Reba Wilcoxon affirms that the "Satyre" rejects Christian eschatology, a position seen to be inspired by the Epicurean critique of religion, but her discussion of the poem generally neglects theology in favor of philosophy. Though the poem's animus against rationalism is acknowledged to include "the unverifiable concepts of religion" and "the fear engendered by religion," these latter insights are not elaborated upon, nor are they traced out more substantively in the genealogy of intellectual precursors reviewed (see "Rochester's Philosophical Premises: A Case for Consistency," *Eighteenth-Century Studies* 8 [1974]: 192, 197). Griffin connects the "Satyre"'s attack on reason and its theriophilia to a philosophically heterodox tradition, but such heterodoxy is explained merely as "bodies of thought [that] ranged themselves against the official position of the Anglican and Catholic churches" (*Satires*, 162, 163–68). Finally, in Thormählen's extensive discussion of the poem's influences, while Hobbes is acknowledged to be an atheist in the eyes of Rochester's contemporaries and the presence of his thinking in the "Satyre" is confirmed, no attempt is made to consider the question of Rochester's infidelity or how it may have been informed by Hobbes. The influence of Montaigne and the skeptics is treated similarly (*Rochester*, 174, 175, 360–61; 183–84, 201).

6. John Wilmot, *The Works of John Wilmot, Earl of Rochester*, ed. Harold Love (Oxford: Oxford University Press, 1999). All subsequent references to Rochester's poetry will follow Love's edition of the poems and be cited by line number in the body of the text.

7. Trotter, "Wanton Expressions," 111–12; Griffin, *Satires*, 201; Hobbes, *Works*, 5:304; Trotter, "Wanton Expressions," 111; Edward Stillingfleet, *Fifty Sermons Preached upon Several Occasions*, in *The works of that Eminent and*

Most Learned Prelate, Dr. Edw. Stillingfleet, Late Lord Bishop of Worcester, 6 vols. (London, 1710), 1:227.

8. See Manning, "Rochester's *Satyr*"; Thormählen, *Rochester*, 171–73; and Griffin, *Satires*, 182–96.

9. Manning, "Rochester's *Satyr*," 103–6.

10. See John Spurr, "'Rational Religion' in Restoration England," *Journal of the History of Ideas* 49 (1988): 563–85; and Stephen, *History of English Thought*, 1:86–92.

11. Stillingfleet, *Fifty Sermons*, 1:227.

12. The Christian humanist tradition had long championed what it called "right reason" as a divinely implanted guide. The later seventeenth century, however, witnessed the divorce of the realms of knowledge and virtue. Even Anglicanism was influenced by reason's newly natural and pragmatic function (see Spurr, "Rational Religion," 570–71).

13. John Standish, *A Sermon Preached before the King at White-Hal, Septem. the 26ᵗʰ, 1675* (London, 1676), 25; Joseph Glanvill, *Logou Threskeia: or, A Seasonable Recommendation, and Defence of Reason, in the Affairs of Religion* (London, 1674), 29, 23; Henry Hallywell, preface to *A Discourse of the Use of Reason in Matters of Religion*, by George Rust (London, 1683), 49.

14. Paulson has argued that this final section (lines 174–225), which in early manuscripts was often circulated as a separate poem (see Wilmot, *Works*, 393n173.2), was composed at a later date than the rest and intended as a rebuttal to Edward Stillingfleet's attack on the "Saytre" ("The Reverend Edward Stillingfleet"). His findings are thought to be inconclusive (see Manning, "Rochester's *Satyr*," 116n6).

15. See Thomas H. Fujimura, "Rochester's 'Satyr against Mankind': An Analysis," in *Attribution in Restoration Poetry: A Study of Rochester's Poems of 1680*, ed. David M. Vieth (New Haven, CT: Yale University Press, 1963), 216–17; and Griffin, *Satires*, 206, 241.

16. Bentley, "Sermon IX," 307–8.

17. See Pinto, *Enthusiast*, 157–58, for the view that the speaker's conditional recantation signals a desire to embrace faith as traditionally defined. My reading of these lines also differs from Thormählen's argument that the speaker would agree to obey a truly pious churchman, not because he shares the latter's faith, but rather because his senses would inform him of the existence of one who is worthy of receiving his subservience (*Rochester*, 237). It is notable that John Toland's deist manifesto, *Christianity Not Mysterious*, similarly pledged deference to an authentically pious churchman. Toland writes: "To all corrupt Clergymen therefore, who make a meer Trade of Religion, and build an unjust Authority upon the abus'd Consciences of the Laity, I'm a profest Adversary. But as I shall always remain a hearty Friend to pure and genuine Religion, so I shall preserve the highest Veneration for the sincere Teachers thereof, than whom there is not a more useful Order of Men, and without whom there could not be any happy Society or well constituted Government in this World" (*Christianity Not Mysterious*, 2nd ed. [London, 1696], xxx).

18. Manning, "Rochester's *Satyr*," 102.

19. Hill, "Freethinking and Libertinism," 61. See also Hill, *The Collected Essays of Christopher Hill*, 3 vols. (Amherst: University of Massachusetts Press, 1985), 1:298–316; Hill, *The World Turned Upside Down: Radical Ideas during the English Revolution* (New York: Penguin, 1975), 197–230. For a view similar to Hill's on the continuity between radical religion in the Interregnum and the Restoration, see George L. Mosse, "Puritan Radicalism and the Enlightenment," *Church History* 29 (1960): 424–39; and Roger L. Emerson, "Heresy, the Social Order, and English Deism," *Church History* 37 (1968): 389–403.

20. By "enthusiastic" I refer to the radical sects' subversive claims to a personal divine inspiration, one whose content was often opposed to the revealed religion sanctioned by Scripture and institutionalized religion.

21. Turner, "Properties of Libertinism," 80. Francis Fane, dedication to *Love in the Dark* (1675), in *Rochester: The Critical Heritage*, ed. David Farley-Hills (London: Routledge, 1972), 37, quoted in Turner, "Properties of Libertinism," 79, and Hill, *Collected Essays*, 1:303.

22. J. G. A. Pocock, "Enthusiasm: The Antiself of Enlightenment," in *Enthusiasm and Enlightenment in Europe, 1650–1850*, ed. Lawrence E. Klein and Anthony J. La Vopa (San Marino, CA: Huntington Library, 1998), 14, 16, 18; Pocock, "Thomas Hobbes: Atheist or Enthusiast? His Place in a Restoration Debate," *History of Political Thought* 11 (1990): 737–49; Ralph Cudworth, *The True Intellectual System of the Universe* (London, 1678), 134; Glanvill, *Logou*, 30–31.

23. Turner, "Properties of Libertinism," 78. On the distinction between sectarian heresy and skeptical irreligion, see Hunter, "Problem of 'Atheism,'" 136–37.

24. Hill, *Collected Essays*, 1:301, 1:298.

25. Turner, "Properties of Libertinism," 80; see also Turner, *Libertines*, 45–46, 120, 225.

26. See John Locke, *An Essay concerning Human Understanding*, ed. Peter H. Nidditch (Oxford: Clarendon Press, 1975), 4.19.9.

27. See Griffin, *Satires*, 186–88, 211; Thormählen, *Rochester*, 194; Wilcoxon, "Rochester's Philosophical Premises," 193.

28. The latitudinarian movement in Anglicanism eventually abandoned its platonist element, but Rochester here refers to a moment when the two were unified in the fight against enthusiasm on the one side and atheism on the other (see Joseph M. Levine, "Latitudinarians, Neoplatonists, and the Ancient Wisdom," in *Philosophy, Science, and Religion in England, 1640–1700*, ed. Richard Kroll, Richard Ashcraft, and Perez Zagorin [Cambridge: Cambridge University Press, 1992], 85–101; Frederick C. Beiser, *The Sovereignty of Reason* [Princeton, NJ: Princeton University Press, 1996], 139, 169–72; and J. G. A. Pocock, "Within the Margins: Definitions of Orthodoxy," in Lund, *Margins of Orthodoxy*, 45).

29. Manning, "Rochester's *Satyr*," 111.

30. See S. F. Crocker, "Rochester's 'Satire against Mankind': A Study of Certain Aspects of the Background," *West Virginia University Studies* 3 (1937): 57–73; Fujimura, "Rochester's 'Satyr'"; Wilcoxon, "Rochester's Philosophical Premises"; Thormählen, *Rochester*, 174–84; and Griffin, *Satires*, 162–73. On

Montaigne's influence on the Restoration libertines, see Bredvold, *Milieu*, 34. On Montaigne as a source for English deism more generally, see Orr, *English Deism*, 45–47.

31. Montaigne, *Works*, 2.12.380.

32. Ibid., 2.12.337; 2.12.321.

33. Hobbes, *Works*, 4:181–82; 4:171; 4:182; Hobbes, *Leviathan*, 3.36.469.

34. On the evils of sectarian strife in England, Montaigne comments: "I have seen [the laws] of our neighbors the English change three or four times; not only in political matters, in which people want to dispense with constancy, but in the most important subject that can be, to wit, religion" (*Works*, 2.12.436).

35. Hobbes's influence on Rochester's thinking about reason thus has implications that reach well beyond epistemology—the emphasis of most accounts of the relationship between the two figures (see Fujimura, "Rochester's 'Satyr,' "206–7; Wilcoxon, "Rochester's Philosophical Premises," 194–95; Thormählen, *Rochester*, 174–78; and Griffin, *Satires*, 168–69).

36. See Edward Herbert, *Pagan Religions: A Translation of 'De Religione Gentilium'* (Ottawa: Dovehouse Editions, 1996), 52, 302–38.

37. Hobbes, *Works*, 4:174.

38. On deism's tendency to reduce religion to a set of simple, common notions, see D. P. Walker, *The Ancient Theology: Studies in Christian Platonism from the Fifteenth to the Eighteenth Century* (Ithaca, NY: Cornell University Press, 1972), 165; Lovejoy, "The Parallel of Deism and Classicism," 204–5.

39. Though Manning refers to contemporaries' use of the term "deism" to describe the religion of the unbelievers ("Rochester's *Satyr*," 102), she does not explore the specificities of this particular tradition or its presence in Rochester's poem.

40. Hill, *Collected Essays*, 1:309.

41. See Robertson, *Dynamics of Religion*, 65–66; Robertson, *History of Freethought*, 2:630, 634.

42. Charles Blount, *Anima Mundi* (London, 1679), A4^v; Hallywell, preface to *Discourse*, A1.

43. Samuel Parker, preface to *Bishop Bramhall's Vindication of Himself*, by John Bramhall (London, 1672), D7^v; Robert South, "A Sermon Preached at Westminster-Abbey, April 30, 1676," in *Twelve Sermons Preached upon Several Occasions* (London, 1692), 439; Allestree, "Sermon X," 179; [Joseph Glanvill], *An Apology and Advice for Some of the Clergy* (London, 1674), 4–6; William Owtram, *Twenty Sermons Preached upon Several Occasions*, 2nd ed. (London, 1681), A5 (italics mine).

44. For Rochester's correspondence with Blount, see Jeremy Treglown, ed., *The Letters of John Wilmot, Earl of Rochester* (Oxford: Basil Blackwell, 1980), 206–16, 234–41. Charles Blount, *Philostratus*, 227. Blount runs together lines 1–34, 76–77, and 80–97 of Rochester's "Satyre." My reading differs from Joseph Levine's, which sees Blount's *Philostratus* and deism generally as resting religion on reason (see "Deists and Anglicans: The Ancient Wisdom and the Idea of Progress," in Lund, *Margins of Orthodoxy*, 228, 230).

45. See Harth, *Contexts for Dryden's Thought*, 75; Pinto, *Enthusiast*, 152.

46. Stephen, *History of English Thought*, 1:79. On the elevation of reason in moderate or "Christian deism," see also Israel, *Radical Enlightenment*, 471–73.

47. As Margaret Wiley argues, Herbert's view that all historical religions were partly true and partly false suggests "the best tradition of genuine scepticism, which is opposed to both dogmatic disbelief and dogmatic belief" (*The Subtle Knot: Creative Scepticism in Seventeenth-Century England* [Cambridge, MA: Harvard University Press, 1952], 98).

48. Herbert, *Pagan Religions*, 54, 55.

49. John Leland, *A View of the Principal Deistical Writers that Have Appeared in England in the Last and Present Century* (London, 1754), 2.

50. Earbery, *Deism Examined and Confuted*, A6^v; Stillingfleet, *Letter to a Deist*, A3^v. On the clandestine circulation of the first Latin editions of Spinoza's *Tractatus* among the nobility, see Israel, *Radical Enlightenment*, 279. On Spinoza and the aristocracy generally, see Popkin, "The Deist Challenge," 209. Israel suggests that "fear of philosophical deism and atheism gained added intensity in the mid-1670s with the arrival in Britain of batches of Spinoza's *Tractatus*" (*Radical Enlightenment*, 603).

51. Spinoza, *Theological-Political Treatise*, 6, 169. For the argument that Rochester was familiar with the writings of Spinoza, see Pinto, *Enthusiast*, 199–200; and Berman, *History of Atheism*, 55.

52. [Charles Blount], *Miracles, No Violations of the Laws of Nature* (London, 1683), iv.

53. Bentley, *Folly of Atheism*, 5–6. Stephens's *Account of the Growth of Deism in England* also contends that "some who pretend themselves Deists" are "meer Sceptics, and practical Atheists, rather than real Deists" (5). Not surprisingly, one of the defining differences between real and counterfeit deists in both Bentley's and Stephens's view is the respective deist's attitude toward reason. Bentley's deists/atheists significantly "are not led astray by their Reasoning." Reckless and debased scoffers in the eyes of their opponents, they are rather "led captive by their Lusts" (*Folly of Atheism*, 14). Whereas Stephens's sham deists "ridicule the reality of all Miracle and Revelation," replacing serious debate with "a witty Jest," his authentic deists, though also skeptical about revelation, are at least "Men of Sobriety and Probity, who with great freedom have let me into their Thoughts, whereby I can very clearly and fully . . . discern the rise and progress of this their Opinion" (*Account*, 5).

54. Bentley, *Folly of Atheism*, 5; Pierre Viret, quoted in Pierre Bayle, *The Dictionary Historical and Critical of Mr. Peter Bayle*, 5 vols., 2nd ed. (London, 1734–38), 482nD. On the rejection of Providence in "Epicurean" deism, see also Samuel Clarke, *A Discourse concerning the Unchangeable Obligations of Natural Religion* [1706] (Stuttgart-Bad Cannstatt: F. Frommann, 1964), 19.

55. See Robertson, *History of Freethought*, 1:198.

56. This is Rochester's translation of Lucretius, *De rerum natura*, 2:646–51.

57. Gilbert Burnet, *Some Passages of the Life and Death of the Right Honourable John, Earl of Rochester* (London, 1692), 52, 72; Lucretius, *De rerum natura. The Way Things Are*, trans. Rolfe Humphries (Bloomington: Indiana University Press, 1968), 1:149–50.

58. Montaigne, *Works*, 1.23.80.

59. Ibid., 2.12.391, 393, 394.

60. Like Montaigne, Blount traces theriophilia back to its roots in antiquity, explaining that "the Heathens [did not] perceive any considerable difference betwixt us and other Creatures, than what is occasion'd by speach [*sic*] and use of letters" (*Anima Mundi*, 40). On theriophilia in ancient philosophy, see also Arthur O. Lovejoy and George Boas, *Primitivism and Related Ideas in Antiquity* (Baltimore: Johns Hopkins University Press, 1997), 389–420.

61. Montaigne, *Works*, 2.12.336. Montaigne cites the following lines from Lucretius: "And all things go their own way, nor forget / Distinctions by the law of nature set" (Lucretius, *De rerum natura*, 5.921–22; cited in Montaigne, *Works*, 2.12.336).

62. Montaigne, *Works*, 2.12.331, 336. On the anti-Christian implications of Montaigne's critique of an anthropocentric universe, see Walker, *Ancient Theology*, 139–41; and George Boas, *The Happy Beast in French Thought of the Seventeenth Century* (Baltimore: Johns Hopkins University Press, 1933), 9.

63. Montaigne, *Works*, 2.12.346. As Montaigne observes, Plato's account of the advantages of the golden age extols the communication that man then enjoyed with beasts. Learning from their example, man "acquired a very perfect intelligence and prudence, and conduct[ed] his life far more happily than we could possibly do [now]" (2.12.331).

64. The speaker of Rochester's "Tunbridge Wells" praises his horse in similar terms: "For he doing only things fitt for his nature / Did seem to me, by much, the wiser Creature" (185–86).

65. Spinoza, *Theological-Political Treatise*, 72; 74 (italics mine).

66. See Bentley, *Folly of Atheism*, 6, for contemporaries' view that the extreme apartness of the Epicurean deities was a ruse intended to leave nature as the sole force in the universe. As Robert South remarks, the "Old Heathen Philosophers . . . adore[d] Eternity, and Immensity in a Brute, or a Plant, or some viler thing" ("Natural Religion, without Revelation," in *Twelve Sermons Preached upon Several Occasions*, 2 vols. [London, 1697], 2:288, 290).

67. Hobbes, *Leviathan*, 1.12.171.

68. See Thomas Tenison, *The Creed of Mr. Hobbes Examined*, 2nd ed. (London, 1671), 12; Anne Conway, *The Principles of the Most Ancient and Modern Philosophy*, ed. Peter Loptson (Boston: Martinus Nijhoff, 1982), 222; Pocock, "Thomas Hobbes," 742, 745; and Rosalie L. Colie, "Spinoza and the Early English Deists," *Journal of the History of Ideas* 20 (1959): 37–38.

69. Bentley, *Folly*, 8–9; Burnet, *Some Passages*, 54, 52, 22.

70. Charles Blount, *Anima Mundi*, 128, 129, 132, 131.

71. Ibid., 132.

72. Montaigne, *Works*, 2.12.369.

73. Ibid., 2.12.374.

74. Charles Blount, *Anima Mundi*, 103.

75. Charles Blount, *Anima Mundi*, 76. See also Blount's claim in the same

text: "I shall not too confidently oppose a Doctrine, which hath been so long entertain'd in the World" (50).

76. Ibid., 128–29.

77. See Rochester's translation from Seneca's *Troades*, reprinted in Blount's *Philostratus*:

> After Death nothing is, and nothing Death,
> The utmost limit of a Gasp of Breath.
> Let the ambitious Zealot lay aside
> His hopes of Heaven; whose Faith is but his Pride.
> Let slavish Souls lay by their Fear,
> Nor be concern'd which way, nor where,
> After this Life they shall be hurl'd;
> Dead, we become the Lumber of the World.
> ("Senec. Troas. Act. 2. Chor.," 1–8)

78. Charles Blount to Rochester, 7 February 1680, in Wilmot, *Letters*, 239–40.

79. Burnet, *Some Passages*, 53, 72–73, 78.

80. Ibid., 23, 35.

81. Ibid., 126, also 44–45.

82. Ibid., 70.

83. Ibid., 51, 65; also 68, 70, 71, 120, 125.

84. Wilmot, *Works*, 395n219.

85. Burnet, *Some Passages*, 100, 69.

86. For the gloss on "prelacy," see Wilmot, *Works*, 394n193; Mark Goldie, "Danby, the Bishops and the Whigs," in *The Politics of Religion in Restoration England*, ed. Tim Harris, Paul Seaward, and Mark Goldie (Oxford: Basil Blackwell, 1990), 80.

87. [Charles Blount], *An Appeal from the Country to the City; for the Preservation of His Majesties Person, Liberty, Property, and the Protestant Religion* (London, 1679), 5. On Blount's argument that the Popish Plot, and its hopes to reestablish absolute monarchy in England, was as much a threat to Charles's power as it was to his subjects' liberty, see Redwood, "Charles Blount," 491. See also Goldie's argument that Shaftesbury's and Buckingham's allies, of whom Rochester and Blount appear to have been two, supported exclusion in 1679–81 "because it would preserve intact the civil supremacy over the church" ("Danby," 89–90).

88. Rochester complained to Burnet that the positing of mysteries in religion "made way for all the Juglings of Priests, for they getting the People under them in that Point, set out to them what they pleased; and giving it a hard Name, and calling it a *Mystery*, the People were tamed, and easily believed it" (Burnet, *Some Passages*, 100). See also his translation of Seneca's *Troades*, in which he argues that future punishments are "Devis'd by Rogues" and "dreaded by Fools" ("Senec. Troas. Act. 2. Chor.," 15).

89. On the politics of "In the Isle of Brittain," see Harold Love, *English Clandestine Satire, 1660–1702* (New York: Oxford University Press, 2004), 59–60.

90. Buckingham seconds this view in a letter to Rochester of 1677 (see "To Rochester from Buckingham," August 1677, in Wilmot, *Rochester's Letters*, 148–49). A similar critique is suggested by Dryden's Absalom in "Absalom and Achitophel" (1681), in which the rebel complains of Charles that "all his pow'r against himself employs" (*Works*, 2:712).

91. Charles Blount, *Philostratus*, 160. I owe this translation from Blount's Latin to Scott McGill. See Montaigne on Pythagoras' skepticism: "Pythagoras came closest to the truth, holding that the knowledge of this first cause and being of beings must be indefinite, without prescription, without declaration" (*Apology*, 75). Charles Blount, *Anima Mundi*, 76.

92. Coleridge famously coined the phrase "the willing suspension of disbelief" in describing the specific character of "poetic faith" (see *Biographia Literaria; or, Biographical Sketches of My Literary Life and Opinions*, ed. James Engell and W. Jackson Bate [Princeton, NJ: Princeton University Press, 1984], 314). Though my use of the phrase in this book is thus strictly speaking anachronistic, the concept itself dates back to antiquity and crucially informs the hoary tradition of the pious fraud: Ovid's conviction that "it is convenient that there should be gods; and, since it is convenient, let us think they exist" requires the same processes of mind implied by Coleridge (Ovid, *Ars amatoria*, trans. J. H. Mozley [Cambridge, MA: Harvard University Press, 1962], 1, 637). For the Enlightenment uses of the concept, see Addison's discussion of the revaluation of legends, prejudices, and superstitions in imaginative writing: "Many," he writes, "are prepossest with such false Opinions, as dispose them to believe these particular Delusions; at least, we have all heard so many pleasing Relations in favour of them, that *we do not care for seeing through the Falshood, and willingly give our selves up to so agreeable an Imposture*" (no. 419 in *The Spectator*, 3:571–72; italics mine). For an extended discussion of the concept of suspended disbelief in the Enlightenment, see McKeon, "Tacit Knowledge: Tradition and Its Aftermath," in Phillips and Schochet, *Questions of Tradition*, 188–96; McKeon, "Historicizing Absalom and Achitophel," in *The New Eighteenth Century*, ed. Felicity Nussbaum and Laura Brown (New York: Methuen, 1987), 23–40; and McKeon, "Politics of Discourses," 35–51.

93. Burnet, *Some Passages*, 120.

94. On enthusiasm and class anxiety, see Hawes, *Mania and Literary Style*, 25–49; and Michael Heyd, "The Reaction to Enthusiasm in the Seventeenth Century," *Journal of Modern History* 53 (1981): 278.

95. See Rochester's alleged comment to Robert Parsons on his deathbed that "the late Mr. Hobbs, and others, had undone him, and many more, of the best parts in the Nation" (*A Sermon Preach'd at the Funeral of the Rt. Honorable John Earl of Rochester* [London, 1707], 15). My reading of Hobbes's influence on English deism differs from Israel's recent claim that the deists preferred Spinoza's more radical republican leanings to Hobbes's absolutism (Israel, *Radical Enlightenment*, 601–3; see also Colie, "Spinoza," 30–31). While Israel is right to emphasize Spinoza's impact on English freethinking, I would argue that he makes English deism too simply radical, neglecting its contradictory conservative tendencies. Hobbes, as I suggest, is suitably radical and conservative and

thus especially compelling to a figure like Rochester. Moreover, the aristocratic freethinkers seemed to have had little trouble adapting Spinoza to a less than fully radical agenda.

96. Lovejoy, "Parallel of Deism and Classicism," 88; William Wotton, *Reflections upon Ancient and Modern Learning* [1694] (Hildesheim: Georg Olms, 1968), 322–23; J. G. A. Pocock, "Conservative Enlightenment and Democratic Revolutions: The American and French Cases in British Perspective," *Government and Opposition* 24 (1989): 87.

Notes to Chapter Two

1. On Fontenelle's surreptitious connection to the radical Enlightenment, see Israel, *Radical Enlightenment*, 359.

2. Although the myth of a golden age was a staple topos of the pastoral poetry so popular among Behn's contemporaries, we must remember that pastoral was a pagan, not a Christian, genre. Though the moderns attempted to Christianize the pastoral, to many it was clear that the myth of the golden age conflicted with the Christian myth of Eden and placed too much emphasis on man's natural instincts ever to be reconciled with the quest for spiritual righteousness. On the pastoral's incompatibility with Christianity, see Levin, *Myth of the Golden Age*, xv; and Renato Poggioli, *The Oaten Flute: Essays on Pastoral Poetry and the Pastoral Ideal* (Cambridge, MA: Harvard University Press, 1975), 16, 19, 21. On the link between pastoral poetry and sexual hedonism, see Poggioli, *Oaten Flute*, 1–63; also Thomas G. Rosenmeyer, *The Green Cabinet* (Berkeley: University of California Press, 1969), 77–85. On the golden age and the pagan roots of libertinism, see Young, *Eros Denied*, 255–56; and Levin, *Myth of the Golden Age*, xvi, 46–50. The fact that no French model has yet been discovered for Behn's paraphrase of Tasso (the full title of Behn's poem is "The Golden Age: A Paraphrase on a Translation out of French") suggests that Behn may have followed a clandestine manuscript translation that circulated among like-minded freethinkers (see Germaine Greer, "*Ame in Liberate Avvezze*: Aphra Behn's Version of Tasso's Golden Age," in *Aphra Behn (1640–1689): Identity, Alterity, Ambiguity*, ed. Mary Ann O'Donnell, B. Dhuicq, and Guyonne Leduc [Paris: Harmattan, 2000], 229–30).

3. Behn's "The Golden Age" departs from Tasso's *Aminta* in two crucial respects. First, she explicitly links sexual freedom to religious freedom and, second, she writes as a man addressing his lover.

4. On the theme of male sexual inconstancy, see Behn's poem "To Alexis in Answer to His Poem against Fruition. Ode." Octavio, the Dutch nobleman who becomes Sylvia's lover in part 3 of *Love-Letters* stands as an important exception to this rule. Indeed, when Octavio argues, like Philander before him, against the sanctity of the marriage vow, "all he spoke was honourable Truth" (2:280).

5. On Behn's involvement in the libertine scene in London, see Todd, *Secret Life*, 290, 433, 470n14.

6. On mechanism in Behn's poem "On a Juniper-Tree, Cut Down to Make

Busks," see Alvin Snider, "Cartesian Bodies," *Modern Philology* 98 (2000): 299–319.

7. Todd, *Secret Life*, 291.

8. Creech was scandalized by Behn's audaciously irreligious attitude, and he changed the more subversive lines of her tribute to conform to orthodox Christianity (Todd, *Secret Life*, 296–97). In the unbowdlerized version, Behn daringly lauds reason's powers to conquer "Beyond poor Feeble Faith's dull Oracles" (1:56), asserting that man worshipped Gods and kings "for fear" and "safety" (1:73–74).

9. Wolseley writes: "Tis truly observed by a learned Author, that the first Atheism we hear of in the world, was in the most blind and superstitious age of Greece. . . . Then it was, (and not till then) that men began to set their wits on work, to solve the Phaenomena of nature without any Deity at all, and derive the world (in its original) from a fortuitous concourse of an infinite company of little particles, which we call Atoms" (*Unreasonableness of Atheism*, 38–39).

10. Quoted in Dale Underwood, *Etherege and the Seventeenth-Century Comedy of Manners* (New Haven, CT: Yale University Press, 1957), 15.

11. The libertine reception of Hobbes is treated with similar condescension: "The Rattle of [*Leviathan*] at Coffee-houses, has taught [the libertine] to Laugh at Spirits, and maintain that there are no Angels but those in Petticoats" (*Character of a Town-Gallant*, 7); see also *Character of a Coffee-House*, 5. This attitude has persisted to the current moment. In his discussion of libertinism's philosophical context, Dale Underwood argues that libertines culled from the philosophical tradition what they thought would support their ethic of sensualism, often distorting complex traditions of thought in the process (*Etherege*, 15–16).

12. Thomas Creech, *T. Lucretius Carus, the Epicurean Philosopher, His Six Books "De Natura Rerum,"* 2nd ed. (Oxford, 1683), A 4; Glanvill, *Seasonable Reflections*, 5; Ellis, *Vanity of Scoffing*, 30. See also Bentley, *Folly of Atheism*, 14; and John Tillotson, *Sermons Preach'd upon Several Occasions* (London, 1671), 88, 104.

13. John Fell, *The Character of the Last Daies* (Oxford, 1675), 16; Wolseley, *Unreasonableness of Atheism*, 37; see also Edwards, *Some Thoughts*, 28–29. By 1704 philosophical freethinking had become a fully established menace in its own right, and one that surpassed the threat of the libertine scoffers. In a taxonomy of atheisms, Samuel Clarke's Boyle Lecture of that year distinguishes between those unbelievers who are "extremely ignorant and stupid," those who are "totally debauched and corrupted in their practice," and those who embrace "speculative reasoning and . . . the principles of philosophy." Significantly, his lecture is directed to "the third sort of atheists only" (*A Demonstration of the Being and Attributes of God*, ed. Ezio Vailati (Cambridge: Cambridge University Press, 1998), 3–4.

14. Line Cottegnies, "Aphra Behn's French Translations," in *The Cambridge Companion to Aphra Behn*, ed. Derek Hughes and Janet Todd (New York: Cambridge University Press, 2004), 221–34, 228.

15. In her translator's preface, Behn remarks that the Marquise "say[s] a great

many very silly things, tho' sometimes she makes Observations so learned, that the greatest Philosophers in Europe could make no better" (*Works*, 4:77). Behn's translations of Fontenelle have received little critical attention and minimal examination of their freethinking content. For an astute summary of some of their heterodox elements, see Cottegnies, "Aphra Behn's French Translations," 221–42; and Cottegnies, "The Translator as Critic: Aphra Behn's Translation of Fontenelle's *Discovery of New Worlds*," *Restoration* 27 (2003): 23–38. For other criticism on Behn's translations, see Sarah Goodfellow, " 'Such Masculine Strokes': Aphra Behn as Translator of *A Discovery of New Worlds*," *Albion* 28 (1996): 229–50; Robert Adams Day, "Aphra Behn and the Works of the Intellect," in *Fetter'd or Free? British Women Novelists, 1670–1815*, ed. Mary Anne Schofield and Cecilia Macheski (Athens: Ohio University Press, 1986), 372–82; and Mirella Agorni, "The Voice of the 'Translatress': From Aphra Behn to Elizabeth Carter," *Yearbook of English Studies* 28 (1998): 181–95.

16. On the links between Copernicanism and philosophical radicalism, see Israel, *Radical Enlightenment*, 27–28. On the irreligious implications of Copernicanism, see Hill, "Irreligion in the 'Puritan' Revolution," 204.

17. Lucretius, *The Way Things Are*, 2:1055–56, 2:1089–91, 2:1094–95.

18. See Boyle, *Free Enquiry*, esp. 39–40.

19. Richard Bentley, *The Works of Richard Bentley*, ed. Alexander Dyce, 3 vols. (London, 1836–38), 3:74. On the reconciliation of science and theology in the period, see Jacob, *The Radical Enlightenment*, 70, 91–92; and Richard S. Westfall, *Science and Religion in Seventeenth-Century England* (New Haven, CT: Yale University Press, 1958), 80, 84.

20. Spinoza, *Theological-Political Treatise*, 72.

21. Westfall, *Science and Religion*, 89; see also James E. Force, "The Nature of Newton's 'Holy Alliance' between Science and Religion: From the Scientific Revolution to Newton (and Back Again)," in *Rethinking the Scientific Revolution*, ed. Margaret J. Osler (Cambridge: Cambridge University Press, 2000), 253–54.

22. Westfall, *Science and Religion*, 79; Barbara J. Shapiro, *John Wilkins, 1614–1672: An Intellectual Biography* (Berkeley: University of California Press, 1969), 237.

23. Shapiro, *John Wilkins*, 35, 38, 52. On Behn's reliance on Wilkins, see Todd, *Works*, 4:79n.

24. John Wilkins, *A Discovery of New Worlds*, 5th ed. (London, 1684), 118; Wilkins, *A Discourse concerning a New Planet*, 5th ed. (London, 1684), 144; Alexander Ross, *The New Planet no Planet* (London, 1646), 2.

25. Freethinkers commonly twisted the more moderate agenda of early scientific writing to their own purposes. Charles Blount, for example, cites Sprat's entirely mainstream attempt to limit the supernatural in his *History of the Royal Society* as support for his denial of miracles (see *Miracles*, 30).

26. For the orthodox position, see Bentley's "A Confutation of Atheism from the Origin and Frame of the World": "Nor do we count it any absurdity, that such a vast and immense universe should be made for the sole use of such mean and unworthy creatures as the children of men. For . . . the soul of one virtuous

and religious man is of greater worth and excellency than the sun and his planets, and all the stars in the world" (*Works*, 3:174).

27. Thomas Burnet, *The Sacred Theory of the Earth*, 3rd ed., 2 vols. (London, [1734]), 1:433, 438; Charles Blount, *Miracles*, 30, 5. On Burnet's link to Blount's circle, see John Redwood, *Reason, Ridicule and Religion* (London: Thames & Hudson, 1976), 118–20; also Thomas Browne, *Miracles Work's Above and Contrary to Nature* (London, 1683), 2–3, 5–9. Both Burnet and Blount, as well as Fontenelle, follow Spinoza's emphasis on man's ignorance of natural causes in their critiques of the miraculous. In *Sacred Theory*, Burnet remarks that "we often make use of [the Power Extraordinary of God] only to conceal our own Ignorance, or to save us the Trouble of inquiring into natural causes" (438–39). Blount similarly comments that men "very often fancy a certain extraordinary divine power in all Contingents which are unusual, and the natural Causes of which they do not comprehend, as if those Contingents certainly proceeded, not from the order of Nature, but from an immediate operation of God transcending or changing that order" (*Miracles*, 3).

28. Charles Blount's *Oracles of Reason* reproduces chapters 7 and 8 of Burnet's *Archiologie Philosophicae* (1692) as further evidence that Copernicanism discredits revealed religion. The fact that Moses' account of the Creation represents the sun as subservient to the earth proves that "it was not this Sacred Author's design to represent the beginning of the World, exactly according to the Physical Truth" (74).

29. Cottegnies, "Aphra Behn's French Translations," 224; Aphra Behn, *A Discovery of New Worlds* (London, 1688).

30. In anticipation of the objections of the pious, Fontenelle boldly claims, "But I have had a Respect, even to the most delicate Niceties of Religion, and would not be guilty of any thing that should shock it in a publick Work, though that Care were contrary to my Opinion. But that which will surprise you is, that Religion is not at all concerned in this System" (Behn, *Works*, 4:90).

31. See Jean Dietz Moss, *Novelties in the Heavens: Rhetoric and Science in the Copernican Controversy* (Chicago: University of Chicago Press, 1993), 45.

32. Israel, *Radical Enlightenment*, 461.

33. Westfall, *Science and Religion*, 80; Israel, *Radical Enlightenment*, 456, 459.

34. My reading of Behn's "Essay on Translated Prose" thus differs significantly from Goodfellow's claim that Behn is an orthodox defender of the faith and "part of a very old Christian tradition of reconciliation" (" 'Such Masculine Strokes,' " 247).

35. Charles Blount, *Miracles*, 1. Behn appears to have been familiar with the writings of both Blount and Burnet. Behn cites Burnet's *Sacred Theory of the Earth* as a precedent in Bible criticism toward the end of her translator's preface, declaring defensively that his work "incroaches as much, if not more, on the holy Scriptures" (4:85). Todd speculates that Behn may have been part of "an atheist conventicle" including Rochester, Blount, and other freethinking libertines of the period (see *Secret Life*, 470n14; also Feldwick and Nederman, " 'Religion Set the World at Odds,' " 218).

36. This separation of the provinces of faith and philosophy is not to be confused with the antiphilosophical strain of Christianity among the Church Fathers (see Harry Wolfson, *The Philosophy of the Church Fathers*, 2 vols., 3rd ed. [Cambridge, MA: Harvard University Press, 1970], 1:102–6). On other examples of an orthodox separation of faith and reason, see Bredvold, *Intellectual Milieu of John Dryden*, 20–27. As Bredvold points out, however, the Church condemned fideism—the position that faith alone leads us to truth—as early as 1348 (20).

37. Spinoza, *Theological-Political Treatise*, 80.

38. Ibid., 28, 83. On the particular significance of the Joshua miracle in Spinoza, see Leo Strauss, *Spinoza's Critique of Religion* (Chicago: University of Chicago Press, 1965), 137.

39. Charles Blount, *Oracles of Reason*, 8, 10.

40. Israel, *Radical Enlightenment*, 208, 455.

41. Charles Blount, *Oracles of Reason*, 54, 74. This was the position of Averroës, the founder of the double truth doctrine, who argued that "many of the first believers used to hold that Scripture has both an apparent and an inner meaning." Not only have the learned classes of all ages recognized this inner meaning, but they also appreciate and respect the importance of keeping it to themselves; for Averroës insists that if the scholars disclose the truth to the unlearned multitude, they are "summoning [them] to unbelief," adding that "he who summons to unbelief is an unbeliever" (Averroës, *On the Harmony of Religion and Philosophy*, trans. George F. Hourani [London: Gibb Memorial Trust, 1976], 52, 61).

42. Behn is nowhere explicit in her rejection of revealed religion. Todd argues that she makes use of "the double tone" as a reaction to Charles Blount's recent run-in with the censor (*Secret Life*, 398; on radical writing in a climate of persecution, see Strauss, *Persecution and the Art of Writing*). The fact that Wilkins served as an acceptably orthodox screen between Behn and Blount, Burnet, and Spinoza made her venture less dangerous. In his discussion of the theological controversy over Copernicanism, Wilkins had argued, before Spinoza's subversion, that "it were happy for us, if we could exempt Scripture from Philosophical Controversies" (*Discourse concerning a New Planet*, 21). Although his separation of theology and philosophy did not intend to jeopardize theology, Wilkins also cited the Joshua miracle as evidence of Scripture's tendency to refer to "the appearance of things, and the false opinion of the Vulgar," as opposed to natural causes (*Discourse concerning a New Planet*, 26; Shapiro, *John Wilkins*, 52–53). Blount, on the contrary, invokes the Joshua miracle to support his defense of Burnet's heterodox suggestion that Scripture is merely "a pious Allegory" (*Oracles of Reason*, 2, 8–10).

43. Hume articulates this position most memorably in his discussion "Of Miracles" in *An Enquiry concerning Human Understanding*. Of the pervasive accounts of supernatural occurrences in "the first histories of all nations," he writes that "we soon learn, that there is nothing mysterious or supernatural in the case, but that all proceeds from the usual propensity of mankind towards the marvelous, and that, though this inclination may at intervals receive a check from sense and learning, it can never be thoroughly extirpated from human

nature" (*Enquiry concerning Human Understanding*, ed. Tom L. Beauchamp [Oxford: Oxford University Press, 1999], 176).

44. Cottegnies, "Aphra Behn's French Translations," 230–31.

45. Aphra Behn, *The City Heiress*, in *Works*, 7:1.1.199–200.

46. A similar distrust of the fickle allegiances of the masses and their inability to follow reason is evident in *Oroonoko*, when the hero castigates his fellow slaves for their cowardice and failure to see through their rebellion (3:109).

47. Elliot Visconsi, "A Degenerate Race: English Barbarism in Aphra Behn's *Oroonoko* and *The Widow Ranter*," *ELH* 69 (2002): 674.

48. Manuel, *Eighteenth Century Confronts the Gods*, 19–22.

49. Other writings on paganism in the period include the English translation of Hugo Grotius, *Against Paganism, Judaism and Mahumentanism* (London, 1676); *A Dictionary of All Religions, Ancient and Modern* (London, 1704); John Turner, *An Attempt towards an Explanation of the Theology and Mythology of the Antient Pagans* (London, 1687); Howard, *History of Religion*; John Trenchard, *Natural History of Superstition* (London, 1709).

50. Manuel, *Eighteenth Century Confronts the Gods*, 21.

51. Popkin, "Deist Challenge," 196–99.

52. Manuel, *Eighteenth Century Confronts the Gods*, 50.

53. The preceding discussion is indebted to Jonathan Israel's recent account of the context surrounding Fontenelle's *Histoire des oracles* (see *Radical Enlightenment*, 359–73; also Manuel, *Eighteenth Century Confronts the Gods*, 41–53; A. B. Drachmann, *Atheism in Pagan Antiquity* ([London: Gyldendal, 1922], 141–42; and Spink, *French Free-Thought*, 285–88). For the first theological objection to Fontenelle's *Oracles*, see Jean-François Baltus, *Réponse à l'histoire des oracles de M. de Fontenelle* (Strasbourg, 1707). An anonymous translation of Baltus's critique appeared in English in 1709.

54. Jean-François Baltus, *An Answer to Mr. De Fontenelle's "History of Oracles"* (London, 1709), 5.

55. See also Sir Thomas Pope Blount's remark that "as to the common observation concerning the Decay of Oracles at the coming of our Blessed Saviour, 'tis but a meer Fancy" (*Essays on Several Subjects*, 3rd ed. [London, 1697], 17).

56. Herbert, *Pagan Religion*, 349, 299, 292, 349.

57. On Charles Blount's and Herbert's influence on Van Dale and Fontenelle, see Israel, *Radical Enlightenment*, 362–64. The first official edition of *A Dialogue between a Tutor and His Pupil* did not appear until 1768.

58. Herbert, *Dialogue*, 94, 42–43.

59. Ibid., 48.

60. Herbert, *Pagan Religion: A Translation of "De Religione Gentilium,"* ed. John Anthony Butler (Ottawa: Dovehouse Editions, 1996), 300.

61. Todd, *Secret Life*, 400.

62. The dedication was thus evidently written before the Glorious Revolution of 1688–89.

63. On the critique of Christianity in *Oroonoko*, see Janet Todd, *Gender, Art and Death* (Oxford: Polity Press, 1993), 44–48; Arlen Feldwick and Cary J. Nederman, " 'Religion Set the World at Odds': Deism and the Climate of Reli-

gious Tolerance in the Works of Aphra Behn," in *Beyond the Persecuting Society: Religious Toleration before the Enlightenment*, ed. John Christian Laursen and Cary J. Nederman (Philadelphia: University of Pennsylvania Press, 1998), 223–27; and Laura J. Rosenthal, "*Oroonoko*: Reception, Ideology, and Narrative Strategy," in Hughes, *Cambridge Companion*, 162–64. Behn's emphasis in *Oroonoko* on pagan over Christian virtue may have been influenced by Machiavelli's argument that the ancients were "greater lovers of liberty" because they valued worldly over other-worldly honor (*Discourses on Livy*, ed. and trans. Julia Conaway Bondanella and Peter Bondanella [New York: Oxford University Press, 1997], 2.2.158; see also Pocock, *Machiavellian Moment*, 192, 202, 214).

64. Charles Blount, *Anima Mundi*, A 5.

65. Charles Blount, *Oracles of Reason*, 11; see also Herbert, *Pagan Religion*, 292, 299–300, 349. The golden age nostalgia of which deism forms a part is, in Rosenmeyer's words, "an aristocratic scheme contrived when new political and social developments threatened to destroy the influence of the noble lords, and caused them to look back with longing to a remembered glory" (*Green Cabinet*, 215).

66. For the view that Behn's royalism compromises her deism, see Arlen and Feldwick, " 'Religion Set the World at Odds,' " 227–28. On Behn's increasing disillusionment with Tory politics, see Zook, "Contextualizing Aphra Behn," 88–90; and Todd, *Secret Life*, 386–92. For the view that Behn harbored a more critical attitude toward royalism as early as 1681, see Anita Pacheco, "Reading Toryism in Aphra Behn's Cit-Cuckolding Comedies," *Review of English Studies* 55 (2004): 690–708.

67. For the view that *Oroonoko* defends royal authority, see George Guffey, "Aphra Behn's *Oroonoko*: Occasion and Accomplishment," in *Two English Novelists: Aphra Behn and Anthony Trollope* (Los Angeles: William Andrews Clark Memorial Library, 1975), 3–41; Richard Kroll, " 'Tales of Love and Gallantry': The Politics of *Oroonoko*," *Huntington Library Quarterly* 67 (2004): 573–605; and Visconsi, "A Degenerate Race," 673–701. For the contrary view that the novella betrays a more ambivalent attitude toward absolute power, see Margaret Reeves, "History, Fiction, and Political Identity: Heroic Rebellion in Aphra Behn's *Love-Letters between a Nobleman and His Sister* and *Oroonoko*," *1650–1850: Ideas, Aesthetics, and Inquiries in the Early Modern Era* 8 (2003): 269–94; Anita Pacheco, "Royalism and Honor in Aphra Behn's *Oroonoko*," *SEL* 34 (1994): 491–506; and Jerry C. Beasley, "Politics and Moral Idealism: The Achievement of Some Early Women Novelists," in Schofield, *Fetter'd or Free?*, 222.

68. Todd, *Secret Life*, 412; Zook, "Contextualizing Aphra Behn," 89–90.

69. [Charles Blount], *Appeal from the Country*, 5. Though Behn appears to have been a critic of the supposed "Popish Plot" of the 1670s (see Ros Ballaster, "Fiction Feigning Femininity: False Counts and Pageant Kings in Aphra Behn's Popish Plot Writings," in Todd, *Aphra Behn Studies*, 50–65), the reality of James's policies may have changed her stance. For the view that Behn's seemingly Catholic sympathies in the 1670s went hand-in-hand with her skeptical freethinking, see Alison Shell, "Popish Plots: *The Feign'd Curtizans* in Context," in Todd, *Aphra Behn Studies*, 45. As Shell argues, Behn "seems to have valued

Catholicism for a number of non-religious reasons: for its visual beauty . . . and for the opportunities it gave her for Tory mischief" (45).

70. Christopher Hill, *The Century of Revolution: 1603–1714*, 2nd ed. (New York: W. W. Norton, 1982), 170.

71. Hill, *Century of Revolution*, 211.

72. Cottegnies, "Aphra Behn's French Translations," in Hughes, *Cambridge Companion*, 231. Note Behn's likely ironic compliment in the dedication: "Nor can the unthinking and most malicious of your Enemies reproach your Lordship with self-interest in any of your Services" (4:170).

73. See "Astrea's Book of Songs and Satyrs," MS Firth c. 16, Bodleian Library, Oxford, fol. 263, 286v, 288v (quoted in Zook, "Contextualizing Aphra Behn," 89).

74. For a reading of the ideological links between Behn's *Oroonoko*, *The Widow Ranter*, and the third part of *Love-Letters*, also published in James's reign, see Todd, *Gender, Art and Death*, 32–62.

75. See Charles L. Batten, "The Source of Aphra Behn's *The Widow Ranter*," *Restoration and 18th-Century Theatre Research* 13 (1974): 12–18. The other accessible source on the Bacon rebellion that Behn likely consulted was *Strange News from Virginia; Being a full and true Account of the Life and Death of Nathaniel Bacon* (London, 1677).

76. *A True Narrative of the Late Rebellion in Virginia, by the Royal Commisioners, 1677*, in *Narratives of the Insurrections, 1675–1690*, ed. Charles M. Andrews (New York: Scribner's, 1915), 110, 111. William Berkeley, the lieutenant governor whose power Bacon opposed, also complained of "his Expressions of Atheisme, tending to take away al Religion and lawes" ("Berkeley's 'Declaration and Remonstrance,' May 29, 1676," in *The Old Dominion in the Seventeenth Century*, ed. Warren M. Billings [Chapel Hill: University of North Carolina Press, 1975], 271).

77. The view of the commissioner's report is voiced by the degenerate colonial council: "Bacon, contrary to Law and Equity, has to satisfie his own Ambition taken up Arms, with a pretence to fight the Indians, but indeed to molest and enslave the whole Colony, and to take away their Liberties and Properties" (Behn, *Works*, 7:3.2.127–30).

78. On Behn and republican politics, see Warren Chernaik, "Captains and Slaves: Aphra Behn and the Rhetoric of Republicanism," *The Seventeenth Century* 17 (2002): 97–107.

79. On the significance of the Widow in the play, see Shannon Ross, "*The Widdow Ranter*: Old World, New World—Exploring an Era's Authority Paradigms," in O'Donnell, Dhuicq, and Leduc, *Aphra Behn*, 86.

Notes to Chapter Three

1. Juste van Effen, translator's preface to *Le conte du tonneau* (1721), in *Swift: The Critical Heritage*, ed. Kathleen Williams (London: Routledge, 1970), 56.

2. Michael DePorte, "Swift, God, and Power," in *Walking Naboth's Vine-*

yard, ed. Christopher Fox and Brenda Tooley (Notre Dame, IN: University of Notre Dame Press, 1995), 75, 73, 81, 88, 89.

3. Cited in Anthony Collins, *A Discourse concerning Ridicule and Irony in Writing* (1729), ed. Edward A. Bloom and Lillian D. Bloom, Augustan Reprint Society, no. 142 (Los Angeles: University of California Press, 1970), 39.

4. Jonathan Smedley, *An Hue and Cry after the Examiner . . . To which is added A Copy of Verses fasten'd to the Gate of St. P—'s C—h . . .* (London, 1727), 14–15.

5. On Swift's use of satiric personae, see, for example, Ricardo Quintana, "Situational Satire: A Commentary on the Method of Swift," *University of Toronto Quarterly* 17 (1948): 130–36; William B. Ewald, *The Masks of Jonathan Swift* (Oxford: Oxford University Press, 1954); Ronald Paulson, *Theme and Structure in Swift's "Tale of a Tub"* (New Haven, CT: Yale University Press, 1960), 25–34, 45–52; and John R. Clark, *Form and Frenzy in Swift's "Tale of a Tub"* (Ithaca, NY: Cornell University Press, 1970), 10–11, 153–55, 161–70.

6. For the view that Swift condemns the positions expressed by his assumed personae in *A Tale*, see, for example, Roger Lund, "Strange Complicities: Atheism and Conspiracy in *A Tale of a Tub*," *Eighteenth-Century Life* 13 (1989): 34–58; Lund, "*A Tale of a Tub*, Swift's Apology, and the Trammels of Christian Wit," in *Augustan Subjects: Essays in Honor of Martin C. Battestin*, ed. Albert J. Rivero (Newark: University of Delaware Press, 1997), 87–109; and Philip Harth, *Swift and Anglican Rationalism: The Religious Background of "A Tale of a Tub"* (Chicago: University of Chicago Press, 1961). For the alternative view that Swift's speakers are a facet of himself unbowdlerized, see Traugott, "*Tale of a Tub*," 83–126; Rawson, "The Character of Swift's Satire," 17–75; DePorte, "Swift, God, and Power," 81–84; Patrick Reilly, *Jonathan Swift: The Brave Desponder* (Carbondale: Southern Illinois University Press, 1982), 57–80; Warren Montag, *The Unthinkable Swift: The Spontaneous Philosophy of a Church of England Man* (New York: Verso, 1994), 86–123; Frank Palmeri, "Satiric Materialism in *A Tale of a Tub*," in *Satire in Narrative* (Austin: University of Texas Press, 1990), 39–63; and Edward Said, "Swift as Intellectual," in *The World, the Text, and the Critic* (Cambridge, MA: Harvard University Press, 2004), 87.

7. Traugott, "*Tale of a Tub*," 96, 83. On Swift's double irony, or tendency to use an absurd persona as a vehicle through which to voice his own beliefs, see Rawson, "The Character of Swift's Satire," 50–58; and David P. French, "Swift, Temple, and 'A Digression on Madness,'" *Texas Studies in Literature and Language* 5 (1963): 52–57.

8. Irvin Ehrenpreis, *Swift: The Man, His Works, and the Age*, 3 vols. (Cambridge, MA: Harvard University Press, 1962–83), 2:331, 334–35.

9. William Wotton, *Observations upon the Tale of a Tub*, in *A Tale of a Tub*, ed. A. C. Guthkelch and D. Nichol Smith, 321–22. For another critique of Swift's irreligion by a well-known orthodox divine, see Samuel Clarke, *A Discourse concerning the Unchangeable Obligations of Natural Religion* [1706] (Stuttgart-Bad Cannstatt: F. Frommann, 1964), 28–29. As Frank T. Boyle points out, "Swift's opponents in the years before the publication of the Apology of

1710 were moderate Anglican divines associated with the Boyle lectures" ("Profane and Debauched Deist: Swift in the Contemporary Response to *A Tale of a Tub*," *Eighteenth-Century Ireland* 3 [1988]: 26).

10. Rawson, "Character of Swift's Satire," 18, 50; Traugott, "*Tale of a Tub*," 88, 85.

11. Traugott, "*Tale of a Tub*," 100; Strauss, *Spinoza's Critique of Religion*, 86.

12. Traugott, "*Tale of a Tub*," 90. To the extent that the errors *A Tale* documents can be discovered in the mind of any man, Traugott argues that investigations of Restoration religious controversy—"a scholar's revelation of ancient days"—provide little insight into Swift's meaning (89). Traugott clearly has the research of Philip Harth in mind, whose carefully documented *Swift and Anglican Rationalism* (1961) groups Swift's *Tale* with the latitudinarian assault on enthusiasm, atheism, and materialism in the period. Traugott's aversion to a historicist approach to *A Tale* stems from his sense that Swift's religious satire revolves around an anachronistic concern with popery and dissent. According to Harth, and, more recently, Roger Lund, however, Swift's attack on both Catholic idolatry and dissenting enthusiasm implicate each in various materialist and pantheistic heterodoxies, threats that were indeed more immediate to contemporaries than the more belated extravagances of Peter and Jack. It will be my argument that the proper theological context for Swift's *Tale* is the history of religion and superstition more generally and is thus far broader than a critique of popery and dissent or of atheism and materialism.

13. Richard Popkin, "Spinoza and Bible Scholarship," in *The Books of Nature and Scripture: Recent Essays on Natural Philosophy, Theology, and Biblical Criticism in the Netherlands of Spinoza's Time and the British Isles of Newton's Time*, ed. James E. Force and Richard H. Popkin (Boston: Kluwer, 1994), 11. See also Popkin, "The Deist Challenge," 196–99.

14. Popkin, "Deist Challenge," 199; Champion, *Pillars of Priestcraft Shaken*, 81–83, 133–69; Harrison, *"Religion" and the Religions*, 131–38; Eamon Duffy, "Primitive Christianity Revived; Religious Renewal in Augustan England," *Studies in Church History* 14 (1977): 287–300; and Gerald R. McDermott, *Jonathan Edwards Confronts the Gods* (Oxford: Oxford University Press, 2000), 177–78.

15. Thomas Hobbes, *A True Ecclesiastical History, from Moses, to the Time of Martin Luther, in Verse* (London, 1722), 87, 106.

16. John Toland, "The Origin of Idolatry and Reasons of Heathenism," in *Letters to Serena* (London, 1704), 71, 114, 115.

17. Warburton, *Divine Legation*, 412–13. See Philip Skelton's comment that "all the Libertine writers pretend to be of our religion, and profess only an intention to recommend a truer idea of it, than that which is vulgarly entertained" (*Ophiomaches*, 2:283).

18. Edmund Curll, "To the Reader," in *A Complete Key to "The Tale of a Tub"* (1710), in Guthkelch and Nichol Smith, *A Tale of a Tub*.

19. Curll, *Complete Key*, 331–32.

20. For the view that the engagement of *A Tale* with the ancients and mod-

erns controversy is disconnected from its satire on religion, see, for example, Clark, *Form and Frenzy*, 93. Though Miriam Starkman similarly argues that "there can scarcely be said to have been an Ancients versus Moderns controversy in religion," she does acknowledge that Temple and Swift's *Tale* link the decay of learning in modernity with nonconformity and dissent (*Swift's Satire on Learning in "A Tale of a Tub"* [New York: Octagon Books, 1968], 3, 14–15).

21. Wotton, preface to *Reflections*. On Wotton's association of the ancient position with irreligion, see Boyle, "Profane and Debauched Deist," 27.

22. Wotton, *Observations*, 319.

23. See also van Effen's view that the brothers' coats in Swift's allegory "stand for the Christian religion in its primitive purity" (Effen, translator's preface, 56). In his sermon "Upon the Excellency of Christianity, in Opposition to Heathen Philosophy," Swift mourns the present absence of Christianity's first wondrous effects, produced "when it was received and embraced in its utmost purity and perfection" (*Prose Works*, 9:250).

24. See the anonymous censure of Swift's *Tale* that referred to "his Pagan way of scandalizing the Sacred Apostles and Scriptures" (*A Morning's Discourse of a Bottomless Tubb* [London, 1712], 6).

25. See Swift, *Prose Works*, 9:73–74, 155–56, 241–50.

26. See ibid., 9:73, 243.

27. For a similar view on why Christianity is to be preferred to paganism, see the comments of the Sceptic in Gastrell, *Principles of Deism Truly Represented*, 60–61.

Swift's animus against the freethinkers' tendency to exalt the wisdom of the ancients stems from his belief that they aim actively to "disparage revealed knowledge, and the consequences of it, among us" ("A Sermon upon the Excellency of Christianity," in *Prose Works*, 9:243). The status of the Gospel as an article of faith is here less important than the moral and ethical "consequences" it produces in civic life. Swift's *Argument against Abolishing Christianity* similarly contends that "Freedom of Action," such as "whor[ing]," "drink[ing]" and "defy[ing] the Parson," "is the sole End, how remote soever, in Appearance, of all Objections against Christianity" (*Prose Works*, 2:38).

28. Duffy, "Primitive Christianity Revived," 298–99.

29. Wotton, *Reflections*, 327.

30. John Edwards, *A Compleat History or Survey of All the Dispensations and Methods of Religion*, 2 vols. (London, 1699), 2:606, quoted in R. S. Crane, "Anglican Apologetics and the Idea of Progress, 1699–1745," in *The Idea of the Humanities*, 2 vols. (Chicago: University of Chicago Press, 1967), 1:231.

31. David Spadafora, *The Idea of Progress in Eighteenth-Century Britain* (New Haven, CT: Yale University Press, 1990), 16–17, 90–92, 97–98; Crane, "Anglican Apologetics," 1:214–87.

32. I borrow Starkman's term for the clothes-worshippers (*Swift's Satire on Learning*, 56–57).

33. This gloss relies on the editors' notes (*Tale of a Tub*, 76).

34. Montag, *Unthinkable Swift*, 97–98.

35. Harth, *Swift and Anglican Rationalism*, 75–85. It is well known that three editions of *Leviathan* were listed among Swift's books in 1715, as well as copies of Hobbes's *De Cive* and *Opera Philosophica* (see William LeFanu, *A Catalogue of Books Belonging to Dr. Jonathan Swift* [Cambridge: Cambridge Bibliographical Society, 1988], 21). As David French points out, Swift thus owned more copies of Hobbes than of any other author ("Swift and Hobbes," 253). For the view that Swift condemns Hobbesian materialism in *A Tale*, see also Starkman, *Swift's Satire on Learning*, 34–38, 57; Robert H. Hopkins, "Personation of Hobbism," 372–78; Alan S. Fisher, "An End to the Renaissance: Erasmus, Hobbes, and *A Tale of a Tub*," *Huntington Library Quarterly* 38 (1974): 1–20; Lund, "Strange Complicities," 47–49; and Montag, *Unthinkable Swift*, 95–102. Montag, however, argues rightly that "something of Hobbes passes into the text *of A Tale*, producing effects which may or may not conform to its general project, that is, which may either strengthen the ironic assault on materialism or weaken it" (95).

36. Harth, *Swift and Anglican Rationalism*, 77.

37. Harth and Lund are right to point out that contemporary theological polemic described atheistic materialists as "enthusiasts" for matter (Harth, *Swift and Anglican Rationalism*, 78–82; Lund, "Strange Complicities," 38–39, 47–50). It is important to recognize, however, that the devotion attributed to materialist unbelievers was an intentional rhetorical strategy adopted by the churchmen. Seventeenth-century materialists, in other words, did not, in fact, worship matter (see Hunter, "Science and Heterodoxy," 448). Indeed, Hobbes takes pains to distinguish his position from that of the pantheist tradition, arguing that "those Philosophers, who sayd the World, or the Soule of the World was God, spake unworthily of him; and denied his Existence" (*Leviathan*, 2.31.401). As Ehrenpreis has argued, a distinction must stand between the worlds of belief and unbelief; all atheists were not enthusiasts and vice versa ("The Doctrine of *A Tale of a Tub*," in *Proceedings of the First Münster Symposium on Jonathan Swift*, ed. Hermann J. Real and Heinz J. Vienken [Munich: Wilhelm Fink, 1985], 67). Moreover, in terms of the historical trajectory of Swift's allegory, atheistic materialism did not lead to the increase of superstition and superfluous rites, ceremonies, and mysteries in Christianity.

38. For a later (and similar) satire of pagan idolatry, see Hume's *The Natural History of Superstition*: "But the vulgar polytheist . . . deifies every part of the universe, and conceives all the conspicuous productions of nature, to be themselves so many real divinities" (in *Principal Writings on Religion*, ed. J. C. A. Gaskin [New York: Oxford University Press, 1993], 150).

39. I disagree here with Starkman's claim that sartorism is a modern error (*Swift's Satire on Learning*, 62). Swift suggests, I would argue, that clothes-worship is an ancient error that bleeds into modernity through Peter's adoption of older forms of superstition.

40. On the critique of Catholicism as a cover for a broader critique of Christianity, see Harrison, *"Religion" and the Religions*, 144–45; and Manuel, *The Eighteenth Century Confronts the Gods*, 22–23. For contemporary examples, see Hobbes, *A True Ecclesiastical History*, 105–7; [Sir Robert Howard], *The*

History of Religion. Written by a Person of Quality (London, 1694), vii; and Sir Thomas Pope Blount, "Essay I: That Interest Governs the World: and That Popery is Nothing but Priestcraft," in *Essays on Several Subjects*, 1–49. Swift acknowledges the covert irreligion in these writings in his impersonation of the freethinking position in "Mr. Collins's Discourse of Free-Thinking" (1713): "those daring Spirits, who first adventured to write against the direct Rules of Gospel . . . had some Measures to keep; and particularly when they railed at Religion, were in the right to use little artful Disguises, by which a Jury could only find them guilty of abusing Heathenism or Popery" (*Prose Works*, 4:27).

41. See Wotton, *Observations*, 319; Craven, "*Tale of a Tub*," 97–110; Craven, *Jonathan Swift and the Millennium of Madness* (New York: E. J. Brill, 1992), 17–55. On Toland as a source for Swift's *Tale*, see also Lund, "*Tale of a Tub*," 91.

42. Toland, *Christianity Not Mysterious*, xx, xxi.

43. Ibid., 152, 152–53, 155–56.

44. See Craven, "*Tale of a Tub*," 100–101; Craven, *Jonathan Swift*, 20–21. Craven argues that though Swift agrees with Toland's preference for the simplicity of early Christian doctrine, as well as his exposure of priestcraft, the two remain fundamentally opposed on the grounds of faith (*Jonathan Swift*, 21).

45. Toland, *Christianity Not Mysterious*, 67, 68.

46. Charles Blount, *Great Is Diana*, 7 (I thank Scott McGill for the translation of Blount's Latin); Charles Blount, *Two First Books*, A4; italics mine. The term "cloak" was also used to refer to a clerical gown and thus became a derogatory epithet for Presbyterian or Independent ministers during the Civil Wars and, later, for religious fanatics during the Exclusion Crisis (see the ballad pamphlet, "The Cloaks Knavery" [London, 1660], reprinted as "The Ballad of the Cloak: or, The Cloaks Knavery" [London, 1679–82]; and "Religion Made a Cloak For Villany" [London, 1681–84]).

47. Toland makes this claim explicit in his later and more radical work, "The Origin of Idolatry, and Reasons of Heathenism." Here he asserts that "almost every Point of those superstitious and idolatrous Religions are in these or grosser Circumstances reviv'd by many Christians in our Western Parts of the World" (*Letters to Serena*, 127).

48. Toland, *Christianity Not Mysterious*, xx, 79, 71. See also Sir Robert Howard's similar claim that "the word Mystery . . . was always used to keep the Vulgar and Profane, so called, from the Knowledg of, and from examining and inquiring into Religion. This was the Use of Mystery, in the Theology of the Gentiles; Mystery was the secret and extravagant Worship of the false Gods" (*History of Religion*, 53).

49. Wotton, *Observations*, 319.

50. It is worth noting that in his official capacity as an Anglican clergyman, Swift condemns the stance of Toland and others that the Christian mysteries are nothing but "Cant, Imposture, and Priest-craft." He also identifies the critique of popery with "those who have Ill-Will to our Church, or a Contempt for all Religion" (*Prose Works*, 9:162, 163).

51. Voltaire, *Oeuvres complètes*, 22:175 (translation mine). Guthkelch and

Nichol Smith note that the likeness of Swift's allegory to the parable of the three rings was first recognized in a French adaptation, entitled, *Les trois justau-corps* (1721). The editors cite the parable as a possible source, among others, for Swift's allegory of the three brothers, though they emphasize the differences more than the similarities between them (see introduction to Swift, *A Tale of a Tub*, xxxvi–xxxviii).

52. H. B. Nisbet, "*De Tribus Impostoribus*: On the Genesis of Lessing's *Nathan der Weise*," *Euphorian* 73 (1979): 367. On the parable of the three rings and deist writing, see also Orr, *English Deism*, 48. On the theory of the three impostors and Enlightenment irreligion, see Israel, *Radical Enlightenment*, 694–700.

53. For the view that Hobbes and Swift shared similar views on politics and religion, see French, "Swift and Hobbes—A Neglected Parallel," 20–55; Ehrenpreis, "Doctrine of *A Tale of a Tub*," 66–69; Palmeri, "Satiric Materialism," 39–63; Basil Hall, "'An Inverted Hypocrite': Swift the Churchman," in *The World of Jonathan Swift*, ed. Brian Vickers (Cambridge, MA: Harvard University Press, 1968), 51–52.

54. Hobbes, introduction to *Leviathan*, 81.

55. Harth, *Swift and Anglican Rationalism*, 85.

56. Richard Bentley commented in a letter in 1692 that "not one English Infidel in a hundred is any other than a Hobbist; which I know to be rank Atheism in the private study and select conversation of those men, whatever it may appear to be abroad" (quoted in Berman, *History of Atheism in Britain*, 50). For a similar reading of Hobbes's and Swift's shared tendency to reduce the spiritual to the physical, see Palmeri, "Satiric Materialism," 44.

57. Charles Gildon suggested as much in his mock dedication to Swift in *The Golden Spy* (London, 1709): "You, Sir, go farther, and Burlesque Religion itself; while speaking and thinking of it in a Good Humour, you have brought it to be no more than an Old Coat, leaving to the Good Friend honest Moderate Martin, scarce so much as a Lappet to cover his Nakedness."

58. Montag, *Unthinkable Swift*, 95, 94.

59. For the view that Martin provides an unconvincing satiric norm in *A Tale*, see Traugott, "*Tale of a Tub*," 86, 100, 124; Rawson, "Character of Swift's Satire," 56–57; and Palmeri, "Satiric Materialism," 49. It is notable as well that Swift pays cursory attention to the phase of Christianity that *A Tale* ostensibly upholds and on which the modern Anglican Church attempts to base its reformation. Swift's narrator declares that he will "not trouble" the reader "with recounting what Adventures [the brothers] met for the first seven Years, any farther than by taking notice, that they carefully observed their Father's Will, and kept their Coates in very good Order" (74). No sooner does Christianity begin than it almost immediately degenerates back into paganism.

60. See the editors' notes in the reprint of Wotton's *Observations* in Guthkelch and Nichol Smith. On Hobbes's literalization of spirit as a source for Swift's aeolists, see Hopkins, "Personation of Hobbism," 372–78; also Montag, *Unthinkable Swift*, 103–4; Lund, "Strange Complicities," 51–53; Palmeri, "Satiric Materialism," 53–55.

61. Hobbes, *Leviathan*, 3.34.440, 441.

62. Ibid., 3.34.441, 440.

63. See especially Lund, "Strange Complicities," 51–53.

64. Hobbes, *Leviathan*, 3.34.441.

65. On aeolism's derivation from the ancient oracles, see Starkman, *Swift's Satire on Learning*, 41.

66. Origen, *Contra Celsum*, and Saint John Chrysostom, *Homilies on the First Epistle of St. Paul the Apostle to the Corinthians*, both quoted in William Kupersmith, "Swift's Aeolists and the Delphic Oracle," *Modern Philology* 82 (1984): 190–94, 192, 193.

67. Kupersmith, "Swift's Aeolists," 194.

68. For a similar reading of the critique of spirit in Swift, see Montag, *Unthinkable Swift*, 106; Palmeri, "Swift's Satiric Materialism," 40; Traugott, "*Tale of a Tub*," 106, 115, 121.

69. Fontenelle, *History of Oracles*, in Behn, *Works*, 4:221; Hobbes, *Leviathan*, 1.12.175–76. Swift's naturalistic account of the pagan oracles could also have been influenced by Thomas Pope Blount's censure of pagan religion ("Essay I," 11–17).

70. Kupersmith, "Swift's Aeolists," 192.

71. Fontenelle, *History of Oracles*, in Behn, *Works*, 4:274.

72. In Diodorus Siculus, the source Swift indicates in the margins of *A Tale* for his discussion of the Bacchic revels (283–84), the revels were linked to the Delphic oracles, and the frenzy of the Pythian priestess was seen to be a version of the Bacchic frenzy (see also Thomas Dempsey, *The Delphic Oracle* [New York: Benjamin Blom, 1972], 33–34; 50–51; Joseph Fontenrose, *The Delphic Oracle* [Berkeley: University of California Press, 1978], 207; and H. W. Parke and D. E. W. Wormell, *The Delphic Oracle*, 2 vols. [Oxford: Basil Blackwell, 1956], 1:331). Toland also linked modern Christian superstition with the Bacchic frenzy: "Thus lest Simplicity, the noblest Ornament of the Truth, should expose it to the Contempt of Unbelievers, Christianity was put upon an equal Level with the Mysteries of Ceres, or the Orgies of Bacchus" (*Christianity Not Mysterious*, 153). Incidentally, Champion notes that Diodorus was also one of Toland's preferred ancient sources (*Pillars of Priestcraft Shaken*, 131, 149).

73. Harth, *Swift and Anglican Rationalism*, 103–11; see also Angus Ross, "*The Anatomy of Melancholy* and Swift," in *Swift and His Contexts*, ed. John Irwin Fischer, Hermann Josef Real, and James D. Woolley (New York: AMS Press, 1989), 133–58; Michael V. DePorte, *Nightmares and Hobbyhorses: Swift, Sterne, and Augustan Ideas of Madness* (San Marino, CA: Huntington Library, 1974), 60–61; and W. Scott Blanchard, "Swift's *Tale*, the Renaissance Anatomy, and Humanist Polemic," in *Representations of Swift*, ed. Brian A. Connery (Newark: University of Delaware Press, 2002), 57–73. See also Temple's comment that "a clear account of enthusiasm and fascination, from their natural causes, . . . might perhaps prevent many public disorders, and save the lives of many innocent, deluded, or deluding people" (Temple, *Five Miscellaneous Essays*, 175–76).

74. Robert Burton, *The Anatomy of Melancholy*, ed. Thomas C. Faulkner, Nicolas K. Kiessling, and Rhonda L. Blair, 3 vols. (Oxford: Clarendon Press, 1989–94), 3.4.1.1.

75. Ibid., 3.4.1.1, 3.4.1.2.

76. Casaubon, *Treatise concerning Enthusiasme*, 22; Henry More, *Enthusiasmus Triumphatus: or, A Discourse of the Nature, Causes, Kinds, and Cure, of Enthusiasme*, ed. G. A. J. Rogers (Bristol: Thoemmes Press, 1997), 19.

77. Burton, *Anatomy of Melancholy*, 3.4.1.2; 1.2.5.2.

78. Henry More, *Enthusiasmus Triumphatus*, 17, 39.

79. Burton, *Anatomy of Melancholy*, 3.4.1.2, see also 1.2.1.2.

80. Casaubon, *Treatise concerning Enthusiasme*, 36, 41, 42; see also 24, 35–36; More, *Enthusiasmus Triumphatus*, 58, 59.

81. More, *Enthusiasmus Triumphatus*, 48. On the Christian orthodoxy of Burton, Casaubon, and More, see Harrison, *"Religion" and the Religions*, 120–25.

82. Edwards, *Some Thoughts*, 100–101.

83. See also Sir Thomas Pope Blount's account of the priestly manipulation of ancient oracles: " 'Tis hard to say, who were guilty of the greater folly, the ignorant Heathen, who believ'd those Praedictions to come from Heaven; or those Superstitious Christians, who thought they came from the Devil; since they were both under a gross Mistake. For certainly to any Man, who is unbiass'd in Opinion, and who dares suffer himself to think beyond, the narrow Rules of his Education, they cannot appear to be any thing but the meer juggling and imposture of the Heathen Priests" ("Essay I," 11–12).

84. Trenchard, *Natural History of Superstition*, 8.

85. See Manuel, *Eighteenth Century Confronts the Gods*, 76; Harrison, *"Religion" and the Religions*, 125.

86. For an English translation of Swift's citation of Horace, see Horace, *Satire, Epistles and Ars Poetica*, trans. H. Rushton Fairclough (Cambridge, MA: Harvard University Press, 1926), 191–92.

87. See Swift's nonsatiric "Thoughts on Religion" for a similar view: "Miserable mortals! can we contribute to *the honour and Glory of God*? I could wish that expression were struck out of our Prayer-books" (*Prose Works*, 9:263).

88. Lucretius, *De rerum natura*, 5.165–67. Traugott points out that Swift cites Lucretius' ironic prayer to Fortune (5.107) at the start of his exposition of the Aeolist religion. Like Lucretius, Swift intends to mock those who believe they enjoy God's special favor ("Tale of a Tub," 111).

89. Montaigne, *Complete Works*, 2.12.394; see also Spinoza, *Theological-Political Treatise*, 180, 78.

90. Hobbes argues similarly that "Ignorance of naturall causes disposeth a man to Credulity, so as to believe many times impossibilities: For such know nothing to the contrary, but that they may be true; being unable to detect the Impossibility" (*Leviathan*, 1.11.166–67).

91. Strauss, *Spinoza's Critique of Religion*, 51.

92. DePorte, "Swift, God, and Power," 87–88.

93. See "Stella's Birthday, 1727," in *Jonathan Swift: The Complete Poems*, ed. Pat Rogers (New York: Penguin Books, 1983).

Notes to Chapter Four

1. See Guthkelch and Nichol Smith, introduction to *A Tale of a Tub*, xxviii–xxx. See also the definition of "a tale of a tub" in the *OED*, s.v. "tub," definition 9.

2. Reprinted in Gillian Manning, "The Deist: A Satyr on the Parsons," *The Seventeenth Century* 8 (1993): 149–60.

3. Sarah Jennings Churchill, Duchess of Marlborough, *Memoirs of Sarah, Duchess of Marlborough*, ed. William King (New York: Kraus Reprint, 1969), 247; Wotton, *Observations*, 317. See also Wotton's later condemnation of Swift's allusions to Toland on the Christian mysteries, "the Word and Thing whereof he [Toland] is known to believe to be no more than a *Tale of a Tub*" (319).

4. *Select Letters Taken from Fog's "Weekly Journal,"* 2 vols. (London, 1732), 2:73, 74.

5. Montag, *Unthinkable Swift*, 99–100.

6. Enthusiasm's threat to the State forms a recurrent theme in Swift's writings on the Church. "On the Testimony of Conscience" contends that the demands of "Fanaticks" for liberty of conscience boil down to their seditious impulses, their desire "to overthrow the Faith which the Laws have already established" (9:151). As his "Sentiments of a Church-of-England Man" argues, any attempt to separate from the established worship of the State, "although to a new one that is more pure and perfect," should be definitively rejected on the grounds that it "may be an Occasion of endangering the Publick Peace" (2:11). The "Ecclesiastical Government" of the Anglican Church is thus "fittest, of all others for preserving Order and Purity, and . . . best calculated for our Civil State" (2:5).

7. Harold D. Kelling, "Reason in Madness: *A Tale of a Tub*," *PMLA* 69 (1954): 204.

8. Ricardo Quintana, "Two Paragraphs in *A Tale of a Tub*, Section IX," *Modern Philology* 73 (1975): 27. On Swift's ironic praise (and thus censure) of delusion in "A Digression concerning Madness," see also Harth, *Swift and Anglican Rationalism*, 132–37; Starkman, *Swift's Satire on Learning*, 41–44; Kelling, "Reason in Madness: *A Tale of a Tub*"; and Robert C. Elliot, "Swift's Tale of a Tub: An Essay in Problems of Structure," *PMLA* 66 (1951): 450–55.

9. F. R. Leavis suggests that "it is as if one found Swift in the place—at the point of view—where one expected to find his butt" ("The Irony of Swift," in *Determinations: Critical Essays* [London: Chatto & Windus, 1934], 98).

10. See Leavis, "Irony of Swift," 101.

11. Sir William Temple, "Of Popular Discontents," in *The Works of Sir William Temple*, 3:44.

12. Horace, *Satire, Epistles, and Ars Poetica*, 2.2.126–40.

13. On Erasmus's *The Praise of Folly* as a source for Swift's *Tale*, see Traugott, *"Tale of a Tub,"* 103–4; Paulson, *Theme and Structure in Swift's "Tale of a Tub,"* 80, 249–53; Eugene R. Hammond, "In Praise of Wisdom and the Will

of God: Erasmus' *Praise of Folly* and Swift's *A Tale of a Tub*," *Studies in Philology* 80 (1983): 253–76; and Fisher, "An End to the Renaissance," 1–20. Whereas the above critics argue that Swift largely parodies Erasmus, thereby rejecting the latter's notion that the world is a theater and that delusion is productive of happiness, I want to suggest that Swift adopts Erasmus' view without irony (see also for this view J. T. Parnell, "Swift, Sterne, and the Skeptical Tradition," *Studies in Eighteenth-Century Culture* 23 [1994]: 221–42). Montaigne's influence on Swift has been less considered than Erasmus'. For a recent exception, see Claude Rawson, *God, Gulliver, and Genocide* (Oxford and New York: Oxford University Press, 2001), esp. 1–91; also Ehrenpreis, *Swift: The Man, His Works, and the Age*, 1:179, 192; Kathleen Williams, *Jonathan Swift and the Age of Compromise* (Lawrence: University of Kansas Press, 1958), 50–51, 87–88; and Parnell, "Swift, Sterne, and the Skeptical Tradition," 230–38.

14. From Erasmus, Swift learned the art of speaking improprieties through adopting an outrageous persona as well as the wisdom that the human mind "is far more taken with appearances than reality" (*The Praise of Folly*, trans. Clarence H. Miller, 2nd ed. [New Haven, CT: Yale University Press, 2003], 71).

15. Viscount Bolingbroke to Swift, 30 September 1729, in Swift, *Correspondence*, 3:348; Montaigne, *Complete Works of Montaigne*, 2.12.366.

16. Erasmus, *Praise of Folly*, 36; Montaigne, *Complete Works*, 2.12.368; Erasmus, *Praise of Folly*, 51. On the virtues of the golden age see also Montaigne, *Complete Works*, 2.12.331.

17. Erasmus, *Praise of Folly*, 44; Montaigne, *Complete Works*, 2.12.366.

18. Erasmus, *Praise of Folly*, 71.

19. Montaigne, *Complete Works*, 2.12.372; see Terence Penelhum, "Skepticism and Fideism," in Burnyeat, *The Skeptical Tradition*, 289.

20. Erasmus, *Praise of Folly*, 58.

21. On Swift and Skepticism, see James Noggle, *The Skeptical Sublime: Aesthetic Ideology in Pope and the Tory Satirists* (Oxford: Oxford University Press, 2001), 71–96; Boyle, "Profane and Debauched Deist," 25–38; Williams, *Jonathan Swift*, esp. 43–90; Parnell, "Swift, Sterne, and the Skeptical Tradition," 221–42; and French, "Swift, Temple, and 'A Digression on Madness,'" 42–57.

22. On the links between Skepticism and antienthusiasm in religion, see Penelhum, "Skepticism and Fideism," 297.

23. On Swift's skeptical attitude toward reason and man's capacity for knowledge, see also his "Ode to the Athenian Society," in Rogers, *Jonathan Swift: The Complete Poems*, 132–52, 176–88. For the contrary reading that Swift advocates the powers of reason in "A Digression concerning Madness," see Harth, *Swift and Anglican Rationalism*, 123–53; Paulson, *Theme and Structure*, 177–87; Quintana, "Two Paragraphs," 15–32; Starkman, *Swift's Satire on Learning*, 24–44; and Kelling, "Reason in Madness," 212, 216.

24. Penelhum "Skepticism and Fideism," 289–90, 292, 316.

25. Ibid., 292. See also Montaigne's comment of Pyrrhonism: "Ignorance that knows itself, that judges itself and condemns itself, is not complete ignorance: to be that, it must be ignorant of itself" (Montaigne, *Complete Works*, 2.12.372).

26. Erasmus, *Praise of Folly*, 65–66. On Erasmus' critique of the truths of religion, see especially *Praise of Folly*, 132.

27. Indeed, for the author, the mischievous pleasure in such ploys was also to scandalize the clerics (by insinuating unbelief) while taking shelter in the defense made possible by the text's more literal meaning ("Deism, Immortality, and the Art of Theological Lying," 72).

28. On the "double truth" and its links to the twofold philosophy, see Harrison, *'Religion' and the Religions*, 86.

29. Bredvold, *Intellectual Milieu of John Dryden*, 21. On the use of double truth doctrine in pious circles, see also Hiram Haydn, *The Counter-Renaissance* (New York: Charles Scribner's Sons, 1950), 101.

30. Bredvold, *Intellectual Milieu of John Dryden*, 21, 73–74.

31. See Schmitt, "Rediscovery of Ancient Skepticism," 229, 240; Bredvold, *Intellectual Milieu of John Dryden*, 73–74; Popkin, *History of Skepticism*, 55; and Alan Kors, *Atheism in France, 1650–1729* (Princeton, NJ: Princeton University Press, 1990), 115–16. Few readers mistook the disdain for religion behind David Hume's claim that "Our most holy religion is founded on *Faith*, not on reason; and it is a sure method of exposing it to put it to such a trial as it is, by no means, fitted to endure" (*Enquiry concerning Human Understanding*, 186). On the links between Skepticism and unbelief, see also Hume's *Dialogues concerning Natural Religion*, in *Principal Writings on Religion, Including Dialogues concerning Natural Religion; and The Natural History of Religion*, ed. J. C. A. Gaskin (Oxford: Oxford University Press, 1998), pt. 4, 60–62.

32. Ehrenpreis aptly suggests that the narrator's tone in *An Argument* hearkens back to the irreverence of the court wits of Rochester's age: "In its air of ease and worldiness the style of the essay captures the manner of a libertine gentleman in a Restoration play, freed from the blinkers of common decency. For the experienced reader this manner has associations opposed to preachments and piety. It recalls a licentious court and an intellectual milieu receptive to dangerous ideas" (*Swift*, 2:285).

33. Ibid., 2:280.

34. On the levels of irony in "An Argument," see Rawson, "Character of Swift's Satire," 41–43, 58–60; Ehrenpreis, *Swift*, 2:276–97. According to Ehrenpreis, Swift's satire in this essay allows the reader to "feel the rash excitement of burning a jail without losing the serene complacency of wearing a policeman's uniform" (2:297).

35. Rawson, "Character of Swift's Satire," 58.

36. Swift here echoes Halifax's similarly pragmatic view that although "in some well chosen and dearly beloved Auditories, good resolute Nonsense back'd with Authority may prevail, yet generally Men are become so good Judges of what they hear, that the Clergy ought to be very wary how they go about to impose upon their Understandings, which are grown less humble than they were in former times" (George Savile, Marquis of Halifax, *The Character of a Trimmer*, 3rd ed. [London, 1697], 45). Halifax's *Trimmer* was included in Temple's

library and was thus available to Swift while he was writing *A Tale* (Ehrenpreis, *Swift*, 1:287).

37. I here follow Rawson's view that "close relationships exist between attitudes which Swift repudiated through ironic mimicry, and attitudes which he held literally." As he contends, "If the scintillating indirections of the *Argument against Abolishing Christianity* tempt us to feel superior to the speaker's boneheaded statesmanliness as he concedes the uses of religion 'for the common People,' we cannot dissociate Swift himself from some non-ridiculed version of the same view" ("Character of Swift's Satire," 58, 59). We might well apply the same reading to Swift's references to the pious fraud in "Mr. Collins's Discourse of Free-Thinking" (4:40) and in *Gulliver's Travels* (New York: Oxford University Press), 1.6.51–52.

38. Montaigne, *Complete Works*, 2.12.379.

39. Erasmus, "Letter to Martin Dorp," in *Praise of Folly*, 143. Erasmus several times compares his praise of delusion to the sweetening properties of honey (see *Praise of Folly*, 47–48, 70–71).

40. I thank Scott McGill for this translation of Lucretius. It is a widely cited fact that Swift read Lucretius three times in 1697, while working on *A Tale* at Moor Park. Henry Craik writes that "of all authors the one quoted most often, and something in the spirit of whose genius seems most in sympathy with that of Swift, is Lucretius. Swift had, indeed, little enough in common with the philosophy of Lucretius. But in both we have the same gloom of cynicism. In both there is the same profound scorn of superstition, and yet the same belief that in superstition we must find the main source of most human action" (*The Life of Jonathan Swift* [London: J. Murray, 1882], 112). On Lucretius as a source for *A Tale*, see also A. H. de Quehen, "Lucretius and Swift's *Tale of a Tub*," *University of Toronto Quarterly* 63 (1993): 287–307; Charles Scruggs, "Swift's Use of Lucretius in *A Tale of a Tub*," *Texas Studies in Literature and Language* 15 (1973): 39–50; Bernard Fleischmann, *Lucretius and English Literature, 1680–1740* (Paris: Librairie Nizet, 1964), 242–51; and Traugott, "*Tale of a Tub*," 109–18.

41. Lucretius, *The Way Things Are*, 1:931–50; see also 4:6–25.

42. On citing the example of the ancients in his praise of the varied pleasures of delusion, Erasmus grants that "perhaps the authority of these writers is not highly regarded among Christians" (*Praise of Folly*, 118). On the attempt among seventeenth- and eighteenth-century freethinkers to insinuate unbelief in writing that ostensibly supported religion, see Berman, "Deism, Immortality, and the Art of Theological Lying," 72–76.

43. Lucretius, *The Way Things Are*, 2:644–45, 653–64. Shaftesbury remarks of Lucretius that "Notwithstanding he denied the principles of religion to be natural, he was forced tacitly to allow there was a wondrous disposition in mankind towards supernatural objects" (*Characteristics*, 25). For the view that Lucretius' poem advocates nonsuperstitious reverence of the Gods, see Most, "Philosophy and Religion," 306.

44. Lucretius, *The Way Things Are*, 4:31, 4:33, 4:64, 4:34–35.

45. Ibid., 4:503–8.

46. See Lund, "Strange Complicities," 46; Harth, *Swift and Anglican Rationalism*, 86–98, 125–27, 137–40; Starkman, *Swift's Satire on Learning*, 30–34, 41–44.

47. Erasmus, *Praise of Folly*, 85–86; Montaigne, *Complete Works*, 2.12.407; 2.12.360. Montaigne satirically asks of Epicurean atomism in his *Apology*, "If the atoms have, by chance, formed so many sorts of figures, why have they never happened to meet to make a house, or a shoe? Why do we not believe likewise that an infinite number of Greek letters scattered about the place would be capable of forming the web of the *Iliad*?" (*Complete Works*, 2.12.407). Swift alludes approvingly to this passage in his "Tritical Essay" (1707), querying, "How can the *Epicureans* Opinion be true, that the Universe was formed by a fortuitous Concourse of Atoms, which I will no more believe, than that the accidental Jumbling of the Letters in the Alphabet, could fall by Chance into a most ingenious and learned Treatise of Philosophy" (*Prose Works* 1:246–47). However, Swift departs from Montaigne in reading Lucretius' discussion of the deception inherent in sensation (*The Way Things Are*, 4:493–507) as a positive example of the possession of being well deceived. Montaigne criticizes the same passage from Lucretius in his *Apology* as proof of the hopeless inadequacy of the senses and thus the impossibility of man's knowing anything. "This desperate and most unphilosophical advice means nothing else than that human knowledge can maintain itself only by unreasonable, mad, and senseless reason; but that still it is better for man, in order to assert himself, to use it and any other remedy, however fantastic, than to admit his necessary stupidity" (*Complete Works*, 2.12.447). It is precisely this paradox that interests Swift; the unavoidable fact of false and uncertain knowledge is that with which man must wrestle and contend. As French writes of "A Digression concerning Madness," "Seeming absurdities may in fact be the only true sanities" ("Swift, Temple, and 'A Digression on Madness,'" 53).

48. Sir William Temple "Upon the Gardens of Epicurus," in *Five Miscellaneous Essays*, 5–6; ibid., 4, 6. See this same view expressed in Herbert of Cherbury's *Dialogue*, 43.

49. On the question of Temple's intellectual influence on Swift, I differ from A. C. Elias, who argues that Swift satirizes his mentor's views in "A Digression concerning Madness" (see *Swift at Moor Park: Problems in Biography and Criticism* [Philadelphia: University of Pennsylvania Press, 1982], 157–83).

50. See also the following passage in "A Digression": "For, to speak a bold Truth, it is a fatal Miscarriage, so ill to order Affairs, as to pass for a Fool in one Company, when in another you might be treated as a *Philosopher*" (168).

51. Strauss, *Spinoza's Critique of Religion*, 96; also Robertson, *History of Freethought*, 2:617.

52. Sir William Temple, "Of Poetry," in Monk, *Five Miscellaneous Essays*, 200; Temple, "Observations upon the United Provinces of the Netherlands," 173–74.

53. See also Swift's "Mr. Collins's Discourse of Free-Thinking," in *Prose Works*, 4:27.

54. See Hobbes, *Leviathan*, 1.12.171; 2.31.404; Montaigne, *Complete Works*, 2.12.368–70, 380–81, 385. Contemporaries read Montaigne's description of God as an incomprehensible power as evidence of his links to radical deism (see Alan M. Boase, *The Fortunes of Montaigne* [London: Methuen, 1935], 35).

55. Thomas Tenison, *The Creed of Mr. Hobbes Examined*, 2nd ed. (London, 1671), 30.

56. Williams, *Jonathan Swift*, 44.

57. Strauss, *Spinoza's Critique of Religion*, 48.

58. Wolesley, *Unreasonableness of Atheism*, 18. For similar contemporary objections to the doctrine of state authority in religion, see John Owen, *A Brief and Impartial Account of the Nature of the Protestant Religion* (London, 1682), 28; and Parker, *Discourse of Ecclesiastical Politie*, 114–15. On the links between the argument for the social, moral, and political role of religion and charges of atheism in the period, see Hunter, "Science and Heterodoxy," 44; and Bredvold, *Intellectual Milieu of John Dryden*, 86.

59. Rawson, "Character of Swift's Satire," 21.

60. Sextus Empiricus, *Against the Physicists*, trans. R.G. Bury, 4 vols. (Cambridge, MA: Harvard University Press, 1933–49), 3:1.54. The view is also discussed by Cotta in Cicero's *On the Nature of the Gods*: "What think you of those, who have asserted that the whole doctrine concerning the immortal Gods was the invention of politicians, whose view was to govern that part of the community by religion, which reason could not influence? Are not their opinions subversive of all religion?" (*The Treatises of M. T. Cicero*, trans. C. D. Yonge [London: Henry G. Bohn, 1853], 1.42). In the period, the Critias fragment is reproduced in full and discussed at length in Warburton's *Divine Legation*, 418–24.

61. Indeed, despite its irreligious origins, the theory of the pious fraud had become so widespread by the late seventeenth century that Anglican apologists attempted to appropriate it for their own purposes (see Hill, "Freethinking and Libertinism," 58–59). One finds the likes of Richard Bentley, for example, observing that "as to the benign Influence of Religion upon Communities and Governments, . . . 'tis so apparent and unquestionable, that *'tis one of the wise Objections of the Atheist,* That it first was contrived and introduced by Politicians to bring the wild and stragling Herds of Mankind under Subjection and Laws" (Bentley, *Folly of Atheism*, 29–30 [italics mine]). As early as 1672, Samuel Parker had also asserted that "if our Religion were nothing else but (as all Religion is lately defined) the Belief of Tales publickly allowed, . . . yet after all this, they are and must be allowed necessary Instruments in the State" (Parker, preface to *Bishop Bramhall's Vindication*, E2^r. See also Tillotson, "Folly of Scoffing at Religion," 38–39; Glanvill, *Seasonable Reflections and Discourses*, 35–36). And yet despite these endeavors to redirect the tradition of unbelief back toward a defense of Christianity, orthodox theologians remained for the most part reluctant to part with more traditional conceptions of spiritual commitment.

Notes to Conclusion

1. Pope to Swift, 28 November 1729, in *The Correspondence of Alexander Pope*, ed. George Sherburn, 5 vols. (Oxford: Clarendon Press, 1956), 3:81. See also Bolingbroke to Swift, 19 November 1729, in which Bolingbroke bids Swift to inquire of Pope about "the Work he is about"; and Pope to Swift, 19 June 1730, in which Pope refers to his work on a book that will "make mankind look upon this life with comfort and pleasure, and put morality in good humour" (Pope, *Correspondence*, 3:71, 117).

2. Swift to Pope, 1 November 1734, in Pope, *Correspondence*, 3:439.

3. Bolingbroke to Swift, 2 August 1731, in Pope, *Correspondence*, 3:213.

4. Bolingbroke to Swift, 30 August–5 October 1729, in Pope, *Correspondence*, 3:48–49; Bolingbroke and Pope to Swift, 20 March 1730/31, in Pope, *Correspondence*, 3:183.

5. Bolingbroke to Swift, 2 August, 1731, in Pope, *Correspondence*, 3:214.

6. It should be noted here that Bolingbroke makes explicit a rejection of a future state that remains more implicit in *An Essay on Man*. As he himself notes in the letter, "You will not understand by what I have said that Pope will go so deep into the argument, or carry it so far, as I have hinted" (Pope, *Correspondence*, 3:214). In later letters, Bolingbroke expresses his hope and conviction that Swift "both understand[s] and approve[s]" Pope's "Ethic Epistles" (Pope, *Correspondence*, 3:404–5; also 3:414).

7. In his *Fragments, or Minutes of Essays*, Bolingbroke writes, "There may be rewards and punishments reserved to another life; but whether there are, or are not, the religion of nature teaches, that morality is our greatest interest, because it tends to the greatest happiness of our whole kind in this life" (*The Works of the Late Right Honourable Henry St. John, Lord Viscount Bolingbroke*, 8 vols. [London, 1809], 8:465).

8. Bolingbroke to Swift, 2 August, 1731, in Pope, *Correspondence*, 3:211.

9. Bolingbroke, *Works*, 5:422, 417–18.

10. Bolingbroke, *Works*, 5:96. For other examples of Bolingbroke's support for pious frauds in religion, see *Works*, 5:417, 421–30; 8:103.

11. Viscount Bolingbroke to Swift, 12 September 1724, in Swift, *Correspondence*, 3:28.

12. Bolingbroke, *Works*, 8:105; see also 5:99–100.

13. Ibid., 5:100.

14. Ibid., 8:164, 165.

15. Ibid., 8:165.

16. Ibid., 8:166, 165.

17. See Maynard Mack, "Introduction to *An Essay on Man*," in *Collected in Himself* (Newark: University of Delaware Press, 1982), 198. Bolingbroke was just beginning to compile his ideas on philosophy and religion as Pope was completing the fourth epistle of *An Essay on Man*. In September of 1734, Bolingbroke told Swift that he had written six and a half letters of what would later be published among Bolingbroke's *Works* of 1754 as *Letters, or Essays, Addressed to Alexander Pope* (see Pope and Bolingbroke to Swift, 15 September 1734, in

Pope, *Correspondence*, 1:432–33). There has been extensive controversy in Pope studies over the extent to which Bolingbroke influenced Pope or vice versa (see esp. Mack, "Introduction," 205–6; Robert W. Rogers, *The Major Satires of Alexander Pope*, Illinois Studies in Language and Literature, vol. 40 [Urbana: University of Illinois Press, 1955], 45–49; Brean S. Hammond, *Pope and Bolingbroke: A Study of Friendship and Influence* [Columbia: University of Missouri Press, 1984], 57–91; and Fred Parker, *Scepticism and Literature: An Essay on Pope, Hume, Sterne, and Johnson* [Oxford: Oxford University Press, 2003], 86–137).

18. This phrase is repeated in *An Essay on Man*, 1:294, 4:145, and 4:394. Leibniz's *Théodicée* of 1710 argued similarly that this was the best of all possible universes. On Leibniz's possible influence on Pope, see Cecil A. Moore, "Did Leibniz Influence Pope's *Essay?*" *Journal of English and Germanic Philology* 16 (1917): 84–102.

19. On Pope's deism in *An Essay on Man*, see Leslie Stephen, *History of English Thought in the Eighteenth Century*, 3rd ed., 2 vols. (London: Smith, Elder, 1902), 2:349–53; Kallich, *Heav'n's First Law*, 3–34; Maynard Mack, *Alexander Pope: A Life* (New Haven, CT: Yale University Press, 1985), 739–41; Hammond, *Pope and Bolingbroke*, 69–91; and Noggle, *The Skeptical Sublime*, 118–19. For a dissenting view, see Nancy K. Lawlor, "Pope's *Essay on Man*: Oblique Light for a False Mirror," *Modern Language Quarterly* 28 (1967): 305–16; and G. Douglas Atkins, "Pope and Deism: A New Analysis," *Huntington Library Quarterly* 35 (1972): 257–78. For a discussion of the parallels between *An Essay on Man* and Lucretius' *De rerum natura* that asserts Pope's religious orthodoxy, see Miriam Leranbaum, *Alexander Pope's "Opus Magnum," 1729–1744* (Oxford: Clarendon Press, 1977), 38–63. Other critics discuss Pope's refusal of Christian revelation and the supernatural without recurring to the deist label; see especially Douglas H. White, *Pope and the Context of Controversy: The Manipulation of Ideas in "An Essay on Man"* (Chicago: University of Chicago Press, 1979); and also Geoffrey Tillotson, *Pope and Human Nature* (Oxford: Clarendon Press, 1958), 41; Thomas R. Edwards, *This Dark Estate: A Reading of Pope* (Berkeley: University of California Press, 1963), 43–44; and Douglas Canfield, "The Fate of the Fall in Pope's *Essay on Man*," *The Eighteenth Century* 23 (1982): 134–50.

20. Voltaire, *Oeuvres complètes*, 22:175, 176. The cosmopolitan afterlife of Pope's *Essay on Man* is indicated not only by the poem's notoriety in France, discussed here, but also by its relevance to the German Enlightenment (see Gotthold Lessing and Moses Mendelssohn's *Pope ein Metaphysiker!* [1755]). This international literary phenomenon culminated in the publication of a polyglot edition of the poem in 1801 (Robert Shackleton, "Pope's *Essay on Man* and the French Enlightenment," in *Studies in the Eighteenth Century: II*, ed. R. F. Brissenden [Toronto: University of Toronto Press, 1973], 1; see also Robert W. Rogers, "Critiques of the *Essay on Man* in France and Germany, 1736–1755," *ELH* 15 [1948]: 176–93).

21. Pope to Caryll, 19 July 1711, in Pope, *Correspondence*, 1:126. Pope's letter documents that, like Swift's satire on religious corruption in *A Tale of a Tub*,

his critique of superstition in *An Essay on Criticism* provoked the charge that he intended all of religion to be encompassed in the denunciation of religious fraud. Though a member of the Catholic Church, Pope stresses repeatedly that he is not a "Papist" but rather "a Catholick, in the strictest sense of the word" (see Pope to Atterbury, 20 November 1717 and Pope to Viscount Harcourt, [6 May 1723], in Pope, *Correspondence*, 1:454; 2:171–72.

22. Pope to Atterbury, 20 November 1717, in Pope, *Correspondence*, 1:453–54.

23. That Christianity's special revelations are absent from this generalist creed is suggested in an anonymous poem published in a miscellany of 1717, very likely edited by Pope. Here the same vacillation between Protestantism and popery mentioned in Pope's letter to Atterbury of that year leads the speaker to atheism:

> See how the wandring *Danube* flows,
>   Realms and Religions parting;
> A friend to all true Christian foes,
>   To *Peter, Jack, and Martin.*
> Now Protestant, and Papist now;
>   Not constant long to either,
> At length an infidel does grow,
>   And ends his journey, neither.
> Thus many a youth I've known set out
>   Half protestant, half papist,
> And rambling long the world about,
>   Turn Infidel or Atheist.

("On the River Danube," in *Poems on Several Occasions* [London, 1717]). On Pope's involvement in this miscellany, see A. E. Case, "Some New Poems by Pope?" *London Mercury* 10 (1924), 614–23; and George Sherburn, *The Early Career of Alexander Pope* (Oxford: Clarendon Press, 1934), 61.

24. Other early clues of Pope's heterodox leanings include several manuscript satires and ballads published piratically by Pope's nemesis, Edmund Curll. Both "A Roman Catholick Version of the First Psalm; for the Use of a Young Lady" and "To the Ingenious Mr. Moore, Author of the Celebrated Worm-Powder" appeared surreptitiously in 1716—to Pope's considerable embarrassment. The former made a burlesque of Scripture by applying Thomas Sternhold's verse adaptation of Psalm 1 to the libertine adventures of a town lady, an expression of impiety that earned Pope this response in *The Flying Post* of 12–14 July 1716:

> No Atheist, Deist, Devil yet,
> Thus rudely touch'd that Lyre;
> To prostitute thus Holy Writ,
> As do's this Popish Squire.

"To the Ingenious Mr. Moore," described by contemporaries as Pope's "satire against mankind," associated Pope with Rochester's alleged atheism and anticipated the rejection of a future state insinuated in *An Essay on Man*: "Man is a very Worm by Birth," Pope writes, "Vile Reptile, weak, and vain!/ A while he crawls upon the Earth,/ Then shrinks to Earth again" (5–8). On evidence of irreligion in Pope's early works, see Sherburn, *Early Career*, 61–62, 95–96, 175–76, 180–84; Mack, *Alexander Pope*, 297–98.

25. Pope, "The Design," 502.

26. Warburton read this passage the other way around: on his Christian reading of the poem, Pope's aim was to show that natural religion depends crucially on revelation without admitting it (see Lawlor, "Pope's *Essay on Man*," 305–16). On Pope's awareness that his poem advocated natural religion above revelation, see Pope to Caryll, 23 October 1733, and Pope to Caryll, 1 January 1733/34, in Pope, *Correspondence*, 3:390, 400.

27. Laura Brown views Pope's theriophilia and critique of anthropocentrism as reinforcing an imperialist program of expansionism and acquisition (*Alexander Pope* [Oxford: Blackwell, 1985], 68–79), a reading that I would argue betrays current critical ideologies more than those of the eighteenth century.

28. See Pope to Caryll, 8 March 1732/33, in Pope, *Correspondence*, 3:354. Note that Pope has not yet claimed authorship of the poem in this letter.

29. See Crousaz's comment that Pope aims "to prove that revelation is of no use, since error and illusion may produce the same effect, and afford us with the tranquillity and peace of mind, which we search for in its doctrines" (*Commentary*, 17:205).

30. For another version of Pope's attack on superstition and praise of the simplicity of natural religion, see the summary of his intended epic poem, *Brutus*, in Owen Ruffhead, *The Life of Alexander Pope* (London, 1769), 409–24.

31. Pope to Caryll, 19 July 1711, in Pope, *Correspondence*, 1:126. Pope significantly omitted "as Christians" from the end of his sentence in his 1735 edition of his letters.

32. Bolingbroke, *Works*, 5:73. On Pope screening himself against charges of heterodoxy, see his letters to Caryll in *Correspondence*, 3:353–54, 390, 400.

33. Samuel Johnson, *The Lives of the Most Eminent English Poets; with Critical Observations on Their Works*, 4 vols. (Oxford: Clarendon Press, 2006), 4:40. See Pope and Bolingbroke to Swift, 15 September 1734: "The design of concealing myself was good, and had its full effect; I was thought a divine, a philosopher, and what not? And my doctrine had a sanction I could not have given to it" (Pope, *Correspondence*, 3:433); also Pope to Caryll, 8 March 1732/33, in Pope, *Correspondence*, 3:354.

34. "On Some Authors leveling the Rational Nature with the Brutal," *Weekly Miscellany*, 11 August 1733; *Weekly Miscellany*, 28 September 1734; *The Prompter*, 2 December 1735; [Mr. Bridges], *Divine Wisdom and Providence; an Essay*, 2nd ed. (London, 1737), i. This text appeared in three editions between 1736 and 1738. Joseph Warton commented similarly that Pope adopted a very different method from Milton's in his justification of the ways of God to man, as he "imagined, that the goodness and justice of the Deity might be defended, *without* having recourse to the doctrine of a future state, and of the depraved state of man" (*Essay on the Genius and Writings of Pope*, 5th ed., 2 vols. [London, 1806], 2:60, and also 2:64, 66).

35. *London Evening-Post*, 15–17 January 1736.

36. Cited in Mack, "Introduction," 201 (translation mine).

37. See Ira O. Wade, *Voltaire and Candide: A Study in the Fusion of History, Art, and Philosophy* (Princeton, NJ: Princeton University Press, 1959), 62–63.

38. Mack, "Introduction," 201.

39. As Crousaz asks, why should the weak of faith be "exposed by Flights of Poetry and magnificent Expressions, to grow familiar with prophane Ideas?" (*Commentary*, 17:79). Du Resnel's translation, on which Crousaz bases his *Commentaire*, is notoriously inaccurate, omitting some passages and expanding others in Pope's original. For this reason, many Pope scholars have considered Crousaz's attacks irrelevant to any correct understanding of Pope (see Mack, "Introduction," 201–2). What such a view has failed to consider, however, is that the broad strokes of Crousaz's commentary are echoed throughout the period by critics in England, who read Pope in his original language (see esp. [Almonides], *Common Sense a Common Delusion* [London, 1751]; and also Bridges, *Divine Wisdom and Providence*, ii–iii; William Ayre, *Truth. A Counterpart to Mr. Pope's Essay on Man, Epistle the First* [London, 1739]; and Johnson, *Lives*, 4:44–45).

40. Numerous editions of Warburton's Pope were published in the eighteenth century. Almost all of them contained his commentary on *An Essay on Man*. Needless to say, such an apparatus "put the poem on the side of religion" (Ruffhead, *Life of Alexander Pope*, 223). For a fascinating discussion of Warburton's editorial revisions of Pope's *Essay on Man*, see James McLaverty, "Warburton's False Comma: Reason and Virtue in Pope's *Essay on Man*," *Modern Philology* (2002): 379–92.

41. Louis Racine, *La religion, poëme* [1742] (Paris, 1785). It is interesting to note that an English translation of the poem published in 1753/54 omits completely all mention of Pope and his philosophy.

42. Rogers, "Critiques of the *Essay on Man*," 181; Shackleton, "Pope's *Essay on Man*," 10–11.

43. Shackleton, "Pope's *Essay on Man*," 6. For evidence that Voltaire had the first two epistles in hand as early as May 1733—seven weeks before he sent the twenty-fifth letter on Pascal to his printer—see Shackleton, "Pope's *Essay on Man*," 4–7; and George R. Havens, "Voltaire's Marginal Comments upon Pope's *Essay on Man*," *Modern Language Notes* 43 (1928): 429.

44. Voltaire, *Oeuvres complètes*, 22:176. Pope's correspondence shows that the two writers esteemed and read one another's work (see Bolingbroke to Pope, 18 February 1724, and Pope to Caryll, 25 December 1725, in Pope, *Correspondence*, 2:222, 354). In 1724, Pope had expressed his admiration of Voltaire's "principled Spirit of true Religion," concluding that the *philosophe* was "at once a Free thinker and a Lover of Quiet; no Bigot, but yet no Heretick: one who honours Authority and National Sanctions without prejudice to Truth or Charity; One who has Study'd Controversy less than Reason, and the Fathers less than Mankind" (Pope to Bolingbroke, 9 April 1724, in Pope, *Correspondence*, 2:229).

45. Voltaire, *Oeuvres complètes*, 22:177, 178, 44, cited in Havens, "Voltaire's Marginal Comments," 432. I thank Daniel Cohen for help with this translation.

Pope's version of Voltaire's sentiment, appearing in epistle I of *An Essay on Man*, goes as follows:

> Presumptuous Man! the reason wouldst thou find,
> Why form'd so weak, so little, and so blind!
> First, if thou canst, the harder reason guess,
> Why form'd no weaker, blinder, and no less!
>   (1.35–38)

46. Havens, "Voltaire's Marginal Comments," 432–33. For a recent denial of Pope's influence, see David Wooton's introduction to *Candide and Related Texts* (Indianapolis, IN: Hackett, 2000), xii; and also Theodore Besterman, *Voltaire* (Chicago: University of Chicago Press, 1976), 367. For the alternative view that Voltaire's debt to Pope's thought is suggested by all the major works between the *Traité de métaphysique* (1734) and the *Poème sur la loi naturelle* (1752)—particularly by Voltaire's *Discours en vers sur l'homme* (1738), an imitation of sorts, as the title suggests, of *An Essay on Man*—see Wade, *Voltaire and Candide*, 62–83; Richard Gilbert Knapp, *The Fortunes of Pope's "Essay on Man" in 18th Century France*, ed. Theodore Besterman, *Studies on Voltaire and the Eighteenth Century*, vol. 82 (Geneva: Institut et Museé Voltaire, 1971), 79–122; and Shackleton, "Pope's *Essay on Man*," 1–15.

47. Shackleton, "Pope's *Essay on Man*," 11–12.

48. On Voltaire's abandonment of optimism, see Theodore Besterman, *Voltaire* (Chicago: University of Chicago Press, 1976), 365–74.

49. Voltaire, *Correspondence*, in *The Complete Works of Voltaire*, ed. Theodore Besterman, vols. 85–135 (Toronto: University of Toronto Press, 1968–), 88: D1342 (translation mine).

50. Warburton argues similarly to Crousaz against the doctrine of fatalism, only in this case vindicating Pope's poem against impiety. "The *Doctrine of Fate*," he writes, "subverts and annihilates *all Religion*: For the Belief of Rewards and Punishments, without which *no Religion* can subsist, is founded on the Principle of Man's being an *accountable* Creature; but when *Freedom of Will* is wanting, Man is no more so than a Clock or Organ" (*A Critical and Philosophical Commentary on Mr. Pope's "Essay on Man"* [New York: Garland Publishing, 1974], xv).

51. Crousaz, *Commentary*, 17:113.

52. Ibid., 17:115–16, 110, 115, 116.

53. Ibid., 17:272, 322.

54. For an illuminating discussion of sex in *Candide*, see Roger Pearson, "The Candid *Conte*," in *The Fables of Reason: A Study of Voltaire's "Contes Philosophiques"* (Oxford: Clarendon Press, 1993), 125–28. For an equally illuminating treatment of Pope's links to a libertine underworld, see James Grantham Turner, "Pope's Libertine Self-Fashioning," *The Eighteenth Century: Theory and Interpretation* 29 (1988): 123–44.

55. Voltaire, *Candide*, 6. Note also Voltaire's related satire on the belief, current among the freethinkers examined here, that the primitive state of mankind was more virtuous because more natural (*Candide*, 32–35).

56. Ibid., 11.

57. Ibid., 10.

58. See Pope's comment to the Bishop of Atterbury: "I hope all churches and all governments are so far of God, as they are rightly understood, and rightly administered: and where they are, or may be wrong, I leave it to God alone to mend or reform them; which whenever he does, it must be by greater instruments than I am" (Pope to Atterbury, 20 November 1717, in Pope, *Correspondence*, 1:454). On Pope's conservative vision in *An Essay on Man*, see Jonathan Lamb, *The Rhetoric of Suffering: Reading the Book of Job in the Eighteenth Century* (Oxford: Oxford University Press, 1995), 71–72. The English version of optimism, as popularized by Pope, was not Voltaire's only target in *Candide*. Leibniz's theodicy was as much if not more censured by Voltaire (see Wooton's introduction to *Candide* for a useful discussion of these various influences [x–xvii]).

59. Rochester in the country to Savile in London, spring 1676, in Wilmot, *Letters*, 119. On optimism and conservatism, see Haydn Mason, *Candide: Optimism Demolished* (New York: Twayne Publishers, 1992), 48.

60. Voltaire, *Candide*, 47, 78.

61. Voltaire, *Correspondence*, 102:D7570. On Voltaire's refusal of a providential God, see Besterman, *Voltaire*, 215–32; Ira O. Wade, *The Intellectual Development of Voltaire* (Princeton, NJ: Princeton University Press, 1969), 667–68; René Pomeau, "Voltaire's Religion," in *Voltaire: A Collection of Critical Essays*, ed. William F. Bottiglia (Englewood Cliffs, NJ: Prentice-Hall, 1968), 140–49; and Pearson, "Candid *Conte*," 115–16. On this front, Voltaire and Pope share a freethinking view abhorred by Crousaz, who rails in his *Commentaire* against the "blasphemy" and "libertine" ethos of "he that ascribes to a spirit of pride the inestimable effects of divine grace" (*Commentary*, 78).

62. Voltaire is far from naïve about the possibilities for freedom of action in a world plagued by corruption and depravity (see *Candide*, 5, 12).

63. Jean Starobinski, "Voltaire's Double-Barreled Musket," in *Blessings in Disguise; or, The Morality of Evil*, trans. Arthur Goldhammer (Cambridge, MA: Harvard University Press, 1993), 89; Voltaire, *Candide, ou l'optimisme*, in *Oeuvres complétes*, 48:260; Wooton, *Candide*, 79. On the significance of work at the close of *Candide*, see the following criticism in English: David Langdon, "On the Meanings of the Conclusion of *Candide*," *Studies on Voltaire and the Eighteenth Century* 238 (1985): 397–432; Patrick Henry, "Sacred and Profane Gardens in *Candide*," *Studies on Voltaire and the Eighteenth Century* 176 (1979): 133–52; Pearson, "Candid *Conte*," 119–21; Ludwig W. Kahn, "Voltaire's *Candide* and the Problem of Secularization," *PMLA* 67 (1952): 886–88; and William F. Bottiglia, "Candide's Garden," *PMLA* 66 (1951): 718–33. More has been written on *Candide*, and particularly its conclusion, than on any other work in Voltaire's corpus. My discussion here seeks not so much to present a new or original reading as to point out that the concluding call to action, noted by numerous critics, should be read as a corrective to the quietism of Pope's optimism and of English freethinking generally.

64. Pope to Caryll, 18 June 1711, in Pope, *Correspondence*, 1:119; see also Pope to Caryll, 19 July 1711, in Pope, *Correspondence*, 1:128. Pope also agreed to revise his "Universal Prayer," originally cast as a hymn, to make it more consistent with orthodox Christian doctrine. The later versions, overseen by Warburton, come closer to admitting supernatural revelation and introduce a new stanza that asserts free will (R. W. Rogers, "Alexander Pope's *Universal Prayer*," in *Essential Articles for the Study of Alexander Pope*, ed. Maynard Mack [Hamden, CT: Archon Books, 1964], 351–67.

65. Ruffhead, *Life of Alexander Pope*, 268; Joseph Spence, *Anecdotes, Observations, and Characters, of Books and Men* (London, 1820), 315. Both Spence and Ruffhead describe how the third of the "Ethic Epistles" on civil and ecclesiastical government was afterward conceived as an epic poem, set in ancient times and based on Brutus' arrival on the islands of the Britons. Never completed, the epic was to end with Brutus conquering superstition and priestcraft in the newly discovered land, establishing the true religion of "one God, and the doctrines of morality" (Spence, *Anecdotes*, 289; see also Ruffhead, *Life of Alexander Pope*, 409–24, for a more extensive description of this intended epic).

66. Warburton, *Critical and Philosophical Commentary*, 88.

67. Jonathan Richardson, *Richardsoniana* (London, 1776), 264–65.

68. Pope to Warburton, 11 April [1739], in Pope, *Correspondence*, 4:171–72.

69. Johnson, *Lives*, 4:59.

70. This reading is supported by Richardson's comment that on talking frequently with Pope of the deistical elements in *An Essay on Man*, Pope never "appear[ed] to understand it otherwise" (*Richardsoniana*, 265). For the contrary reading that Warburton's Christian reading of Pope is the correct one and that Pope sincerely embraced Warburton's championing of his orthodoxy, see Mack, "Introduction," 202; and Lawlor, "Pope's *Essay on Man*," 305–16.

71. Pope to Caryll, 18 June 1711, and Pope to Caryll, 19 July 1711, in Pope, *Correspondence*, 1:118, 128. See also Pope to Louis Racine, 1 September 1742, in which Pope expresses a similar deference "in submitting all my Opinions to the Decision of the Church" (Pope, *Correspondence*, 4:416).

72. For a recent account of the contradictory nature of Pope's skeptical conservatism in *An Essay on Man*, see Noggle, *Skeptical Sublime*, 97–127.

73. Voltaire, *Candide*, 78.

74. Berman, "Deism, Immortality, and the Art of Theological Lying," in Lemay, *Deism, Masonry, and the Enlightenment*, 72.

75. See Lucretius, *The Way Things Are*, 4:20–26.

76. Such a desire, John Traugott argues, informs Swift's famous *Drapiers Letters* (1724–25), written in the voice of a tradesman persona second only to the Hack of *A Tale*, to oppose the introduction into Ireland of a debased coinage of half-pence. Here, as in *A Tale*, the inciting effects of art and irony take on a life of their own, reaching fulfillment in their daring to teach, contrary to the colonial apparatus, that the Irish people are "free thinkers with solidarity in their immediate political purpose" (" 'Shall Jonathan Die?': Swift, Irony, and a Failed Revolution in Ireland," in *The Politics of Irony: Essays in Self-Betrayal*, ed. Daniel W. Conway and John E. Seery [New York: St. Martin's Press, 1992],

36). On the tension between liberty and authority in Swift's politics, see also David Nokes, "The Radical Conservatism of Swift's Irish Pamphlets," *British Journal for Eighteenth-Century Studies* 7 (1984): 169–76; Carole Fabricant, "Speaking for the Irish Nation: The Drapier, the Bishop, and the Problems of Colonial Representation," *ELH* 66 (1999): 337–72; and Claude Rawson, "The Injured Lady and the Drapier: A Reading of Swift's Irish Tracts," *Prose Studies* 3 (1980): 15–43. For recent work on Swift's anticolonialism, see Clement Hawes, "Swift's Immanent Critique of Colonial Modernity," in *The British Eighteenth Century and Global Critique* (New York: Palgrave, 2005), 139–68.

Bibliography

Addison, Joseph. *The Spectator*. Edited by Donald F. Bond. 5 vols. Oxford: Clarendon Press, 1965.

Agorni, Mirella. "The Voice of the 'Translatress': From Aphra Behn to Elizabeth Carter." *Yearbook of English Studies* 28 (1998): 181–95.

Allestree, Richard. *Eighteen Sermons*. London, 1669.

[Almonides]. *Common Sense a Common Delusion*. London, 1751.

Anderson, Perry. *English Questions*. New York: Verso, 1992.

Andrews, Charles M., ed. *Narratives of the Insurrections, 1675–1690*. New York: Scribner's, 1915.

Anonymous. "The Ballad of the Cloak; or, the Cloaks Knavery." [London, 1679–82].

Anonymous. *The Character of a Coffee-House*. London, 1673.

Anonymous. *The Character of a Town-Gallant, Exposing the Extravagant Fopperies of Some Vain Self-Conceited Pretenders to Gentility and Good Breeding*. London, 1675.

Anonymous. *A Dictionary of All Religions, Ancient and Modern*. London, 1704.

Anonymous. *A Morning's Discourse of a Bottomless Tub*. London, 1712.

Anonymous. "Religion Made a Cloak For Villany." [London, 1681–84].

Anonymous. *Select Letters Taken from Fog's "Weekly Journal."* 2 vols. London, 1732.

Anonymous. *Strange News From Virginia; Being a Full and True Account of the Life and Death of Nathaniel Bacon*. London, 1677.

Assheton, William. *An Admonition to a Deist, Occasioned by Some Passages in Discourse with the Same Person*. London, 1685.

Atkins, G. Douglas. "Pope and Deism: A New Analysis." *Huntington Library Quarterly* 35 (1972): 257–78.

Averroës. *On the Harmony of Religion and Philosophy*. Translated by George F. Hourani. London: Gibb Memorial Trust, 1976.

Ayre, William. *Truth. A Counterpart to Mr. Pope's Essay on Man, Epistle the First*. London, 1739.

Ayres, Philip. *Classical Culture and the Idea of Rome in Eighteenth-Century England*. New York: Cambridge University Press, 1997.

Baltus, Jean-François. *Réponse à l'histoire des oracles de M. de Fontenelle* [An Answer to Mr. De Fontenelle's History of Oracles]. Strasbourg, 1707.

Barnett, S. J. *The Enlightenment and Religion: The Myths of Modernity*. New York: Palgrave, 2003.

Barrow, Isaac. *The Works of the Learned Isaac Barrow*. Edited by John Tillotson and Abraham Hill. 4 vols. 2nd ed. London, 1687.

Batten, Charles L. "The Source of Aphra Behn's *The Widow Ranter*." *Restoration and 18th-Century Theatre Research* 13 (1974): 12–18.

Baxter, Richard. *More Reasons For the Christian Religion, and No Reason Against It*. London, 1672.

Baxter, Stephen. *England's Rise to Greatness, 1660–1763*. Berkeley: University of California Press, 1983.

Bayle, Pierre. *The Dictionary Historical and Critical of Mr. Peter Bayle*. 5 vols. 2nd ed. London, 1734–8.

Behn, Aphra. *The Works of Aphra Behn*. Edited by Janet Todd. 7 vols. London: William Pickering, 1992–96.

Beiser, Frederick C. *The Sovereignty of Reason*. Princeton, NJ: Princeton University Press, 1996.

Bentley, Richard. *Eight Sermons*. 6th ed. Cambridge, 1735.

———. *The Folly of Atheism, and (What Is Now Called) Deism*. 2nd ed. London, 1692.

———. *The Works of Richard Bentley*. Edited by Alexander Dyce. 3 vols. London, 1836–38.

Berman, David. *A History of Atheism in Britain: From Hobbes to Russell*. New York: Croom Helm, 1988.

Berti, Silvia, Françoise Charles-Daubert, and Richard H. Popkin, eds. *Heterodoxy, Spinozism, and Free Thought in Early-Eighteenth-Century Europe*. Boston: Kluwer Academic Publishers, 1996.

Besterman, Theodore. *Voltaire*. Chicago: University of Chicago Press, 1976.

Billings, Warren M., ed. *The Old Dominion in the Seventeenth Century*. Chapel Hill: University of North Carolina Press, 1975.

[Blount, Charles]. *An Appeal from the Country to the City; for the Preservation of His Majesties Person, Liberty, Property, and the Protestant Religion*. London, 1679.

———. *Miracles, No Violations of the Laws of Nature*. London, 1683.

Blount, Charles. *The Miscellaneous Works of Charles Blount*. 2nd ed. London, 1695.

———. *The Oracles of Reason*. London, 1693.

———. *The Two First Books of Philostratus, concerning the Life of Apollonius Tyaneus*. London, 1680.

Blount, Sir Thomas Pope. *Essays on Several Subjects*. London, 1691.

Boas, George. *The Happy Beast in French Thought of the Seventeenth Century*. Baltimore: Johns Hopkins University Press, 1933.

Boase, Alan M. *The Fortunes of Montaigne*. London: Methuen, 1935.

Bolingbroke, Henry St. John Viscount. *The Works of the Late Right Honourable Henry St. John, Lord Viscount Bolingbroke*. 8 vols. London, 1809.

Bottiglia, William F. "Candide's Garden." *PMLA* 66 (1951): 718–33.

———. *Voltaire: A Collection of Critical Essays.* Englewood Cliffs, NJ: Prentice-Hall, 1968.

Boyle, Frank T. "Profane and Debauched Deist: Swift in the Contemporary Response to *A Tale of a Tub.*" *Eighteenth-Century Ireland* 3 (1988): 25–38.

Boyle, Robert. *A Free Enquiry into the Vulgarly Received Notion of Nature.* 1686. Edited by Edward B. Davis and Michael Hunter. New York: Cambridge University Press, 1996.

Branch, Lori. *Rituals of Spontaneity: Sentiment and Secularism from Free Prayer to Wordsworth.* Waco, TX: Baylor University Press, 2006.

Bredvold, Louis I. *The Intellectual Milieu of John Dryden: Studies in Some Aspects of Seventeenth-Century Thought.* Ann Arbor: University of Michigan Press, 1956.

[Bridges, Mr.]. *Divine Wisdom and Providence.* 2nd ed. London, 1737.

Brown, Laura. *Alexander Pope.* Oxford: Blackwell, 1985.

Brown, Thomas. *The Late Converts Exposed, or, the Reasons of Mr. Bays's Changing His Religion: Part the Second.* London, 1690.

Browne, Thomas. *Miracles, Work's Above and Contrary to Nature.* London, 1683.

Budick, Sanford. *Dryden and the Abyss of Light.* New Haven, CT: Yale University Press, 1970.

Burnet, Gilbert. *Bishop Burnet's History of His Own Time.* 6 vols. Oxford, 1883.

———. *Some Passages of the Life and Death of the Right Honourable John, Earl of Rochester.* London, 1693.

Burns, Edward, ed. *Reading Rochester.* Liverpool, UK: Liverpool University Press, 1995.

Burnyeat, Myles, ed. *The Skeptical Tradition.* Berkeley: University of California Press, 1983.

Burton, Robert. *The Anatomy of Melancholy.* Edited by Thomas C. Faulkner, Nicolas K. Kiessling, and Rhonda L. Blair. 3 vols. Oxford: Clarendon Press, 1989–94.

Canfield, Douglas. "The Fate of the Fall in Pope's *Essay on Man.*" *The Eighteenth Century* 23 (1982): 134–50.

———, and Deborah C. Payne, eds. *Cultural Readings of Restoration and Eighteenth-Century English Theater.* Athens: University of Georgia Press, 1995.

Casaubon, Meric. *A Treatise concerning Enthusiasme, as it is an Effect of Nature.* 1656. 2nd ed. Edited by Paul J. Korshin. Gainesville, FL: Scholars' Facsimiles & Reprints, 1970.

Case, A. E. "Some New Poems by Pope?" *The London Mercury* 10 (1924): 614–23.

Champion, J. A. I., *The Pillars of Priestcraft Shaken: The Church of England and Its Enemies, 1660–1730.* Cambridge: Cambridge University Press, 1992.

———. " 'Religion's Safe, with Priestcraft Is the War': Augustan Anticlericalism and the Legacy of the English Revolution, 1660–1720." *The European Legacy* 5 (2000): 547–61.

Chernaik, Warren. "Captains and Slaves: Aphra Behn and the Rhetoric of Republicanism." *The Seventeenth Century* 17 (2002): 97–107.

———. *Sexual Freedom in Restoration Literature.* Cambridge: Cambridge University Press, 1995.

Churchill, Sarah Jennings, Duchess of Marlborough. *Memoirs of Sarah, Duchess of Marlborough.* Edited by William King. New York: Kraus Reprint, 1969.

Clark, J. C. D. *English Society, 1688–1832: Religion, Ideology, and Politics during the Ancien Regime.* Cambridge: Cambridge University Press, 2000.

Clark, John R. *Form and Frenzy in Swift's Tale of a Tub.* Ithaca, NY: Cornell University Press, 1970.

Clarke, Samuel. *A Demonstration of the Being and Attributes of God.* Edited by Ezio Vailati. Cambridge: Cambridge University Press, 1998.

———. *A Discourse concerning the Unchangeable Obligations of Natural Religion.* 1706. Stuttgart-Bad Cannstatt: F. Frommann, 1964.

Coleridge, Samuel Taylor. *Biographia Literaria, or Biographical Sketches of My Literary Life and Opinions.* Edited by James Engell and W. Jackson Bate. Princeton, NJ: Princeton University Press, 1984.

Colie, Rosalie L. "Spinoza and the Early English Deists." *Journal of the History of Ideas* 20 (1959): 23–46.

Collins, Anthony. *A Discourse Concerning Ridicule and Irony in Writing.* 1729. Edited by Edward A. Bloom and Lillian D. Bloom. Augustan Reprint Society, no. 142. Los Angeles: University of California Press, 1970.

Coltharp, Duane. "Rivall Fops, Rambling Rakes, Wild Women: Homosocial Desire and Courtly Crisis in Rochester's Poetry." *The Eighteenth Century* 38 (1997): 23–42.

Connery, Brian A., ed. *Representations of Swift.* Newark: University of Delaware Press, 2002.

Conway, Anne. *The Principles of the Most Ancient and Modern Philosophy.* Edited by Peter Loptson. Boston: Martinus Nijhoff, 1982.

Conway, Daniel W., and John E. Seery, eds. *The Politics of Irony: Essays in Self-Betrayal.* New York: St. Martin's Press, 1992.

Cooper, Anthony Ashley. *Characteristics.* Edited by Lawrence E. Klein. Cambridge and New York: Cambridge University Press, 1999.

Cottegnies, Line. "The Translator as Critic: Aphra Behn's Translation of Fontenelle's *Discovery of New Worlds* [1688]." *Restoration* 27 (2003): 23–38.

Craik, Henry. *The Life of Jonathan Swift.* London: J. Murray, 1882.

Crane, R. S. *The Idea of the Humanities.* 2 vols. Chicago: University of Chicago Press, 1967.

Craven, Kenneth. *Jonathan Swift and the Millennium of Madness.* New York: E. J. Brill, 1992.

———. "*A Tale of a Tub* and the 1697 Dublin Controversy." *Eighteenth-Century Ireland* 1 (1986): 97–110.

Creech, Thomas. *T. Lucretius Carus. The Epicurean Philosopher, His Six Books De Natura Rerum.* 2nd ed. Oxford, 1683.

Crocker, L. G., ed. *L'età dei lumi: Studi storici sul settecento europeo in onore di Franco Venturi.* Vol. 2. Naples: Jovene, 1985.

Crocker, S. F. "Rochester's 'Satire against Mankind': A Study of Certain Aspects of the Background." *West Virginia University Studies* 3 (1937): 57–73.

Crousaz, J. P. *A Commentary on Mr. Pope's Principles of Morality, or Essay on Man* [1739]. Translated by Samuel Johnson. Vol. 17. *The Yale Edition of the Works of Samuel Johnson.* Edited by J. H. Middendorf. 18 vols. New Haven, CT: Yale University Press, 1958–2004.

Cryle, Peter, and Lisa O'Connell, eds. *Libertine Enlightenment: Sex, Liberty and License in the Eighteenth Century.* New York: Palgrave, 2004.

Cudworth, Ralph. *The True Intellectual System of the Universe.* London, 1678.

Dempsey, Thomas. *The Delphic Oracle.* New York: Benjamin Blom, 1972.

DePorte, Michael. *Nightmares and Hobbyhorses: Swift, Sterne, and Augustan Ideas of Madness.* San Marino, CA: Huntington Library, 1974.

Dowling, William. *The Epistolary Moment: The Poetics of the Eighteenth-Century Verse Epistle.* Princeton, NJ: Princeton University Press, 1991.

Drachmann, A. B. *Atheism in Pagan Antiquity.* London: Gyldendal, 1922.

Dryden, John. *The Works of John Dryden.* Edited by Edward Niles Hooker, H. T. Swedenberg, Jr., and Vinton A. Dearing. 20 vols. Berkeley: University of California Press, 1956–2000.

Duffy, Eamon. "Primitive Christianity Revived: Religious Renewal in Augustan England." *Studies in Church History* 14 (1977): 287–300.

Earbery, Matthias. *Deism Examin'd and Confuted, in an Answer to a Book intitled, "Tractatus Theologico Politicus."* London, 1697.

Edwards, John. *A Compleat History or Survey of All Dispensations and Methods of Religion.* 2 vols. London, 1699.

———. *Some Thoughts concerning the Several Causes and Occasions of Atheism, Especially in the Present Age.* London, 1695.

Edwards, Thomas R. *This Dark Estate: A Reading of Pope.* Berkeley: University of California Press, 1963.

Ehrenpreis, Irvin. *Swift: The Man, His Works, and the Age.* 3 vols. Cambridge, MA: Harvard University Press, 1962–83.

Elliot, Robert C. "Swift's *Tale of a Tub*: An Essay in Problems of Structure." *PMLA* 66 (1951): 441–55.

[Ellis, Clement]. *The Gentile Sinner, or England's Brave Gentleman.* 2nd ed. Oxford, 1661.

———. *The Vanity of Scoffing.* London, 1674.

Emerson, Roger L. "Heresy, the Social Order, and English Deism." *Church History* 37 (1968): 389–403.

Empson, William. "Dryden's Apparent Scepticism." *Essays in Criticism* 20 (1970): 172–81.

Erasmus, Desiderius. *The Praise of Folly.* Translated by Clarence H. Miller. 2nd edition. New Haven, CT: Yale University Press, 2003.

Ewald, William B. *The Masks of Jonathan Swift.* Oxford: Oxford University Press, 1954.

Fabricant, Carole. "Speaking for the Irish Nation: The Drapier, the Bishop, and the Problems of Colonial Representation." *ELH* 66 (1999): 337–72.

Farley-Hills, David, ed. *Rochester: The Critical Heritage*. London: Routledge, 1972.

Feeney, Denis. *Literature and Religion at Rome*. Cambridge: Cambridge University Press, 1998.

Fell, John. *The Character of the Last Daies*. Oxford, 1675.

Fischer, John Irwin, Hermann Josef Real, and James D. Woolley, eds. *Swift and His Contexts*. New York: AMS Press, 1989.

Fisher, Alan S. "An End to the Renaissance: Erasmus, Hobbes, and *A Tale of the Tub*." *Huntington Library Quarterly* 38 (1974): 1–20.

Fisher, Nicholas. "The Contemporary Reception of Rochester's *A Satyr Against Mankind*." *RES* 57 (2006): 185-205.

———, ed. *That Second Bottle: Essays on John Wilmot, Earl of Rochester*. Manchester, UK: Manchester University Press, 2000.

Fleischmann, Bernard. *Lucretius and English Literature, 1680–1740*. Paris: Librairie Nizet, 1964.

Foisneau, Luc, and George Wright, eds. *New Critical Perspectives on Hobbes's "Leviathan."* Milan: FrancoAngeli, 2004.

Fontenrose, Joseph. *The Delphic Oracle*. Berkeley: University of California Press, 1978.

Force, James E., and Richard H. Popkin, eds. *The Books of Nature and Scripture: Recent Essays on Natural Philosophy, Theology, and Biblical Criticism in the Netherlands of Spinoza's Time and the British Isles of Newton's Time*. Boston: Kluwer, 1994.

Fox, Christopher, ed. *The Cambridge Companion to Jonathan Swift*. New York: Cambridge University Press, 2003.

———, and Brenda Tooley, eds. *Walking Naboth's Vineyard*. Notre Dame, IN: University of Notre Dame Press, 1995.

French, David. "Swift and Hobbes—A Neglected Parallel." *Boston University Studies in English* 3 (1957): 243–55.

———. "Swift, Temple, and 'A Digression on Madness.'" *Texas Studies in Literature and Language* 5 (1963): 42–57.

Fujimura, Thomas H. "Dryden's *Religio Laici*: An Anglican Poem." *PMLA* 76 (1961): 205-17.

Gastrell, Francis. *The Principles of Deism Truly Represented and Set in a Clear Light; in Two Dialogues between a Sceptick and a Deist*. London, 1708.

Gay, Peter. *The Enlightenment: An Interpretation*. 2 vols. New York: Alfred A. Knopf, 1966.

Gildon, Charles. *The Golden Spy*. London, 1709.

Gill, Christopher, and T. P. Wiseman, eds. *Lies and Fiction in the Ancient World*. Austin: University of Texas Press, 1993.

[Glanvill, Joseph]. *An Apology and Advice for Some of the Clergy*. London, 1674.

———. *Logou Threskeia, or, A Seasonable Recommendation, and Defence of Reason, in the Affairs of Religion*. London, 1674.

———. *Seasonable Reflections and Discourses in Order to the Conviction, & Cure of the Scoffing, & Infidelity of a Degenerate Age*. London, 1676.

Goodfellow, Sarah. " 'Such Masculine Strokes': Aphra Behn as Translator of *A Discovery of New Worlds.*" *Albion* 28 (1996): 229–50.

Goodman, John. *The Old Religion, Demonstrated in Its Principles, and Described in the Life and Practice Thereof*. London, 1684.

Grell, Ole Peter, Jonathan I. Israel, and Nicholas Tyacke, eds. *From Persecution to Toleration: The Glorious Revolution and Religion in England*. Oxford: Clarendon Press, 1991.

Griffin, Dustin. *Satires against Man: The Poems of Rochester*. Berkeley: University of California Press, 1973.

Grotius, Hugo. *Against Paganism, Judaism and Mahumentanism*. Translated by Clement Barksdale. London, 1676.

Guffey, George. *Two English Novelists: Aphra Behn and Anthony Trollope*. Los Angeles, CA: William Andrews Clark Memorial Library, 1975.

Guilhamet, Leon M. "Dryden's Debasement of Scripture in *Absalom and Achitophel.*" *SEL* 9 (1969): 395–413.

Hallywell, Henry. Preface to *A Discourse of the Use of Reason in Matters of Religion*, by George Rust. London, 1683.

Hammond, Brean S. *Pope and Bolingbroke: A Study of Friendship and Influence*. Columbia: University of Missouri Press, 1984.

Hammond, Eugene R. "In Praise of Wisdom and the Will of God: Erasmus' *Praise of Folly* and Swift's *A Tale of a Tub.*" *Studies in Philology* 80 (1983): 253–76.

Harris, Tim, Paul Seaward, and Mark Goldie, eds. *The Politics of Religion in Restoration England*. Oxford: Basil Blackwell, 1990.

Harrison, Peter. *"Religion" and the Religions in the English Enlightenment*. Cambridge and New York: Cambridge University Press, 1990.

Harth, Philip. *Contexts of Dryden's Thought*. Chicago: University of Chicago Press, 1968.

———. *Swift and Anglican Rationalism: The Religious Background of "A Tale of a Tub."* Chicago: University of Chicago Press, 1961.

Havens, George R. "Voltaire's Marginal Comments Upon Pope's *Essay on Man.*" *Modern Language Notes* 43 (1928): 429–39.

Hawes, Clement. *The British Eighteenth Century and Global Critique*. New York: Palgrave, 2005.

———. *Mania and Literary Style: The Rhetoric of Enthusiasm from the Ranters to Christopher Smart*. Cambridge: Cambridge University Press, 1996.

Haydn, Hiram. *The Counter-Renaissance*. New York: Charles Scribner's Sons, 1950.

Henry, Patrick. "Sacred and Profane Gardens in *Candide.*" *Studies in Voltaire and the Eighteenth Century* (1979): 133–52.

Herbert of Cherbury, Edward. *The Antient Religion of the Gentiles*. London, 1705.

———. *Pagan Religion: A Translation of De Religione Gentilium*. Translated by John Anthony Butler. Ottawa: Dovehouse, 1996.

———. *A Dialogue between a Tutor and His Pupil.* London, 1768.

Heyd, Michael. "The Reaction to Enthusiasm in the Seventeenth Century." *Journal of Modern History* 53 (1981): 258–80.

Hill, Christopher. *The Century of Revolution: 1603–1714.* 2nd ed. New York: W. W. Norton, 1982.

———. *The Collected Essays of Christopher Hill.* 3 vols. Amherst: University of Massachusetts Press, 1985.

———. *Reformation to Industrial Revolution: A Social and Economic History of Britain, 1530–1780.* London: Weidenfeld & Nicolson, 1967.

———. *The World Turned Upside Down: Radical Ideas during the English Revolution.* New York: Viking Press, 1975.

Hobbes, Thomas. *The English Works of Thomas Hobbes of Malmesbury.* Edited by Sir William Molesworth. 12 vols. London: Thoemmes, 1839–45.

———. *A True Ecclesiastical History from Moses to the Time of Martin Luther, in Verse.* Translated by John Rooke. London, 1722.

———. *Leviathan.* Edited by C. B. Macpherson. New York: Penguin Books, 1968.

Hopkins, Robert H. "The Personation of Hobbism in Swift's *Tale of a Tub* and *Mechanical Operation of the Spirit.*" *Philological Quarterly* 45 (1966): 372–78.

Horace. *Satire, Epistles, and Ars Poetica.* Translated by H. Rushton Fairclough. Cambridge, MA: Harvard University Press, 1926.

[Howard, Sir Robert]. *The History of Religion.* London, 1694.

Hughes, Derek, and Janet Todd, eds. *The Cambridge Companion to Aphra Behn.* New York: Cambridge University Press, 2004.

Hume, David. *An Enquiry concerning Human Understanding.* Edited by Tom L. Beauchamp. Oxford: Oxford University Press, 1999.

———. *Principal Writings Upon Religion Including "Dialogues concerning Natural Religion" and "The Natural History of Religion."* Edited by J. C. A. Gaskin. Oxford: Oxford University Press, 1998.

Hunt, Lynn, ed. *The Invention of Pornography.* New York: Zone Books, 1993.

Hunter, Michael. "The Problem of 'Atheism' in Early Modern England." *Transactions of the Royal Historical Society* 35 (1985): 136–37.

———. *Science and Society in Restoration England.* Cambridge: Cambridge University Press, 1981.

———, and David Wootton, eds. *Atheism from the Reformation to the Enlightenment.* Oxford: Clarendon Press, 1992.

Hutcheson, Harold. *Lord Herbert of Cherbury's "De Religione Laici."* New Haven, CT: Yale University Press, 1944.

Hutner, Heidi, ed. *Rereading Aphra Behn.* Charlottesville: University Press of Virginia, 1993.

Irlam, Shaun. *Elations: The Poetics of Enthusiasm in Eighteenth-Century Britain.* Stanford, CA: Stanford University Press, 1999.

Israel, Jonathan I. *Radical Enlightenment: Philosophy and the Making of Modernity, 1650–1750.* Oxford: Oxford University Press, 2001.

Jacob, Margaret. *The Radical Enlightenment: Pantheists, Freemasons, and Republicans.* London: George Allen & Unwin, 1981.

Jocelyn, H. D. "The Roman Nobility and the Religion of the Republican State." *Journal of Religious History* 4 (1966): 89–104.

Johnson, Samuel. *The Lives of the Most Eminent Poets; With Critical Observations on Their Works.* Edited by Roger Lonsdale. 4 vols. Oxford: Clarendon Press, 2006.

Johnson, William. *The Formation of English Neo-Classical Thought.* Princeton, NJ: Princeton University Press, 1967.

Kahn, Ludwig W. "Voltaire's *Candide* and the Problem of Secularization." *PMLA* 67 (1952): 886–8.

Kallich, Martin. *Heav'n's First Law: Rhetoric and Order in Pope's Essay on Man.* DeKalb: Northern Illinois University Press, 1967.

Kaufman, Anthony. " 'The Perils of Florinda': Aphra Behn, Rape, and the Subversion of Libertinism in *The Rover, Part I.*" *Restoration and 18th-Century Theatre Research* 11 (1996): 1–21.

Kelling, Harold D. "Reason in Madness: *A Tale of a Tub.*" *PMLA* 69 (1954): 198–222.

Kenshur, Oscar. "Scriptural Deism and the Politics of Dryden's *Religio Laici.*" *ELH* 54 (1987): 869–92.

Ker, W. P., ed. *Essays of John Dryden.* 2 vols. Oxford: Clarendon Press, 1900.

King, William. *The Original Works of William King.* 3 vols. London, 1776.

Klein, Lawrence E., and Anthony J. La Vopa, eds. *Enthusiasm and Enlightenment in Europe, 1650–1850.* San Marino, CA: Huntington Library, 1998.

Knapp, Richard Gilbert. "The Fortune of Pope's *Essay on Man* in 18th Century France." Studies on Voltaire in the Eighteenth Century, vol. 82. Edited by Theodore Besterman. Geneva: Institut et Museé Voltaire, 1971.

Kors, Alan. *Atheism in France, 1650–1729.* Princeton, NJ: Princeton University Press, 1990.

Kramnick, Isaac. *Bolingbroke and His Circle: The Politics of Nostalgia in the Age of Walpole.* Ithaca, NY: Cornell University Press, 1968.

Kramnick, Jonathan Brody. "Rochester and the History of Sexuality." *ELH* 69 (2002): 277–301.

Kroll, Richard. *The Material Word: Literate Culture in the Restoration and Early Eighteenth Century.* Baltimore: Johns Hopkins University Press, 1991.

———. " 'Tales of Love and Gallantry': The Politics of *Oroonoko.*" *Huntington Library Quarterly* 67 (2004): 573–605.

———, Richard Ashcraft, and Perez Zarogin, eds. *Philosophy, Science, and Religion in England, 1640–1700.* Cambridge: Cambridge University Press, 1992.

Kubek, Elizabeth Bennett. " 'Night Mares of the Commonwealth': Royalist Passion and Female Ambition in Aphra Behn's *The Roundheads.*" *Restoration* 17 (1993): 88–103.

Kupersmith, William. "Swift's Aeolists and the Delphic Oracle." *Modern Philology* 82 (1984): 190–94.

Lamb, Jonathan. *The Rhetoric of Suffering: Reading the Book of Job in the Eighteenth Century*. Oxford: Oxford University Press, 1995.

Langdon, David. "On the Meanings of the Conclusion of *Candide*." *Studies in Voltaire and the Eighteenth Century* 238 (1985): 397–432.

Laursen, John Christian, and Cary J. Nederman, eds. *Beyond the Persecuting Society: Religious Toleration Before the Enlightenment*. Philadelphia: University of Pennsylvania Press, 1998.

Lawlor, Nancy K. "Pope's *Essay on Man*: Oblique Light for a False Mirror." *Modern Language Quarterly* 28 (1967): 305–16.

Leavis, F. R. *Determinations*. London: Chatto & Windus, 1934.

LeFanu, William. *A Catalogue of Books Belonging to Mr. Jonathan Swift*. Cambridge: Cambridge Bibliographical Society, 1988.

Leland, John. *A View of the Principal Deistical Writers That Have Appeared in England in the Last and Present Century*. London, 1754.

Lemay, J. A. Leo, ed. *Deism, Masonry, and the Enlightenment*. Newark: University of Delaware Press, 1987.

Leranbaum, Miriam. *Alexander Pope's "Opus Magnum," 1729–1744*. Oxford: Clarendon Press, 1977.

Levin, Carole, and Patricia A. Sullivan, eds. *Political Rhetoric, Power, and Renaissance Women*. Albany, NY: SUNY Press, 1995.

Levin, Harry. *The Myth of the Golden Age in the Renaissance*. Bloomington: Indiana University Press, 1969.

Levine, Joseph M. *The Battle of the Books: History and Literature in the Augustan Age*. Ithaca, NY: Cornell University Press, 1991.

———. *Between the Ancients and the Moderns: Baroque Culture in Restoration England*. New Haven, CT: Yale University Press, 1999.

Lindberg, David C., and Robert S. Westman, eds. *Reappraisals of the Scientific Revolution*. Cambridge and New York: Cambridge University Press, 1990.

Locke, John. *An Essay Concerning Human Understanding*. Edited by Peter H. Nidditch. Oxford: Clarendon Press, 1975.

Love, Harold. *English Clandestine Satire, 1660–1702*. New York: Oxford University Press, 2004.

Lovejoy, Arthur O. *Essays in the History of Ideas*. Baltimore: Johns Hopkins University Press, 1948.

———, and George Boas. *Primitivism and Related Ideas in Antiquity*. Baltimore: Johns Hopkins University Press, 1997.

Lucretius Carus, Titus. *De rerum natura. The Way Things Are*. Translated by Rolfe Humphries. Bloomington: Indiana University Press, 1968.

Lund, Roger D., ed. *The Margins of Orthodoxy*. Cambridge: Cambridge University Press, 1995.

———. "Strange Complicities: Atheism and Conspiracy in *A Tale of a Tub*." *Eighteenth-Century Life* 13 (1989): 34–58.

Machiavelli, Niccolò. *Discourses on Livy*. Translated by Julia Conaway Bondanella and Peter Bondanella. Oxford: Oxford University Press, 1997.

Mack, Maynard. *Alexander Pope: A Life*. New Haven, CT: Yale University Press, 1985.

————. *Collected in Himself.* Newark: University of Delaware Press, 1982.

————, ed. *Essential Articles for the Study of Alexander Pope.* Hamden, CT: Archon Books, 1964.

Manning, Gillian. "The Deist: A Satyr on the Parsons." *The Seventeenth Century* 8 (1993): 149–60.

————. "Rochester's *Satyr against Reason and Mankind* and Contemporary Religious Debate." *The Seventeenth Century* 8 (1993): 99–121.

Manuel, Frank Edward. *The Eighteenth Century Confronts the Gods.* Cambridge, MA: Harvard University Press, 1959.

Marlborough, Sarah Jennings Churchill. *Memoirs of Sarah, Duchess of Marlborough.* Edited by William King. New York: Kraus Reprint, 1969.

Mason, Haydn. *Candide: Optimism Demolished.* New York: Twayne Publishers, 1992.

Mayo, Thomas Franklin. *Epicurus in England, 1650–1725.* Dallas, TX: Southwest Press, 1934.

McDermott, Gerald R. *Jonathan Edwards Confronts the Gods.* Oxford: Oxford University Press, 2000.

McGregor, J. F., and B. Reay. *Radical Religion in the English Revolution.* London: Oxford University Press, 1984.

McKeon, Michael. *Origins of the English Novel.* Baltimore: Johns Hopkins University Press, 1987.

McLaverty, James. "Warburton's False Comma: Reason and Virtue in Pope's *Essay on Man.*" *Modern Philology* (2002): 379–92.

Miller, Peter N. " 'Freethinking' and 'Freedom of Thought' in Eighteenth-Century Britain." *The Historical Journal* 36 (1993): 599–617.

Mintz, Samuel I. *The Hunting of Leviathan.* Bristol, UK: Thoemmes Press, 1996.

Montag, Warren. *The Unthinkable Swift: The Spontaneous Philosophy of a Church of England Man.* New York: Verso, 1994.

Montaigne, Michel de. *The Complete Works of Montaigne.* Translated by Donald M. Frame. Stanford, CA: Stanford University Press, 1957.

Moore, Cecil A. "Did Leibniz Influence Pope's *Essay?*" *Journal of English and Germanic Philology* 16 (1917): 84–102.

More, Henry. *Enthusiasmus Triumphatus: or, A Discourse of the Nature, Causes, Kinds, and Cure, of Enthusiasme.* Edited by G. A. J. Rogers. Bristol: Thoemmes Press, 1997.

Morton, Timothy, and Nigel Smith, eds. *Radicalism in British Literary Culture, 1650–1830.* New York: Cambridge University Press, 2002.

Moss, Jean Dietz. *Novelties in the Heavens: Rhetoric and Science in the Copernican Controversy.* Chicago: University of Chicago Press, 1993.

Mosse, George L. "Puritan Radicalism and the Enlightenment." *Church History* 29 (1960): 424–39.

Murdock, Kenneth. *The Sun at Noon.* New York: Macmillan, 1939.

Nisbet, H.B. "*De Tribus Impostoribus*: On the Genesis of Lessing's *Nathan der Weise.*" *Euphorian* 73 (1979): 365–87.

———, and Claude Rawson, eds. *The Cambridge History of Literary Criticism.* Vol. 4 of *The Eighteenth Century.* Cambridge: Cambridge University Press, 1997.

Noggle, James. *The Skeptical Sublime: Aesthetic Ideology in Pope and the Tory Satirists.* Oxford: Oxford University Press, 2001.

Nokes, David. "The Radical Conservatism of Swift's Irish Pamphlets." *British Journal for Eighteenth-Century Studies* 7 (1984): 169–76.

Nokes, G. D. *A History of the Crime of Blasphemy.* London: Sweet & Maxwell, 1928.

Nussbaum, Felicity, and Laura Brown, eds. *The New Eighteenth Century.* New York: Methuen, 1987.

O'Donnell, Mary Ann, B. Dhuicq, and Guyonne Leduc, eds. *Aphra Behn (1640–1689): Identity, Alterity, Ambiguity.* Paris: Harmattan, 2000.

Orr, John. *English Deism: Its Roots and Its Fruits.* Grand Rapids, MI: Eerdmans, 1934.

Osler, Margaret J., ed. *Rethinking the Scientific Revolution.* Cambridge: Cambridge University Press, 2000.

Owen, John. *A Brief and Impartial Account of the Nature of the Protestant Religion.* London, 1682.

Owen, Susan. " 'Suspect My Loyalty When I Lose My Virtue': Sexual Politics and Party in Aphra Behn's Plays of the Exclusion Crisis." *Restoration* 18 (1994): 37–47.

Ovid. *Ars amatoria.* Translated by J. H. Mozley. Cambridge, MA: Harvard University Press, 1962.

Owtram, William. *Twenty Sermons Preached upon Several Occasions.* London, 1669.

Pacheco, Anita. "Reading Toryism in Aphra Behn's Cit-Cuckolding Comedies." *The Review of English Studies* 55 (2004): 690–708.

———. "Royalism and Honor in Aphra Behn's *Oroonoko*." *SEL* 34 (1994): 491–506.

Palmeri, Frank. *Satire and Narrative.* Austin: University of Texas Press, 1990.

Parke, H. W., and D. E. W. Wormell. *The Delphic Oracle.* 2 vols. Oxford: Basil Blackwell, 1956.

Parker, Fred. *Scepticism and Literature: An Essay on Pope, Hume, Sterne, and Johnson.* Oxford: Oxford University Press, 2003.

Parker, Samuel. *Bishop Bramhall's Vindication of Himself.* London, 1672.

———. *A Discourse of Ecclesiastical Politie.* London, 1670.

Parnell, J. T. "Swift, Sterne, and the Skeptical Tradition." *Studies in Eighteenth-Century Culture* 23 (1994): 221–42.

Patterson, Annabel. *Censorship and Interpretation: The Conditions of Writing and Reading in Early Modern England.* Madison: University of Wisconsin Press, 1984.

Paulson, Kristoffer S. "The Reverend Edward Stillingfleet and the 'Epilogue' to Rochester's *A Satyr against Reason and Mankind*." *Philological Quarterly* 50 (1971): 657–63.

Paulson, Ronald. *Theme and Structure in Swift's "Tale of a Tub."* New Haven, CT: Yale University Press, 1960.

Pearson, Roger. *The Fables of Reason: A Study of Voltaire's "Contes Philosophiques."* Oxford: Clarendon Press, 1993.

Pennington, Donald, and Keith Thomas, eds. *Puritans and Revolutionaries.* Oxford: Clarendon Press, 1978.

Phillips, Mark Salber, and Gordon Schochet, eds. *Questions of Tradition.* Toronto: University of Toronto Press, 2004.

Phillipson, Nicholas, and Quentin Skinner, eds. *Political Discourse in Early Modern Britain.* Cambridge: Cambridge University Press, 1993.

Pinto, Vivian DeSola. *Enthusiast in Wit: A Portrait of John Wilmot, Earl of Rochester 1647–1680.* Lincoln: University of Nebraska Press, 1962.

Pocock, J. G. A. "Conservative Enlightenment and Democratic Revolutions: The American and French Cases in British Perspective." *Government and Opposition* 24 (1989): 81–105.

———. *The Machiavellian Moment: Florentine Political Thought and the Atlantic Republican Tradition.* Princeton, NJ: Princeton University Press, 1975.

———. "Thomas Hobbes: Atheist or Enthusiast? His Place in a Restoration Debate." *History of Political Thought* 11 (1990): 737–49.

Poggioli, Renato. *The Oaten Flute.* Cambridge, MA: Harvard University Press, 1975.

Pope, Alexander. *The Correspondence of Alexander Pope.* Edited by George Sherburn. 5 vols. Oxford: Clarendon Press, 1956.

———. *The Poems of Alexander Pope.* Edited by John Butt. New Haven, CT: Yale University Press, 1963.

[Pope, Alexander, ed.]. *Poems on Several Occasions.* London, 1717.

Popkin, Richard H. *History of Skepticism from Erasmus to Spinoza.* Berkeley: University of California Press, 1979.

Porter, Roy. *The Creation of the Modern World: The Untold Story of the British Enlightenment.* New York: W. W. Norton, 2000.

Quehen, A. H. de. "Lucretius and Swift's *Tale of a Tub.*" *University of Toronto Quarterly* 63 (1993): 287–307.

Quintana, Ricardo. "Situational Satire: A Commentary on the Method of Swift." *University of Toronto Quarterly* 17 (1948): 130–36.

———. "Two Paragraphs in *A Tale of a Tub*, Section IX." *Modern Philology* 73 (1975): 15–32.

Racine, Louis. *La Religion, Poëme* [1742]. Paris, 1785.

Rawson, Claude, ed. *The Character of Swift's Satire.* Newark: University of Delaware Press, 1983.

———. *God, Gulliver, and Genocide.* Oxford and New York: Oxford University Press, 2001.

———. "The Injured Lady and the Drapier: A Reading of Swift's Irish Tracts." *Prose Studies* 3 (1980): 15–43.

———. *Swift.* London: Sphere Books, 1971.

Real, Hermann J., and Heinz J. Vienken, eds. *Proceedings of the First Münster Symposium on Jonathan Swift.* München: Wilhelm Fins, 1985.

Redwood, John. "Charles Blount, Deism, and English Free Thought." *Journal of the History of Ideas* 35 (1974): 490–98.

———. *Reason, Ridicule and Religion.* London: Thames & Hudson, 1976.

Reeves, Margaret. "History, Fiction, and Political Identity: Heroic Rebellion in Aphra Behn's *Love-Letters between a Nobleman and His Sister* and *Oroonoko.*" *1650–1850: Ideas, Aesthetics, and Inquiries in the Early Modern Era* 8 (2003): 269–94.

Reilly, Patrick. *Jonathan Swift: The Brave Desponder.* Carbondale: Southern Illinois University Press, 1982.

Richardson, Jonathan. *Richardsonia.* London, 1776.

Rivero, Albert J., ed. *Augustan Subjects: Essays in Honor of Martin C. Battestin.* Newark: University of Delaware Press, 1997.

Robertson, J. M. *The Dynamics of Religion.* 2nd ed. London: Watts, 1926.

———. *A History of Freethought, Ancient and Modern, to the Period of the French Revolution.* 4th ed. 2 vols. London: Watts, 1936.

Rogers, Robert W. "Critiques of the *Essay on Man* in France and Germany, 1736–1755." *ELH* 15 (1948): 176–93.

———. *The Major Satires of Alexander Pope.* Illinois Studies in Language and Literature 40. Urbana: University of Illinois Press, 1955.

Rooke, John. Preface to *A True Ecclesiastical History from Moses to the Time of Martin Luther,* by Thomas Hobbes. London, 1722.

Rosenmeyer, Thomas G. *The Green Cabinet.* Berkeley: University of California Press, 1969.

Ross, Alexander. *The New Planet No Planet.* London, 1646.

Ruffhead, Owen. *The Life of Alexander Pope.* London, 1769.

Said, Edward. *The World, the Text, and the Critic.* Cambridge, MA: Harvard University Press, 1984.

Savile, George, Marquis of Halifax. *The Character of a Trimmer.* 3rd ed. London, 1697.

Schofield, Mary Anne, and Cecilia Macheski, eds. *Fetter'd or Free? British Women Novelists, 1670–1815.* Athens: Ohio University Press, 1986.

Scott, Jonathan. "Review Essay: Radicalism and Restoration: The Shape of the Stuart Experience." *The Historical Journal* 31 (1988): 453–67.

Scott, Sir Walter. *The Life of John Dryden.* Edited by Bernard Kreissman. Lincoln: University of Nebraska Press, 1963.

Scruggs, Charles. "Swift's Use of Lucretius in *A Tale of a Tub.*" *Texas Studies in Literature and Language* 15 (1973): 39–50.

Sedley, David, ed. *The Cambridge Companion to Greek and Roman Philosophy.* Cambridge: Cambridge University Press, 2003.

Shackleton, Robert. "Pope's *Essay on Man* and the French Enlightenment." *Studies in the Eighteenth Century II.* Edited by R. F. Brissenden. Toronto: University of Toronto Press, 1973.

Shapiro, Barbara J. *John Wilkins, 1614–1672: An Intellectual Biography.* Berkeley: University of California Press, 1969.

Sharpe, Kevin, and Steven N. Zwicker, eds. *Politics of Discourse*. Berkeley: University of California Press, 1987.

Sheehan, Jonathan. *The Enlightenment Bible: Translation, Scholarship, Culture*. Princeton, NJ: Princeton University Press, 2005.

Sherburn, George. *The Early Career of Alexander Pope*. Oxford: Clarendon Press, 1934.

Skelton, Philip. *Ophiomaches: or Deism Revealed*. 1749. 2 vols. Bristol, UK: Thoemmes, 1990.

Smedley, Jonathan. *An Hue and Cry after the Examiner . . . To Which Is Added a Copy of Verses Fasten'd to the Gate of St. P--'s C--h . . .* London, 1727.

Smith, Hilda L., ed. *Women Writers and the Early Modern British Political Tradition*. Cambridge: Cambridge University Press, 1998.

Snider, Alvin. "Cartesian Bodies." *Modern Philology* 98 (2000): 299–319.

South, Robert. *Twelve Sermons Preached upon Several Occasions*. 2 vols. London, 1697.

Spadafora, David. *The Idea of Progress in Eighteenth-Century Britain*. New Haven, CT: Yale University Press, 1990.

Spence, Joseph. *Anecdotes, Observations, and Characters, of Books and Men*. London, 1820.

Spencer, John. *De Legibus Hebraeorum*. Cambridge, 1685.

Spink, J. D. *French Free-Thought from Gassendi to Voltaire*. London: Athlone Press, 1960.

Spinoza, Baruch. *Theological-Political Treatise*. Translated by Samuel Shirley. Indianapolis: Hackett, 1998.

Sprat, Thomas. *History of the Royal Society*. 1667. Edited by Jackson I. Cope and Harold Whitmore Jones. Saint Louis, MO: Washington University Studies, 1958.

Spurr, John. "'Rational Religion' in Restoration England." *Journal of the History of Ideas* 49 (1988): 563–85.

Standish, John. *A Sermon Preached before the King at White-Hal, Septem. the 26th, 1675*. London, 1676.

Stapleton, M. L. "Aphra Behn, Libertine." *Restoration* 24 (2000): 75–97.

Starkman, Miriam. *Swift's Satire on Learning in "A Tale of a Tub."* New York: Octagon Books, 1968.

Starobinski, Jean. *Blessings in Disguise: Or, The Morality of Evil*. Translated by Arthur Goldhammer. Cambridge: Cambridge University Press, 1993.

Steele, Richard. *The Tatler*. Edited by Donald F. Bond. 3 vols. Oxford: Clarendon Press, 1987.

———. *The Guardian*. 2 vols. London, 1767.

Stephen, Leslie. *History of English Thought in the Eighteenth Century*. 3rd ed. 2 vols. London: Smith, Elder, 1902.

Stephens, William. *An Account of the Growth of Deism in England*. London, 1696.

Stewart, Ann Marie. "Rape, Patriarchy, and the Libertine Ethos: The Function of Sexual Violence in Aphra Behn's 'The Golden Age' and *The Rover, Part I*." *Restoration and 18th-Century Theatre Research* 12 (1997): 26–39.

Stillingfleet, Edward. *A Letter to a Deist, in Answer to Several Objections against the Truth and Authority of the Scriptures.* London, 1677.

———. *Origines Sacraes.* London, 1662.

———. *The Works of that Eminent and Most Learned Prelate, Dr. Edw. Stillingfleet, Late Lord Bishop of Worcester.* Edited by Richard Bentley and John Russell Bedford. 6 vols. London, 1710.

Stone, Lawrence. *The Crisis of the Aristocracy, 1558–1641.* Oxford: Oxford University Press, 1965.

Strauss, Leo. *Persecution and the Art of Writing.* Glencoe, IL: Free Press, 1952.

———. *Spinoza's Critique of Religion.* Translated by E. M. Sinclair. Chicago: University of Chicago Press, 1965.

Swift, Jonathan. *The Correspondence of Jonathan Swift.* Edited by Harold Williams. 5 vols. Oxford: Clarendon Press, 1963–65.

———. *Gulliver's Travels.* Edited by Claude Rawson and Ian Higgins. New York: Oxford University Press, 2005.

———. *Jonathan Swift: The Complete Poems.* Edited by Pat Rogers. New York: Penguin Books, 1983.

———. *The Prose Works of Jonathan Swift.* Edited by Herbert Davis. 14 vols. Oxford: Basil Blackwell, 1939–68.

———. *A Tale of a Tub.* Edited by A. C. Guthkelch and D. Nichol Smith. 2nd ed. Oxford: Clarendon Press, 1958.

Temple, Sir William. *Five Miscellaneous Essays.* Edited by Samuel Holt Monk. Ann Arbor: University of Michigan Press, 1963.

———. *The Works of Sir William Temple.* Edited by Jonathan Swift. 4 vols. London, 1757.

Tension, Thomas. *The Creed of Mr. Hobbes Examined.* 2nd ed. London, 1671.

Thompson, E. P. *The Poverty of Theory.* New York: Monthly Review Press, 1978.

Thormählen, Marianne. *Rochester: The Poems in Context.* New York: Cambridge University Press, 1993.

Tillotson, Geoffrey. *Pope and Human Nature.* Oxford: Clarendon Press, 1958.

Tillotson, John. *Sermons Preach'd Upon Several Occasions.* London, 1671.

———. *The Works of the Most Reverend Dr. John Tillotson.* London, 1696.

Tindal, Matthew. *Christianity as Old as the Creation.* London, 1730.

———. *Rights of the Christian Church Asserted.* London, 1706.

Todd, Janet, ed. *Aphra Behn Studies.* Cambridge: Cambridge University Press, 1996.

———. *Gender, Art and Death.* Oxford: Polity Press, 1993.

———. *The Secret Life of Aphra Behn.* New Brunswick, NJ: Rutgers University Press, 1996.

Toland, John. *Christianity Not Mysterious.* 2nd ed. London, 1696.

———. *Letters to Serena.* London, 1704.

———. *Pantheisticon.* 1751. New York: Garland Publishing, 1976.

Treglown, Jeremy, ed. *Spirit of Wit: Reconsiderations of Rochester.* Hamden, CT: Archon Books, 1982.

Trenchard, John. *The Natural History of Superstition.* London, 1709.

Turner, James G. *Libertines and Radicals in Early Modern London: Sexuality, Politics, and Literary Culture, 1630–1685.* Cambridge: Cambridge University Press, 2002.

———. "Pope's Libertine Self-Fashioning." *The Eighteenth Century: Theory and Interpretation* 29 (1988): 123–44.

———. "The Properties of Libertinism." *Eighteenth-Century Life* 9 (1985): 75–87.

Turner, John. *An Attempt towards an Explanation of the Theology and Mythology of the Ancient Pagans.* London, 1687.

Underwood, Dale. *Etherege and the Seventeenth Century Comedy of Manners.* New Haven, CT: Yale University Press, 1957.

Velissariou, Aspasia. " 'Tis Pity That When Laws Are Faulty They Should Not Be Mended or Abolisht': Authority, Legitimation, and Honor in Aphra Behn's *The Widdow Ranter.*" *PLL* 38 (2002): 137–66.

Verrall, A. W. *Lectures on Dryden.* Edited by Margaret De G. Verrall. Cambridge: Cambridge University Press, 1914.

Vickers, Brian, ed. *The World of Jonathan Swift.* Cambridge, MA: Harvard University Press, 1968.

Vieth, David M. *Attribution in Restoration Poetry: A Study of Rochester's 'Poems' of 1680.* New Haven, CT: Yale University Press, 1963.

———. *John Wilmot, Earl of Rochester: Critical Essays.* New York: Garland Press, 1988.

Villiers, George. *The Works of His Grace, George Villiers, Late Duke of Buckingham.* 3rd ed. 2 vols. London, 1715.

Visconsi, Eliott. "A Degenerate Race: English Barbarism in Aphra Behn's *Oroonoko* and *The Widow Ranter.*" *ELH* 69 (2002): 673–701.

Voltaire. *Candide and Related Texts.* Edited and intro. by David Wooton. Indianapolis, IN: Hackett, 2000.

———. *Correspondence.* In *The Complete Works of Voltaire.* Edited by Theodore Besterman. Vols. 85–135. Toronto: University of Toronto Press, 1968–.

———. *Oeuvres Complètes.* Edited by Louis Moland. 52 vols. Paris: Garnier Frères, 1877–85.

Wade, Ira O. *The Intellectual Development of Voltaire.* Princeton, NJ: Princeton University Press, 1969.

———. *Voltaire and Candide: A Study in the Fusion of History, Art, and Philosophy.* Princeton, NJ: Princeton University Press, 1959.

Walker, D. P. *The Ancient Theology: Studies in Christian Platonism from the Fifteenth to the Eighteenth Century.* Ithaca, NY: Cornell University Press, 1972.

Warburton, William. *A Critical and Philosophical Commentary on Mr. Pope's 'Essay on Man.'* New York: Garland, 1974.

————. *The Divine Legation of Moses Demonstrated: On the Principles of a Religious Deist, from the Omission of the Doctrine of a Future State of Reward and Punishment in the Jewish Dispensation*. London, 1738.

————. *The Divine Legation of Moses Demonstrated*. 2 vols. London, 1837.

Warton, Joseph. *An Essay on the Genius and Writings of Pope*. 5th ed. 2 vols. London, 1806.

Waterland, Daniel. *Christianity Vindicated against Infidelity*. London, 1732.

Weber, Harold. "Drudging in Fair Aurelia's Womb: Constructing Homosexual Economies in Rochester's Poetry." *The Eighteenth Century* 33 (1992): 99–117.

Wehrs, Donald R. "*Eros*, Ethics, Identity: Royalist Feminism and the Politics of Desire in Aphra Behn's *Love-Letters*." *SEL* 32.3 (1992): 461–78.

Weinbrot, Howard D. *Augustus Caesar in 'Augustan' England: The Decline of a Classical Norm*. Princeton, NJ: Princeton University Press, 1978.

————. "The Pattern of Formal Verse Satire in the Restoration and the Eighteenth Century." *PMLA* 80 (1965): 394–401.

————. "The Swelling Volume: The Apocalyptic Satire of Rochester's *Letter from Artemisia in the Town to Chloe in the Country*." *Studies in the Literary Imagination* 5 (1972): 19–21.

Westfall, Richard S. *Science and Religion in Seventeenth-Century England*. New Haven, CT: Yale University Press, 1958.

Whitby, Daniel. *A Discourse of the Necessity and Usefulness of the Christian Revelation*. London: A. & J. Churchill, 1705.

White, Douglas H. *Pope and the Context of Controversy: The Manipulation of Ideas in An Essay on Man*. Chicago: University of Chicago Press, 1979.

Wilcoxon, Reba. "Rochester's Philosophical Premises: A Case for Consistency." *Eighteenth-Century Studies* 8 (1974–75): 183–201.

————. "Rochester's Sexual Politics." *Studies in Eighteenth-Century Culture* 8 (1979): 137–49.

Wiley, Margaret. *The Subtle Knot: Creative Skepticism in Seventeenth-Century England*. Cambridge, MA: Harvard University Press, 1952.

Wilkins, John. *A Discourse concerning a New Planet*. 5th ed. London, 1684.

————. *A Discovery of New Worlds*. 5th ed. London, 1684.

Williams, Kathleen. *Jonathan Swift and the Age of Compromise*. Lawrence: University of Kansas Press, 1958.

————. *Swift: The Critical Heritage*. London: Routledge, 1970.

Williamson, George. *The Proper Wit of Poetry*. Chicago: University of Chicago Press, 1961.

Wilmot, John, Second Earl of Rochester. *The Letters of John Wilmot, Earl of Rochester*. Edited by Jeremy Treglown. Oxford: Basil Blackwell, 1980.

————. *The Works of John Wilmot, Earl of Rochester*. Edited by Harold Love. Oxford: Oxford University Press, 1999.

Winstanley, Gerrard. *The Works of Gerrard Winstanley*. Edited by George H. Sabine. New York: Russell & Russell, 1965.

Wolfson, Harry. *The Philosophy of the Church Fathers*. 3rd ed. 2 vols. Cambridge, MA: Harvard University Press, 1970.

Wolseley, Sir Charles. *The Unreasonableness of Atheism Made Manifest in a Discourse Written by the Command of a Person of Honour.* London, 1675.

Wooton, David. "Unbelief in Early Modern Europe." *History Workshop Journal* 20 (1985): 82–100.

Wotton, William. *Reflections upon Ancient and Modern Learning.* 1694. Hildesheim: Georg Olms, 1968.

Young, Wayland. *Eros Denied.* London: Weidenfeld & Nicholson, 1964.

Zagorin, Perez, ed. *Culture and Politics from Puritanism to the Enlightenment.* Berkeley: University of California Press, 1980.

Zaller, Robert. "The Continuity of British Radicalism in the Seventeenth and Eighteenth Centuries." *Eighteenth-Century Life* 6 (1981): 17–38.

Zwicker, Steven N., ed. *The Cambridge Companion to John Dryden.* Cambridge: Cambridge University Press, 2004.

———. *Politics and Language in Dryden's Poetry.* Princeton, NJ: Princeton University Press, 1984.

Index